LIVING UNDER FIVE FLAGS.

MY LIFE & MINISTRY IN CHALLENGING TIMES.

BOOK TWO

CALLED, ANOINTED, & COMMISSIONED.

RHODESIA TO ZIMBABWE

By

Alan (AB) Robertson

Living Under Five Flags-Book Two

© **2021 by Alan (AB) Robertson**
ISBN 978-1-8384255-5-5
Published by Caracal Books
United Kingdom. https://www.facebook.com/CaracalBooks

All rights reserved. No part of this publication may be reproduced, stored in a retrieval system, or transmitted in any form or by any means—for example, electronic, photocopy, recording—without the prior written permission of the publisher. The only exception is brief quotations in printed reviews.

The internet addresses, email addresses, and phone numbers in this book are accurate at the time of publication.

Photos-Maps-© Colin Weyer
www.rhodesia.me.uk

Scripture- New King James Version®. Copyright © 1982 by Thomas Nelson. Used by permission. All rights reserved.

Foreword

The title of this account is very apt for it covers a generation of great change and upheaval in central Africa. Southern Rhodesia was a British colony and, as such, had over a few brief decades, established a substantial infra-structure of towns, roads, railways, farms, mines, hospitals, schools, manufacturing enterprises and much more, all from absolutely nothing but uncultivated bush.

In the early 1950s the country was incorporated into the Federation of Rhodesia and Nyasaland which was extremely successful and catapulted the nations into tremendous agricultural, manufacturing and economic growth. This was brought to a halt when nationalist movements agitated for independence and the three nations that had comprised the Federation separated.

Two of them were granted almost immediate independence from Britain but Rhodesia had a unique history and was so successful that it had achieved self-government back in the 1920s. There was disagreement between the existing local national administration and the British home government and subsequently when talks broke down Rhodesia declared independence.

The result was that the once peaceful nation slid into an internal conflict in which people suffered and faced tremendous upheavals and dangers. It was a time of uncertainty in which people of all ethnic groups became open to the Gospel and began to seek spiritual truth. As people sought God there were tremendous evidences of the working of the Holy Spirit and people were miraculously convicted, converted and healed by

The Lord.

There was a great need for "labourers to be sent out into the harvest" and it was to this that Alan responded and tirelessly functioned, often in circumstances of great difficulty and very real danger. (Matthew 9:37,38)

I can recommend this account which is well worth the read in more ways than one. It is full of anecdotes, amazing and interesting people and wonderful records of how The Lord moved in power and grace despite the difficult circumstances.

I have had the pleasure and privilege of knowing Alan for over five decades. He must be one of the most astounding and outstanding men I have known. His commitment to The Lord and steadfast faith, often in the face of overwhelming difficulties, opposition and peril, has never wavered.

As you read this account it will become more and more apparent that his one main aim through life has been to win people to Christ and to then establish them in their faith. To this end he has been prepared to lay down his life in more ways than one. He did all this without wavering in his love and commitment to his family who faced many challenges and trials in very trying and dangerous times, both during the upheavals in Rhodesia/Zimbabwe, and then in having to leave the land of their birth and forge a new life in a new land.

Alan's ministry has impacted many people from all walks of life, ethnic groups and ages. There will undoubtedly be a notable eternal harvest through his amazing life of service to The Lord.

I have witnessed his endurance in adversity, his

compassion in caring, his brokenness in bereavement, his faithfulness in service, his determination in difficulty and his courage in the face of very real danger. Utterly dependable and reliable, he is a man of The WORD.

I can say with conviction that Alan is one in a thousand. If The Lord asked me, who would I want to stand with me in a time of trouble I would choose Alan. God bless you, Alan.

Roland Pletts.
Basingstoke England.

Roland has authored a number of books, his wonderful paintings adorn the living room walls of many ex-Zimbabweans, he is also an anointed minister of the Gospel and a long-time friend. Thank you, Roland!

Foreword 2

The three volumes of LIVING UNDER FIVE FLAGS are an autobiography that not only offers richly stored memories of Rhodesian life, 1944-1989, but also generously shares Alan's intimate family life, with its attendant joys and sorrows.

This is a story that invites the reader into the personal space of one, called by God into Ministry, with the choices and responsibilities that such a commitment involves. Within the narrative we are introduced to the variety of characters who became entwined with this faith-filled family. Glimpses of the inevitable ups and downs of church life, are generously portrayed.

'LIVING UNDER FIVE FLAGS', has the added richness of insight into the social history of 20th century Rhodesia/Zimbabwe. Years of contentment and peace, years of war and strife.

Read these vividly recalled memories and be impressed! A remarkable labour of love for both his family, his friends and the wider community. An inspiring witness to the faith that Alan professes. Hallelujah

Jenny Leason, Benidorm

Jenny is currently an active member of my congregation in Benidorm who has sought to serve The Lord her entire life. I am greatly indebted to her for proof reading the whole manuscript before I sent it to the printers. Thank you, Jenny.
Alan (AB) Robertson

FLAGS & MAPS

FEDERATION OF RHODESIA AND NYASALAND

RHODESIA

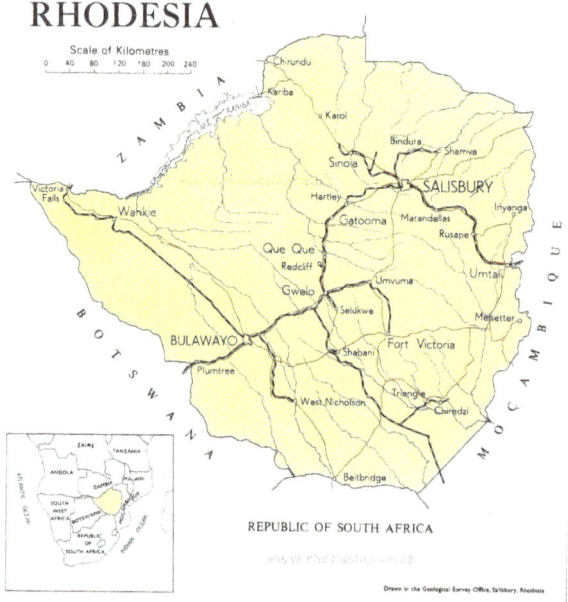

INTRODUCTION

As mentioned in the introduction to Book One, I was asked to write the "foreword" of **"IN SEARCH OF OPHIR,"** a book by Tim King dealing with the history of the Assemblies of God in Rhodesia/Zimbabwe between 1952-1985. I did as I was requested, but also provided information about my own ministry up and down Zimbabwe. As his book was already written, Tim suggested that I write my own book, and **'LIVING UNDER FIVE FLAGS'** is the result.

In Book One, I dealt with my early years, living under the Southern Rhodesian flag. This was followed by details of how The Lord called me into the ministry during the days when the Rhodesian flag flew confidently over our country. In Book Two I deal with my life as a Minister of the Gospel from 1972 until to the end of 1980 when we moved to Bulawayo. During those years I lived under the flags of Rhodesia, Zimbabwe-Rhodesia, the Union Jack (for a short season) and finally the flag of Zimbabwe.

As you will discover I was privileged to minister in a number of different towns up and down the country. I have dealt with each congregation as I remember it and have tried to mention people by name, but sadly some of the 'names' have been forgotten.

I have written my story from memory with very little help from anywhere else. However, God has been good, as believe it or not, I still have three 'Newsletters' in my possession written in 1973 and 1974. I also possess an address list dating back to the 1980s which helped to fill in a few gaps in my memory. Having said that, my apologies if I have not mentioned you by name!

As can be expected, there were a few 'difficult' situations to deal with during those years, but I have either not mentioned them at all, or not mentioned the person or people concerned. However, in order tell the story, on rare occasions, I have mentioned the names of the people concerned. In that case I trust that I have also mentioned that any problem that occurred was also as a result of failures by myself. Praise God for His great grace and His willingness to forgive!

I count it an incredible privilege to have grown up in Rhodesia and to have come to Christ in my late teens. I praise God that I was called into the Ministry with the Assemblies of God and had the privilege of serving my Lord in my homeland during those years. I was also privileged to be married to Mally who gave me three wonderful sons. I could not have done the work I did without their backing and love. Thank you, Lord, for giving me Mally, as my wife, and Mark, Matthew and Jonathan as my sons, I have truly been blessed!

In addition to my own family, I have also been blessed to work with some wonderful people. Some of them taught me the Word of God, and others I was privileged to lead to The Lord. Of those I led to The Lord some have done amazing things in the decades since they came to Christ. It has been a great honour to know that we had a part in bringing them to The Lord. My life has not always been easy but it has without doubt been interesting. I trust that the reader will be blessed as we travel down this road together.

Yours in the service of King Jesus.
Alan (AB) Robertson

Chapter 1 - ASSISTANT MINISTER.

THE LAYING ON OF HANDS.
SUNDAY 2nd April 1972

As already mentioned in book one, the Easter Convention was held at McChlery Avenue from Friday 31st March until Monday 3rd April in 1972 and as usual we had a very good turnout. Our own Minister John Stegman was there as was John Bond and other Ministers from around the country. At the close of the Sunday morning service, I was called to the front of the Assembly and the Ministers and elders present, gathered around, laid hands on me and prayed for God to use me in the days that lay ahead. What I remember most about that day was that I had the full backing of the entire congregation and in the days that were ahead I knew that many would be praying for me.

However, having returned from my wonderful holiday in South Africa, in order to work as an assistant to John Stegmann I was in for a surprise. Instead of getting involved with the work in Salisbury I was sent off to Gwelo to assist Bill and Fiona Stevenson. They had returned to Rhodesia with their five sons after spending some time in Queenstown in South Africa and were now ministering in Gwelo and Selukwe and needed some help.

A) GWELO & SELUKWE IN 1972

The 'work' in Gwelo included an outreach in Selukwe a

mining town some twenty-three miles away. As a result, Bill was responsible for two Sunday services, a Sunday School, Youth Work and a Bible Study, in Gwelo, plus a Sunday Afternoon Service and midweek Bible Study in Selukwe. I believe Bill was convinced that with a little bit of effort a new Assembly could be established in Selukwe. As a result, he had approached the oversight in Salisbury and asked if they could spare me for a short while to see what would happen if someone was able to concentrate most of his efforts upon the town.

The Oversight in Salisbury agreed to Bill's request and as a result I packed my bags and moved down to Selukwe where I was provided with accommodation by Mr. and Mrs. Sleigh who were members of the fellowship. They could not have been kinder to their new lodger and I felt immediately at home. My main preaching responsibility was to take the Sunday afternoon service and the midweek Bible Study in Selukwe. It was also my responsibility to visit all the contacts that we had in the area and hopefully increase the numbers attending the local meetings. In addition, I was expected to attend the Gwelo meetings and give support wherever it was needed.

The older Stevenson's were very good to me; however, their sons had the rather annoying habit of referring to me as **"AB baby."**

Can you imagine what that did to the 'dignity,' of one so recently exalted to the position of a full time Minister of the Assemblies of God? Only joking, I was not at all worried really, I mean others had referred to me as **"Abie my boy."**

The only difference to being called **"AB baby,"**

and **"Abie my boy,"** is a few years and the spelling. By the way they were all great kids and a blessing to me personally while I was with them. One thing that I remember about them was their knowledge of the Bible. They were able to recite all the books of the Bible in song, which I have never been able to do. Some years before, for a short while, I had the two oldest boys in my Sunday School class, while I briefly stood in for another teacher. I was also blessed to have two of the sons of Brother Ashkenazi in my class at the same time. Brother Ashkenazi was a very committed Jewish believer in Jesus the Jewish Messiah and a member of our congregation in Salisbury.

Nevertheless, one morning while taking this particular Sunday School class, I had just finished the 'lesson,' when one of the boys said, **"That is just like --------, isn't it?**

To be quite honest I had no idea what he was talking about and so replied, **"Let us just stick to the lesson today please!"**

With a class of boys like that, you really had to be on your toes, and so I was quite relieved when their regular teacher returned!

The congregation in Selukwe was really quite small, and I only remember a few of the members. One of the most likeable men was Kurt Pietersen who had come to Rhodesia from Denmark. He worked on the chrome mines, as did most people in the town, and was exceptionally strong and able to bend a rod of iron with ease. Kurt and his wife and family were a real blessing to me, as were the Sleighs the people that I was living with. In spite of the size of the congregation I applied myself to the work with enthusiasm and made a lot of contacts whilst living there

One day Bill asked me if I would take care of the meetings in Gwelo as he and his wife planned to take some time off and have a short holiday. I was only too happy to oblige, however, when the time came, he changed his mind and never went away. As he was not going to be away, I knew that he would be taking both of the Sunday services in Gwelo and presumed, that he would also be taking the Bible Study that Wednesday evening. On that particular evening, two full carloads of people accompanied me from Selukwe. I am confident that it was the best turnout for a midweek meeting during the entire time that I was assisting in the area. As I **knew** that Bill would be speaking, I only took my Bible and did not even take my notebook.

As was his custom, Bill led the worship and prayers on that memorable evening. It was a good evening assisted by the fact that we had a very good turnout. However, after leading the worship and prayer time Bill announced that Brother Robertson would be taking the Bible Study. On hearing what he said, I was horrified, and have seldom been more surprised in all my life. I was totally unprepared and had nothing to say except something like the following, **"I am sorry Bill but as you never went away, I presumed that you would be taking the Bible Study tonight. I am terribly embarrassed as I am completely unprepared.**

Well, as can be expected when your assistant lets you down, the Senior Minister, took over. However, this very new Minister made up his mind that he would never, ever, be unprepared again. I determined that evening that if I was ever in a similar position, I would ask The Lord to help me, open my Bible and speak. I had been completely humiliated, but what a lesson I learned that evening! That lesson has served me well during the 49 years that I have been in the ministry, at the time of writing this story.

Back in Selukwe, on the evenings when we had our own Bible Study, I usually went and picked up people for the meeting. One evening when I arrived at the home of a couple who had asked for a lift the man of the house had not returned from work. His wife informed me that she would therefore not be attending the meeting that evening as she had better remain so that she could give him his supper when he arrived. She then asked whether I would be willing to take her twin sons to the Bible Study as they had been so excited about going to the meeting all day. The two boys were possibly around six or seven years old at the time, however, what could I say but yes! As we were going to the door one of the boys asked his grandmother if she would like to come. She declined and the little boy said, **"Do you love TV more than God?"**

I instinctively responded with, **"Preach it son!"**

Perhaps I said it a little too loud, but what a preacher that little boy was, he hit the nail on the head! I would love to know how he turned out!

One night Bill asked me to assist with contact visitation in Gwelo and when I saw the names of the contacts that he possessed, I recognised the names of people that I had not seen in years. I asked if I could visit a family who had lived down the road from us when I was a kid in Bulawayo. As an 11-year-old I had been very keen on their daughter who was at school with me. Mr. Beddingfield was a professional musician and every Saturday night many people would attend the Braai (barbecue) that they organised at their home. They provided their guests with large fires made in pits dug in the ground with steel gauze right over the top where they were able to cook their meat. There would be a party atmosphere where he provided the music and a lot of food and 'beer' was consumed. This now older couple were living in Gwelo and I thought it would be great to visit and hopefully see them come to The Lord.

There were two of us in each visitation group and we had just arrived and introduced ourselves, when the phone rang. It was Bill's wife Fiona who had been unable to reach Bill and therefore she phoned us. She had received a message from a couple in QueQue, a town 40 miles away, asking us to pray for their grandchild. This couple's family were visiting from South Africa and their little baby was now desperately ill, suffering from meningitis, in intensive care in the QueQue hospital. She understood from what they said that they wanted us to go to the hospital and pray for the child. We asked the Beddingfields to excuse us and set out immediately. On arrival at the hospital the people were surprised, but grateful, as they had only contacted us in order to ask us for prayer and had not expected us to travel all the way from Gwelo to pray for the child.

The hospital staff were very supportive and allowed us to enter the room with the parents in order to pray for the baby's healing. We gathered around the baby's cot in intensive care and after we had all prayed, we were asked to leave the room. The parents of the child were very appreciative and after a short conversation we returned to Gwelo. It was only a few days later that we learned that God had answered prayer and the parents and their child were already safely back home in South Africa. Praise God, we serve a God of miracles! Hallelujah!

However, I was not going to be a part of the Gwelo & Selukwe fellowship for long. When my friend Peter King, an Elder in Cape Town, said that they must need me if the Assembly in Salisbury were willing to put me into the ministry as an assistant, he was once again proved to be correct. In fact, it was only a few months after going to the area that I had to return to Salisbury.

With a heavy heart, as I had grown to love the people with whom I was ministering, I went around saying goodbye to the members of the Assembly and all the contacts that I had made in the area. However, it seems that I had not really made a good impression on **all** of my contacts. When I visited one elderly gentleman to let him know that I was leaving he responded by saying, **"Not before time."**

What can you say to such a response? I know that I laughed and have laughed about that statement on many occasions. I had obviously made a great impression on this gentleman, so much so that he felt that a few months was far too long to have to put up with me!

And so, after my brief stay in Selukwe as an assistant to Bill Stevenson it was back to Salisbury and to my home Assembly. I would now be working as an assistant to an exceptional Bible Teacher and Minister, John Stegman and his lovely wife Yvonne.

B) McCHLERY AVENUE SALISBURY IN 1972

Although my time as an Assistant to John Stegman was almost as short as my stay in the Midlands there are a number of things that I want to mention which took place during that brief period.

One of the things that I remember with some sadness, was that in spite of my now being a recognised Minister, albeit an Assistant, I was never invited to the regular Oversight Meetings which were held every week in Dave Onion's office in Salisbury. In fact, I was rather annoyed to learn that there was opposition from one or possibly more of the Elders to my attendance at the weekly meeting. Surely as the Assistant Minister, I had a right to be considered as an integral part of the leadership team, and as an 'assistant' surely it ought to have been viewed as part of my ongoing training? It was a puzzle to me that I was never allowed into that meeting in spite of my changed circumstances. Nevertheless, maybe I ought to have been grateful as there was much to keep me busy without having to attend that particular meeting!

Among the many other activities that came my way, I had the job of leading one of the house groups that were operating at the time. I am not sure when the 'house group' at Betty Willis's home commenced, but it was in operation when I was Assistant Minister. It was an amazing group, and after all these years it was without doubt the most successful 'house group' in which I have ever been involved. Possibly the reason for its success, was that every week it was packed with young adults, and our host made us very welcome in her home. Every week, we had great times of worship, testimony, fellowship, and Bible teaching.

In spite of the obvious success of this group, John Stegman decided to change things. He felt the need of a house group in another part of town. The new venue was located in Greendale in the home of Andrè and Pat Silcox and their family. I must admit that I was not too keen on the idea of moving a successful house group to another area, as I felt that there was a lot of truth in the saying, **"If it ain't broke don't fix it!"**

In spite of this, there were a number of reasons for John Stegman's decision, and it was not only the need to reach out into another part of town. Our group was flourishing; however, it was 'only' young adults and John did not want a 'young people's church' he wanted to reach young and old, married and single. And so it was, that in due season, the house group was relocated to the Silcox home in Greendale.

Most evenings when I arrived, I would briefly see Andre before he disappeared into his study leaving his wife to be our host. The reason for his disappearance was that he was studying for some very important exams. As he was holding down a full-time job, the only time he had to study was in the evenings when he got home from work. Although I did not know this at the time, the fact that he took those exams and passed them, made him a suitable candidate to be appointed Post Master General of Zimbabwe about eight years later. However, at the time I must admit that I was puzzled that he was not present, when we were having a house group in his home. Praise God that in spite of the relocation of the house group, most of the group continued to attend, and it continued to be very successful, with a few additional faces.

In 1972 the ministry of John Stegman and our Assembly was reaching out in one way or another to the whole country. As an example, regular meetings were being held in Marandellas a town some 45 miles from Salisbury with different members of our congregation taking meetings in the town every week. In addition, we had a special outreach to the Jewish community which took place over several Sunday evenings. Sadly, a Jewish Doctor, was killed in a road accident somewhere outside Salisbury on the day, or a few days before he was due to attend those special meetings.

Every Sunday evening a number of us took turns in leading the worship prior to the preacher delivering the Word of God. I was due to lead the worship during the outreach to the Jewish community and John Stegman gave me very clear instructions on what 'songs' to choose. For those special meetings I was instructed to choose hymns about the glory of God the Father, His wonderful Creation, His majesty, rather than sing some of the lively "Christian" Choruses that we loved to sing.

We naturally had lots of songs that met those criteria and so that was easy and I did as he requested. However, I had a feeling that in some way we were 'letting the side down.' I felt that it was important to let these Jewish people know by our singing that we worshipped Jesus, the Messiah of Israel.

Although I now understand what he was trying to do during this outreach, at the time I did not fully understand. He was not ashamed of Jesus, rather He was trusting in the Word of God, the Bible, and the message that he would be preaching, to reveal to these people who their Messiah really was. I believe John had a great love for the Jewish people and I believe that my own love for Israel and God's Chosen people, is largely down to what he taught me. I did what he requested, as it is vital for the musicians and worship leaders to recognise that they are not 'in charge,' the Minister, the anointed preacher of the Gospel is the 'leader,' under God, of every meeting and not the musicians or the song or worship leader!

Another thing that was taking place was that John Stegman was producing a weekly Newsletter. This was sent out to every contact, with whom he had an address, and each letter was addressed by hand, with a stamp, in order to make it look as personal as possible to the receiver, when it was delivered. Each Newsletter drew attention to what he would be preaching on the following Sunday. This was a costly exercise but did not come out of 'Church funds' as one of the congregants generously paid for all the costs involved. In addition, volunteers arrived each week to make it happen. This project was without doubt a success. Partly as a result of this regular mailing, the Sunday evening services were packed and each week there were decisions for Christ.

It was around this time that I had a talk with John Stegman in the Assembly car park. He asked me what I thought about the idea of building a large new place of worship where we were standing. Before I give my answer, it is important that I give a little history about the existing Assembly building. It is also important to understand that I only found out about this 'history,' sometime after this conversation.

When the original building was put up, the leaders at the time always understood it to be the 'Minor Hall' as they planned eventually to erect the main Assembly building on what became the car park. However, over time a 'minor hall' was erected next to the Assembly and most people did not know about the original plans. As a result, the only 'vision' of which I was aware, was the plan to establish seven Assemblies in the surrounding suburbs of Salisbury, as well as the main Assembly, McChlery Avenue Assembly in Eastlea.

Not knowing the original plan, when John Stegman asked me whether it was time to do what the leaders had always envisioned, in my ignorance, I did not encourage him to proceed. In fact, I did exactly the opposite and encouraged him to rather keep to the vision, a much 'newer vision' of establishing these suburban Assemblies. Looking back upon that incident I feel that I should have been like Jonathan's armour bearer who encouraged Jonathan to attack the Philistines when he said,

**"Do all that is in your heart. Go then; here I am with you, according to your heart."
1 Samuel 14.7**

As I look back upon this incident, I feel that it is possible that had I supported John Stegman at that time he may have been able to persuade the entire Oversight of the Assembly to adopt the same vision that he had. Had that happened, McChlery Avenue Assembly may well have continued to grow, and as a result been better equipped to establish seven suburban Assemblies in Salisbury as well as continue to establish new Assemblies right across the land. However sadly I was not the encouragement and support that he needed that day!

As I have already mentioned there was a major outreach taking place not only in Salisbury but further afield. On one occasion I was asked by John Stegman to take a Bible Study in Sinoia which was some 70 miles from Salisbury. He had been a few times already, when certain Christians in the area had requested teaching on the Baptism of the Holy Spirit. When he had taken the meeting, I learned that even the local Anglican Vicar had attended. As he had a lot on his plate at the time, he asked me to go in his place and I felt very privileged at the honour of being asked. Sadly, I do not think that the meeting went quite as well as it had, when he had taken it, and I do not remember going a second time.

It was clear that other fellowships were needed around the country to deal with the growing need and interest of the 'white' community. As a result, one day John Stegman asked me to accompany Les Helen in order to see what sort of facilities were available for us to start new congregations in the country. That day we travelled to Sinoia, and then on to Karoi, and finally we ended up in Mangula before returning home. Although I never thought that our expedition produced any results at the time, in the years that lay ahead new Assemblies were started in Sinoia and Karoi.

When many of our faithful young people started work, they often ended up securing jobs in other parts of the country. Others applied for and gained positions in some of the smaller towns because that is where jobs were available. Two of these couples were Brian Boshoff who had married Margaret Willis and Seymour and Dianne Edwards. They moved to QueQue, which was around 140 miles from Salisbury and ended up attending the local Full Gospel Church, however they missed the fellowship they had enjoyed in Salisbury. As a result, one weekend, I arranged to go and visit them with a full carload which included two of Margy Boshoff's sisters.

One of the meetings was held at the home of Brian and Margy who were living out of town at the time. QueQue was a growing town and houses to rent were very hard to find. It was the rainy season, and there had been a storm the night before with very heavy rain. As a result, when we arrived at the low level 'drift' which we had to cross in order to get to their home, it was covered by fast moving water. After waiting for some time for the level of the river to go down, we finally decided to leave the car, and wade across the stream to the other side taking great care I can assure you.

Brian was waiting on the other side and he ferried us to his home which was not far from the river. As we were, by this time, running very late we did not have time to smarten up and so we sat around The Lord's table in bare feet enjoying Breaking Bread together. After a great weekend sadly, it was soon time to head off home.

As it happened it was not too long before I was back in QueQue, this time to arrange a Youth Camp. We had decided that the Camp that year needed to cater for all the young people, in congregations right across the country. As a result, it was important to include Bethshan in Bulawayo and McChlery Avenue in Salisbury in our planning as they were the two largest congregations with the most number of young people. It was because of this that we decided on QueQue, as the town was about the same distance from Bulawayo as it was from Salisbury. I praise God that I was put in touch with Courtney Ferguson, who had a long relationship with the AOG, as without him we could not have done what we did.

The youth camp took place over the 'Rhodes and Founders' weekend and we had a good crowd from the two main Assemblies. I travelled down early in the week to see that everything was organised for the arrival of the young people. The camp site that had been selected was right out in the bush but near the river. Water was pumped from the river, into a large water tank that my friend Courtney and his workers had erected, where it was treated before it could be used. The toilets were very basic pit-latrines surrounded by hessian. The showers were also surrounded by hessian, with the 'shower' being a hose pipe linked up to the water tank with a shower head on the end. The water in the tank was fine for washing, but was not suitable for drinking. The drinking water came in a tanker.

There were separate tent areas for the men and the women and a marquee for the services. I am amazed when I look back at what Courtney and his workers did for us, as to provide all the equipment and have it all set up for our youth camp was an incredible achievement. I know that I thanked Courtney at the time, but thinking of it now, I feel that I just was not appreciative enough. What he did enabled life changing decisions to be taken by many people that weekend.

Our guest speaker was Reg Bendixon who had come up from South Africa with his wife for the weekend. He was a great preacher and had an amazing voice and I have never forgotten him singing 'THE KING IS COMING' and 'HIS EYE IS ON THE SPARROW.' His ministry that weekend was really life transforming for many of those who attended, in particular those who came from Bethshan in Bulawayo. I think I am correct in saying that the youth work in Bulawayo really took off after that camp. People like Craig Friend, Gary Smith, and Patrick Humberstone all subsequently went into the ministry. Patrick moved to Australia where he ministered God's Word for many years, but at the time of writing, I understand he is back in Africa and ministering in Zambia. He was one of those who came to know The Lord at that Youth Camp among many others who had real encounters with God.

The weekend was soon over and we all packed up and made our way back to our various Assemblies. It had been hard work to have a Youth Camp, so far from a functioning Assembly, but it had really paid off. Praise God!

Shortly after I had spent that lovely weekend in QueQue with Brian and Margy, and Seymour and Dianne, a new Assembly was commenced in the town. It was started by Bill Plews who had, some years before, pioneered a Baptist Church in the town. He had since been filled with the Holy Spirit and was in fellowship with the Assembly in Gwelo. He volunteered to go to QueQue in order to start an Assembly. Some years before, whilst he was pioneering the Baptist Church in the town, he had come across a number of people who claimed allegiance to the

Assemblies of God. These people indicated that they might be willing to support a new Assembly and so with that in mind he set out for QueQue to pioneer a new congregation in the town.

Sadly, not long after Bill Plews had started the new fellowship, he was unable to continue, due to certain changes in his own life which resulted in me getting a phone call one memorable Saturday afternoon. I was at home when my mother called me to the phone to speak to John Stegman and the conversation went something like this,

John said, **"AB there is a problem in QueQue and Bill Plews is no longer able to continue to pastor the Assembly. Would you be willing to move to QueQue and take over the responsibility of running the fellowship?"**

"I would be happy to do so." I replied.

John asked, **"How soon would you be willing to go?"**

"What about the end of next week?" I replied.

John responded, **"That would be great."**

"Who is taking the meeting tomorrow?" I asked.

John said, **"No one is available."**

To which I replied, **"No problem, I will go, what time is the meeting and where do they meet?**

And so it was that my 'assistant' days came suddenly to an end, and I was moving to QueQue to pastor my first congregation on my own. The following morning, I set out early to travel the 140 or so miles to the town in order to arrive in time for the morning meeting. Sad to say, that morning, the total congregation, including myself, consisted of five or six people. My good friend Bill Stevenson, (whose sons called me 'AB baby') made a special effort to be there to introduce me to the congregation, such as it was, whilst his wife Fiona took the meeting in Gwelo. In addition to Bill, there was Dianne Edwards and their baby Melony, (her husband Seymour was at work) and Wayne Ferguson (Courtney's brother). Having introduced me to the congregation, as soon as the meeting came to an end, Bill left us to return to Gwelo, no doubt to take the afternoon service in Selukwe and then the evening service in Gwelo.

After the meeting, Wayne, whom I had first met at the Youth Camp not long before, asked me where I would be living when I moved to QueQue. As I only knew the day before that I would be moving to QueQue, I told him that I had no idea, and that was something I needed to find out very soon. When he heard what I had to say he told me that he was renting a two bedroomed flat, and had a servant who looked after him, and if I was interested, I would be welcome to have the second bedroom. The only thing he asked of me was that I gave something extra to his servant as a result of the extra work that I would be creating.

I was overjoyed at how quickly The Lord had met my need of accommodation and accepted his offer at once. He would be out every day from very early in the morning as he and his brother were developing a gold mine out of town and as a result, I would have the place to myself every day. What an amazing God, He had gone ahead and provided me with a home, before I even began to ask or look. As it happened, I stayed with Wayne, or he stayed with me (I will explain later) the whole time I was living in QueQue on that first occasion. Sadly, although I was very appreciative, I possibly never thanked Wayne properly, for all that he did for me. There is no doubt that he was a real blessing to me.

I headed back to Salisbury, after ministering in QueQue, knowing that I only had a week to sort out my affairs. As time was so short and I would not be present at the coming Sunday services, and as I was being sent out from that Assembly to preach the Gospel, I was prayed for at the prayer meeting that Wednesday afternoon. I need to add that I was always conscious of the prayer support of my home Assembly, for which I praise God.

In addition to the prayer meeting, I had one last House Group to lead and one last group of people to inform that I was on my way to QueQue. The meeting was great as usual and when we came to the end, I said that our final song would be: -

"IF WE NEVER MEET AGAIN THIS SIDE OF HEAVEN."

Having announced the song I then announced that I was leaving for QueQue before the end of the week. I explained that they needed a Minister for the new work that had just begun and that I had been asked to fill the position. The news came as quite a shock to most of those who were there and, as a result, my last house group at the Silcox home ended on quite an emotional note.

After I left, my friend Roland Pletts took over the leadership of the house group and I have no doubt that it continued to flourish. Strangely enough Roland also found lodging with my mother as around that time he needed somewhere to stay. Since that time, on certain occasions, a few people have mistaken me for Roland or the other way around and my only explanation has to be my mother's cooking. Although he did not have the privilege of enjoying my mother's cooking for as long as I did, I believe it is the only explanation for this mistaking me for Roland or indeed the other way around.

    The year 1972 was a very eventful year and it was still not quite over. What a year it had been and now for the remainder of the year I was about to 'Pastor' my very first congregation! Sadly, it was only going to last for 15 months before John Stegman would ask me to move again. My next move would be to Hatfield in Salisbury, however, I have still to tell the story of QueQue and in spite of the shortness of my stay it would leave me with many, many, great memories.

Chapter 2   MY OWN CHURCH

1) QUEQUE ASSEMBLY. 1972-1973

I moved to QueQue towards the end of September 1972 and soon after I was settled into Wayne Ferguson's apartment, I had a visit from Bill Plews. He was keen to acquaint me with the situation in the town. He had a list of the names and addresses of the contacts that he had made and wanted to share a little background information about each of the people concerned. Having heard what he had to say, I thanked him, and promised to continue his work and visit each and every contact that he had given to me.

As it happened, the regulars were all known to me, some I had known for many years, and others I had met as a result of the youth camp. Among these were Brian and Margy, Seymour and Dianne, and the Ferguson's; Courtney and Gail and their lovely family, and Wayne and his girlfriend Sylvia whom he later married. All of these people were a real blessing to me and I thank God for their encouragement and love during that very interesting time in QueQue.

Sadly, most of the remaining contacts that Bill had given me, never became part of the congregation. But as I was not to know how things would turn out, I set about visiting them all. The following relates to two ladies and one family that were included on the list that

Bill had given to me. The first one was a young single woman whom we shall call Miss. X.

On arriving at her flat I introduced myself and she welcomed me into her home. After a brief chat, I said something like this, **"Are you a committed believer Miss X?"**

She replied, **"Yes I gave my life to Jesus on ----."**

"Praise God! That is great." I responded.

Miss X said, **"I am due to be married next month."**

"That's wonderful, where are you getting married? I replied.

She said, **"The minister of the Full Gospel Church has agreed to marry us in their Church."**

I asked, **"Is your fiancé a believer?"**

Miss X replied saying, **"Sadly he is not, however I am trusting that he will get saved."**

"I am sorry to hear that, and as a Minister of the Gospel I could never marry you to an unbeliever as it is contrary to the Word of God." I told her.

As can be expected my visit was short and it was not long before I left her home. She was a lovely girl and I really felt sorry for her; however, the Word of God is very clear.

"Do not be unequally yoked together with unbelievers. For what fellowship has righteousness with lawlessness? And what communion has light with darkness?" 2 Corinthians 6.14

You may feel that I was very blunt and had no right to speak as I did, however, years later in South Africa, this same lady went to see Alan Keeling, who was ministering in the town where she was living. Whilst she was there, she said, "**I do wish that I had listened to A.B. Robertson when he visited me before I got married in QueQue. My husband did not come to know Jesus as his Saviour as I had hoped. In fact, after our children were born, he would not let me send them to Sunday School, neither would he allow me to pray or read the Bible when he was around. In fact, he has made it almost impossible for me to serve God in any way."**

I do not tell this story in any way to prove that I was right. I am really very sad that her life turned out the way that it did. Sadly, too many Christians fail to read the Bible, and when they do, they want to select verses that they like, and ignore those verses where God is actually speaking into their circumstances. It is heartbreaking to discover that around the world, millions of Christian young men and women, are making the same mistake as this woman made, by choosing to ignore the clear warning of Scripture and marry outside the faith.

Of even greater concern are the many older Christians who should know better, who are also marrying outside the faith. Many years later when I was ministering in England, I officiated at the funeral of a lovely Christian woman. One of her sons spoke at the funeral and it was obvious that he was a long-standing believer. Sometime later his wife, also a very committed Christian, died and the man and his unmarried daughter continued to live in the family home.

It was at this time that he began to spend time with a lady who wanted nothing to do with the things of God. Not long afterwards his attendance at 'church' became less and less regular and his lovely 'born-again' very committed daughter became increasingly concerned. As far as I am aware he later just dropped out of the picture altogether because he became increasingly "**unequally yoked with**" an unbeliever in total disobedience to the Word of God!

Moving on from there the next "contact" that I had been given was a mature lady possibly a widow but I cannot remember. She had attended a number of services when Bill was the Minister, at the Globe and Phoenix Hall where our new Assembly was located. On her very first visit, according to Bill, she had proclaimed publicly that God had shown her that she should become part of the Assembly. However, sometime later when Bill visited her, he discovered that she was reading 'The Plain Truth Magazine,' a publication produced by Herbert W Armstrong. As Bill was familiar with the magazine, he proceeded to warn her about the dangers of the teaching presented in the magazine as any good 'shepherd' would do. Her response was not good and she became very annoyed and said, **"You are not my teacher, the Holy Spirit is my teacher. I will read what I like and let the Holy Spirit be my guide."**

After trying to reason with her, he realised that it was pointless and he took his leave. The lady never came back to the Assembly, in spite of having so recently declared that it was where God had sent her. When he passed on her name and address to me, he advised me not to bother, as she was not willing to accept any guidance at all. However, I was the 'New Minister' and I felt that I should continue to show her that we loved her and pop around every now and then and see what God would do.

As a result, every week or so I would drop in and have a cup of tea with her trusting that God would open the door for a meaningful chat, somewhere along the way. However, one memorable day when I arrived, she told me that if I chose to do so, I could join her as she was about to have a Bible Study with a well-known Jehovah Witness. On hearing this I retrieved my Bible from the car and went into her home. The next hour was a disaster as Chris ---- held the floor and presented his study with some authority. Sadly, each time I wanted to correct something that he had said, I was unable to find what I was looking for in the Scriptures. I just could not find a thing! It was a real disaster as I have already said, in fact, during the whole time he was there, I failed to say anything relevant or convincing.

At the end of his presentation, our host asked me if I would pray for us all but Chris replied, **"I cannot pray with him as we do not serve the same God!"**

That was possibly the only time that I was able to agree with what he said the whole afternoon.
However, he had one last thing to say to me, **"A.B. If you have a question about what we have discussed, and you see me around town, please do not hesitate to stop and ask, as I have been responsible for helping more than one Minister to see the light."**

In spite of feeling completely humiliated, I prayed with and for the lady of the house and then left, I must add, never to return.

I had never been to Bible College as I had always felt that my Bible College was my local Church. In my home Assembly I had received wonderful teaching from the likes of John Stegman, who was an excellent Bible Teacher, and Bill Mundell, who was a great evangelist. There were also a great many others who played an important role in preparing me for my life's work. Nevertheless, that evening, I wondered whether I had made the right choice by not attending Bible College?

As a direct result of this encounter, I spent a lot of time researching what the JW's believed. Not only what they believed, but more importantly how to reply, as I did not want to be humiliated a second time. Interestingly enough, God had not finished with this particular episode in my life, as Chris --- and I were to meet twice more before I left town. On those occasions, our meetings were to be under very different circumstances, for which I truly praise God.

I believe that it must have been some months later, when I met up with Courtney Ferguson whilst I was in town. After spending some time in 'fellowship' he mentioned that he had agreed to Chris --- the JW, the man who had left me feeling completely humiliated, giving a Bible Study in his home.

On being told this bit of news, I was frankly horrified and failed to understand why any well-established Christian as Courtney evidently was, would invite a JW to give a Bible Study in his home. I then asked whether he felt it was a wise thing to do as he was inviting a man who taught false doctrine to hold a Bible study in his home? He replied that he was well prepared for the encounter and mentioned various Bible helps that he had in his home.

Having heard what he had to say, and just before we parted, I asked whether he would like me to attend. Although I was loathe to actually say the words, and was really hoping that he would say no, as his 'pastor' I could not just walk away and said, **"Courtney, would you like me to attend?"**

But Courtney replied, **"It would be great if you came."**

I immediately realised that I was in trouble, and that I really needed God's help, and prayed that He would give me the wisdom that I needed. As the day approached, I asked the leader of a successful youth group in the town, who had a reputation of being able to handle the JW's, if he would attend with me. I was much relieved when he agreed to attend, and so there were the two of us, plus Courtney and his wife Gail, and a young man who was a very new Christian. I was not happy with this young man attending, but he did not want to stay away, and so the troops were assembled.

When Chris ---- and his wife arrived and saw me, I am sure that he relaxed completely, remembering our previous encounter. The meeting began after introductions had been made, and he laid out his teaching. He did a very good job, and Courtney told me later that Chris was like a snake charmer and he, Courtney, was like a snake being charmed. However, God was at work and somewhere in the course of his presentation, I was able to interrupt and as it were 'break the spell.' From then onwards it was Chris and I going backwards and forwards until the end of the evening. My friend, the Youth leader, whom I had asked to assist me, never had a look in, as Chris and I debated back and forth. Yet, I am sure that he was praying throughout the encounter for which I was extremely grateful.

At the conclusion of the evening, it was decided

to schedule another meeting for the same time the following week. At the appointed time, Chris --- arrived accompanied by another man instead of his wife. Once again, after a few minutes, the two of us became heavily engaged as we debated the Scriptures. Sometime during the course of the evening, he made a comment implying that the healing gifts are not for today, and anything related to what we call 'Divine healing' is of the devil. When he made that comment, I immediately challenged him, and warned him, that by saying such things, he was in danger of sinning against the Holy Spirit, which is the only unforgivable sin. I reminded him that 'healing' was one of the things that 'believers' were commanded to do after Jesus ascended into heaven and God worked with those early believers with 'signs' following. Many of those 'signs' were miracles of Divine healing. We need to remember that Jesus said: -

"Go into all the world and preach the gospel to every creature. ------And these signs will follow those who believe; In my Name they will -------lay hands on the sick, and they will recover." Mark 16.15-18

Because of a very real 'anointing of the Holy Spirit' upon the words that I spoke, at that point Chris backtracked a little. He was not ignorant of the Scriptures; in fact, he was well instructed in God's Word and ought to have known better. After the meeting Gail Ferguson informed me, that a cold shiver ran down her spine when I spoke as it seemed as if God Himself was reinforcing those words. The evening was almost over and in closing Courtney said, **"Chris, it will not be long before you join us."**

It was unbelievable how different my first encounter with Chris, which was a disaster, and the two evenings that we had in the home of Courtney and Gail were. In the years that followed I often pondered over WHY those encounters were so different. It is true that on our first encounter I was taken completely by surprise and was ill-prepared. I arrived at an elderly lady's home fully expecting to share a cup of tea with her but not expecting to have an encounter with an experienced JW! It is also true that when we met again in Courtney and Gail's home, I was more prepared, however, I was not that much more prepared so why had things turned out so differently?

    The conclusion that I finally arrived at is as follows. When I first met up with Chris – we met in the home of a lady who apparently did not want to know the TRUTH. After publicly declaring that God had brought her to the Assembly, when the Minister of that fellowship, warned her of the dangers of reading a certain publication she rejected his advice outright and refused to accept his teaching. She then left the fellowship and later was willing to invite a JW into her home to instruct her. She did not want a 'born-again believer' to instruct her, but was very willing to open her home to any and every false teacher that was available either in person, like Chris, or in a magazine such as THE PLAIN TRUTH! When I tried to counter the arguments put forward by her new 'teacher,' I was not able to say anything of value because she had already proved that she was not willing to listen.

    When we met some months later in the Ferguson's home, we met in a home where everyone present wanted the truth. Not only Courtney and Gail, but the other believers who were there as well. On that occasion, I am sure that all the 'believers,' were praying that they would not be deceived; they wanted the TRUTH.

Sadly, today there is a message being proclaimed that says that 'love' is the only thing that matters. Not the TRUTH only LOVE! However, we need to remember that if we are followers of Jesus, the Messiah of Israel, He said: -

"I am the way, the truth, and the life. No one comes to the Father except through Me."
John 14.6

God's love for His creation led Him to 'give' His Son for your redemption. However, God's Son is **'The Truth'** that we so desperately need to bring us to God! We do not need just any old teaching; we need THE TRUTH!

Moving on from there, I would now like to conclude my memories of the 'contacts' that I had been given by mentioning a particular family that was on my list, a man and his wife and two lovely teenage children, a boy and a girl.

In fact, this particular family who we will now call family 'Y' was one of the main reasons that Bill was willing to travel to QueQue in the first place in order to 'plant' an Assembly in the town. This family claimed to have come to know The Lord in an Assembly in another town, possibly in South Africa. He met them some years before when he was starting a Baptist Church, and 'Y' advised him that they did not want to attend a non-Pentecostal fellowship. However, when

Bill returned and told them that he was establishing a Pentecostal fellowship, he had not shown much enthusiasm. In fact, I am not sure he attended a single meeting while Bill was in town!

Nevertheless, when I visited, I was well received, and a few weeks later they arrived in force for the Sunday evening service, at the Globe and Phoenix Hall. There were eight of them, 'Y' and his wife, son and daughter, and his brother, and his wife and two children. That night the congregation could not have been more than ten people before they arrived, so their arrival almost doubled our numbers. It was great to see these two families in Church, however, I had already discovered that 'Y' could be very critical. As a result, I was very concerned about how things would turn out that evening, as the addition of two families like theirs would really help us to get established in the town. It was therefore vital that they were not offended by anything that evening.

By this time, we possibly had an accomplished musician and most likely Alison Hardwicke was on the piano so the music would have been more than acceptable, and Wayne Ferguson was leading the meeting. However, when I looked at Wayne, after the two families had arrived, I realised that **his hair was really long** and he needed a haircut desperately. He had explained to me that because he was working so far out of town, establishing a gold mine with his brother, he was never in town long enough, and at the right time, to get a haircut. As I looked at my 'worship leader' I began to wonder how 'Y' and his family were reacting?

After leading a few inspiring choruses Wayne

asked if anyone had a testimony to give that evening. The only person to respond was his girlfriend Sylvia who rose to her feet and came up to the front. Now it is important that you realise that Sylvia was a tall lady and that night she was wearing a **very short mini skirt** standing up at the front giving her testimony. Sadly, I must confess, that I am not sure that I heard Sylvia's testimony, as I was more concerned with how 'Y' and his family were responding to '**long hair and mini skirts'** that evening.

It was around that time that I began to get quite angry. Although 'Y' and his family had not said anything **'I KNEW'** what they were thinking and thought to myself, **"What right have THEY to be critical, they do not know Wayne or Sylvia."**

Shortly after that, it was time for me to get up and preach. As I stood to my feet, to my shame, I knew that I had to say something about the importance of not being critical and judgmental. As a result, as I have just said, to my shame, I did include words to that effect in my message that were aimed at 'Y' and his family and not anyone else. How bad is that? However, I am pretty sure that I can honestly say it never took place again. It is not the preacher's job to 'convict' men and woman of their sin; it is the work of the Holy Spirit!

It was not long afterwards that I was in town one morning when I saw 'Y' and his wife on the other side of the road. I immediately crossed over the road to speak to them with a warm greeting on my lips. However, to my surprise 'Y' responded by saying, **"It is because of Ministers like you that I am not in Church every Sunday. How can you walk around town like that?"**

In the height of Summer QueQue and much of Rhodesia had the capacity to become very hot as many reading this account will know. At that time many men had taken to wearing what were called Safari Suits, which were really very suitable for the climate and quite smart as well. You could buy suits with long trousers or short trousers and that morning I was wearing a short safari suit because of the heat. Because of the response to my presence and his evident hostility I did not spend much time in conversation and stepped aside to let them get on their way.

Sometime later, when I arrived home and meditated on what had taken place, I decided to pay 'Y' and his family a visit that same evening. Because of the comments that morning, I arrived at their home wearing a collar and tie and wearing **'long'** trousers. When I was met at the door by 'Y', he greeted me with what I felt was a rather 'smug' look on his face. It made me feel as if he was congratulating himself on succeeding in bringing this young minister into line by teaching him how to dress.

After a short conversation, I made the reason for my visit very plain, by making a suggestion to 'Y' which went something like the following, **"'Y' I have taken note of what you said, and I am therefore prepared to make a deal with you, that is, if you are willing to accept it. Because you have been offended by how I dress in public, I will never be seen in public wearing shorts as long as I am the Minister of the Assembly in QueQue, however if I am going to do this, I expect to see you in Church every week. Those are my conditions."**

Without giving my proposal much consideration 'Y' replied that he was not prepared to accept my proposal. As a result, I then said, **"If you are not willing to accept my proposition then I will continue to dress as I feel fit as a Minister of the Gospel."**

With that I said goodbye and sadly, we never had the pleasure of seeing them in the Assembly again.

Having said what I have just said, I feel it is important that I add something in case you misunderstand what I am trying to convey. I do not agree with the idea that is so prevalent at this time that 'dress' is not important. Many people today excuse their 'sloppy' dress by saying, **"God looks on the heart, not on what you wear."**

Well of course that is true up to a point, however, many have taken liberties which are far removed from what that statement is supposed to convey. Why do we think it is acceptable to a Holy God to stand on a platform representing the King of kings and The Lord of lords in dirty, scruffy, or damaged clothing? In most businesses that deal with the public, that is still totally unacceptable, even in this very permissive age. However, in spite of this, some appear to think that being dressed for the beach, the garden, or the workshop is good enough for a man or woman of God to stand as a representative of the Church of the living God.

When I get up to preach, I try to make sure that I am dressed in a way fitting to represent my **LORD!** I usually still wear a tie and jacket depending on the time of the year, it gets very hot in Benidorm and in the height of Summer, I forgo the jacket. At the Bible Study midweek, I generally dispense with the tie and jacket, but still make sure that I am smartly dressed---- for goodness' sake I represent The Lord of Heaven and

Earth, why would I dress in scruffy, dirty, or damaged clothing?

While I am on the subject, what is wrong with the leaders of so many congregations today who allow the musicians to dress so inappropriately when leading the worship? When has it become acceptable for a worship leader to wear a cap (indoors) when leading the worship? That may well be how 'secular musicians' dress, however they generally have no desire or interest in representing the God who Created them so they can represent the prince of the power of darkness if they so wish! However, surely 'CHRISTIAN WORSHIP LEADERS' should show more respect for the God who Created them, as when they lead worship they represent 'HEAVEN.' The angels of God are careful when in the presence of God, why do we think we can dress just any old how. Brethren, it is time we smartened up, we are 'THE AMBASSADORS OF HEAVEN!'

There is so much more that I want to say on this subject and I have mentioned to some of my friends that I would like to write a book entitled, **'WHY?'** Why are we doing these things? **WHY?**

Having mentioned some of the 'contacts' that I 'inherited,' when I arrived in QueQue we can now begin to look at what took place during my first stay in the town.

Having taken the Sunday morning and evening services for the first time in my new Assembly, it was time for my first mid-week Bible Study. This was attended by the grand total of five people. The study that I gave that evening was on the importance of building on the correct foundation which is, of course,

The Lord Jesus Christ. Once this is laid, and we are saved and part of the 'church,' we ought to be careful how we 'build' on this wonderful foundation. As an example, we need to avoid building with wood, hay, and straw, as the fire of God's judgement will reveal it when He returns and it will all be burned up.

Having spoken about the importance of not using certain materials I then stressed that we ought to build with gold, silver, and precious stones because then we will be rewarded when Jesus returns. That evening I made it clear that my aim was to build with gold, silver, and precious stones in this pioneer work in QueQue. In fact, that evening I made it clear that we were going to build as revealed in the Scriptures and understood by their new minister, one A.B.Robertson. **I Corinthians 3.1-17**

During those first few days I made a point of visiting the rest of the contacts that I had been given. After visiting a number of homes, the one thing that became clear to me was that the people were very confused about the Holy Spirit and in particular the 'Baptism of the Holy Spirit.' As a result, I announced on my second weekend in town that at the next Bible Study, I would be speaking on the 'Baptism of the Holy Spirit.

Once the news got out, I was informed that a number of people from other Churches were planning to come and listen to what I had to say on the subject. Among them was the Youth Leader, that I have already mentioned, another was Richard Morley, an Elder in the Baptist Church, and another was the Dutch Reformed Minister.

When I learned of the interest being shown in

my chosen topic, I became very concerned and felt quite inadequate for the task. I prepared the teaching that I was going to give very carefully, and it caused me to be much in prayer for the coming evening. In fact, I realised that I needed God's help more than ever before for the upcoming study, in particular after my 'brave' words at the Bible Study the week before.

When the evening arrived, instead of there being only five people who arrived at the Bible Study the week before, I found myself facing a congregation of around twenty people. As anticipated, they included the local Dutch Reformed Minister, a Baptist Elder, the Youth Worker previously mentioned and the leader of the Scripture Union in Rhodesia who happened to be in town that day and staying with him. I was truly amazed to see the congregation that had arrived, and with a certain amount of trepidation proceeded to bring the Bible Study that I had prepared.

At the end of the study, I asked if there were any questions and as far as I can remember there was only one. Having received the question, I proceeded to answer it and was rather surprised when the man who had asked the question then said, **"Twist that again."**

In fact, I was more than 'surprised', I was 'shocked' at his response, and also a little annoyed. But I did as he requested and repeated what I had already said and, in his words, proceeded to **"twist it again."**

The meeting ended soon after that, and we all made our way home. During the short time that I was in QueQue, everything that I believed about the Holy Spirit, and indeed everything else, was challenged repeatedly by all sorts of different people. I believe that the man who asked the question was subsequently baptised in the Holy Spirit and many years later he contacted me in England and asked me to visit his brother who had been diagnosed with cancer which I was only too happy to do.

When Roland Pletts read these notes, he provided me with some interesting detail about the Baptist Elder who attended the meeting that evening. Roland was to follow me in QueQue and got to know him very well. The following is what Roland had to say,

"Comment on Richard Morley- during my time in QueQue he was regular in fellowship and fully supported us. Being a construction engineer he also helped in the planning and construction of the new church building that we built. He basically helped oversee the entire process, no mean task for people like us and, although many others helped, I can say confidently it would not have been achieved without him."

I am grateful to Roland for this bit of information and want to make it very clear that Richard and his wife were lovely Christians who did a great work in the town. We got on very well and I highly respected him.

Getting back to my story, during my time in QueQue as I have already said, I was challenged on everything that I believed. As an example, I had many talks with the Dutch Reformed Minister who really felt that he would be doing The Lord a favour if he 'converted' me to Calvinism. He told me of his own experience with The Lord and said that when he was first converted, he **'clutched at any straw'** and went to the Full Gospel Church, which being a Pentecostal Church was very similar to the Assemblies of God. However, when he grew wiser, he moved to the Baptist

Church and became a Baptist Minister. Much later, he advised me, he really **'arrived'** when he joined the Dutch Reformed Church and became one of their Ministers! It seemed from my humble perspective that he had started well but something had gone wrong! However, we became good friends and we had some good conversations which I really enjoyed.

As you are now possibly wondering, you may or may not be pleased to know that he failed to 'convert' me to Calvinism! However, he did introduce me to many of the amazing books written by the Puritans many years before. These books were all very challenging and due to his influence, I read a number of them at that time.

The hall that we used for our meetings was not suitable in many ways; however, it was all that was available when we began our work in QueQue. One side of the building was closed in with large roll down tarpaulins which made it easy for mosquitoes and other insects to gain entrance. It belonged to the Globe and Phoenix gold mine who usually used it for events on a Saturday night where a lot of alcohol was consumed and a great number of cigarettes were smoked. As a result, there was the smell of beer and cigarettes every Sunday morning when I arrived to open up. The hall then had to be swept and tidied up and the chairs arranged in order for our meetings.

My usual Sunday morning would begin when I travelled the short distance to the meeting place, where I would open the hall, sweep up, put the chairs in order, and place the song books on the seats. I would then, usually, get in my car and go and pick up a few people for the meeting. Once back, I would welcome the people, pick up my piano accordion and begin the service. After the worship, I would preach the message and then play my accordion for the closing hymn and then go to the door to say goodbye to the congregation. After this I would collect the song books and take certain people home. In time, praise God, others got on board, like Wayne who would lead the worship, and Alison who played the piano, and I was no longer a one-man band.

That year, 1972, Christmas day fell on a Monday and we had a reasonable turnout for the Sunday morning service on the 24th and for our Christmas Day service on the Monday. As I was on my own, the Ferguson family graciously invited me to join them for a family Christmas lunch in Gwelo on the Sunday afternoon. However, I declined to accompany them as I was not prepared to cancel the Sunday evening service.

That evening as I waited for the congregation to arrive, I was pleasantly surprised to see a young woman arrive accompanied by her Greek boyfriend. She had been to our services on a number of occasions but it was the first time that he had been. I picked up my piano accordion and led a number of songs in worship to The Lord. I am sure that some were Carols as it was, after all, Christmas Day; however, I am sure I included others as well. Having led the singing, I then ministered God's Word to my very small congregation of one believer and one unsaved man.

After the meeting I invited them up to my apartment (Wayne was in Gwelo), so that we could enjoy a coffee together and so that I would have more of an opportunity to speak to this young man of Greek origin. That evening I tried in vain to produce a Cappuccino coffee without the necessary ingredients, which I found to be impossible. However, we all had a good evening.

One Sunday afternoon sometime later, whilst preparing for the evening meeting, I felt The Lord directing me to speak on the 'flood' of Noah's day. The Scripture verses could well have been the following: -

"But as the days of Noah were, so also will the coming of the Son of Man be, for as in the days before the flood, they were eating and drinking, marrying and giving in marriage, until the day that Noah entered the ark, and did not know until the flood came and took them all away, so also will the coming of the Son of Man be." Matthew 24.37-39

But when I began to think about it, I felt that if I was going to preach on Noah's Ark and the 'flood' I really needed to include a lot more detail in the message than I could possibly prepare for that evening's service. The more I thought of it the more I was convinced that preaching on THE FLOOD OF NOAH was for another day and not for that Sunday evening.

As it happened, there was something else on my heart and I spent a lot of time preparing that message. It was not long before I had a great introduction, which is always a good idea, as if you lose the congregation during the introduction, you have possibly lost them for the entire service. A little later I was satisfied that the main body of the message was more than satisfactory, however no matter how hard I tried I was not able to put together a satisfactory conclusion.
Finally, after struggling for a long time I realised that

the time had gone, and in disgust I threw the whole lot in the waste-paper basket. I then jotted down a few verses on a piece of paper including **Matthew 24.37-39**, handed everything over to The Lord, went and had a bath, got dressed and left for the meeting.

At that time, our evening congregation was very small with no more than ten people attending. However, that evening it appeared that revival had broken out as around 15 people arrived for the meeting, five of them, first time visitors. As I saw the **'crowd'** arrive I was really quite concerned as this was our biggest Sunday Evening turnout since I had been in town. The problem was that I basically had nothing to say, just a few verses jotted down on a piece of paper. But The Lord was good to me, as I saw the answer to my problems coming towards the door in the form of one Brian Boshoff.

Sometime before, Brian suggested that we ask different members of the congregation to give their personal testimonies at the service on the Sunday evening. Although I had agreed with him, I had never done anything about it. That evening when I saw Brian coming towards the door, I realised that the time had arrived, and Brian was the ideal person to put 'his' idea into practice. As a result, I was very relieved and praised God when he agreed to give his testimony that evening. And so it was that after some choruses and most likely a hymn I asked Brian to give his testimony.

When he got up to speak that evening, he took the opportunity with both hands, and gave a very full testimony of his life. As can be expected, this took some time, but, as I felt that I had nothing to say, I was quite happy when his testimony continued for some time. In fact, as I listened, I encouraged him under my breath to take all the time he needed, and if he took up all the time that evening, I would be very happy.

It was some weeks before that a young schoolgirl by the name of Alison Hardwicke had begun to attend our meetings. When I discovered that she was an accomplished musician I asked her if she would like to play for us. She was a 'spiritual girl' and instead of saying "yes", or "no", she replied that she would pray about it. The following Sunday, I was really struggling to play the hymns and choruses on my piano accordion, (not on purpose I must add) and after the service she came to me and said that she would be willing to be our pianist. As a result of my poor performance, it is possible that she may well have said that 'The Lord had spoken to her,' however, she was truly a blessing on the piano and became one of our most faithful members.

Our new pianist, had a younger sister by the name of Penny who had also started attending the meetings. On this particular evening another young woman was in the meeting and she was sitting next to Penny. I had known her in Salisbury where she and her husband (boyfriend) had stolen the car belonging to two Salvation Army Missionaries. She was now living in QueQue and her 'husband,' whether the same man I do not know, was in jail. Among the other newcomers was Mrs. Clark, her daughter Cynthia, and her fiancé Rob Cloete, who were all attending for the first time.

After some time, Brian finally finished his very interesting testimony and it was time for me to speak. Although I knew that I had very little to say, as I began to speak the Holy Spirit took over and I preached one of the most anointed messages of my life. In spite of this, as I was ministering under the power of the spirit, I saw the young woman sitting next to Penny not listening and causing a disturbance by talking while I was speaking. When I saw this, I pointed my finger at her, told her in no uncertain terms that the message was for her, and that she had better listen, keep quiet, or leave. After the meeting a number of people told me that it was not only this young woman, who sat up and took notice when I spoke, but the whole congregation. I have no doubt whatsoever that The Lord was anointing His Word in a special way that night.

I only preached for a short time that evening, and it was not long afterwards that I made an appeal and out of that small congregation 5 people made some sort of decision for Jesus. One of them was Mrs. Clark who went on to serve Jesus for the rest of her life. When her husband Ernie found out, he was not impressed, and wanted to stop his wife going to church. Despite his opposition, she was not put off and not long before he died, he eventually came to Christ. What a meeting that was, possibly a meeting that transformed that little fellowship. Praise God for Brian's testimony and for The Lord's anointing upon a young Minister of the Gospel who only had a couple of verses of Scripture and nothing much else to say.

I was enjoying living in the flat, but one day there was a real commotion in our block which turned out to be some domestic problem. I became involved with my immediate neighbours in trying to help in the situation. This resulted in the neighbours getting to know who I was and sometime later they came to the door with a request that I take the funeral of their father who had just died. I had, up to that point, never taken a funeral and so I did my best to direct them in another direction.

My neighbour said, **"My father has just died and we wanted to know whether you would do the funeral for us?**

"I am sorry to hear that, and offer you my deepest condolences, but I will be out of town from this afternoon for a few days." I replied.

"That is not a problem as the funeral can only take place at the beginning of next week." (I am not too sure of all the details) he said.

I asked, **"Was your dad connected in any way to one of the local Churches?"**

He said, **"Yes, he was Christened in the Congregational Church."** (Not sure which one.)

I suggested, **"Surely it would be better to ask them to take the funeral as your dad had some connection to that Church. Have you asked them if they will conduct the ceremony?"**

He replied, **"They do not have a minister at present and no services have been held in the building for some time."**

"What about the other churches in town, have you asked them?" I asked.

"No, but we would really rather have you do it if you can, please."

By that time, I realised that whether I liked it or not, I would be taking the funeral service. As I was leaving town that afternoon, I agreed to visit them as soon as I returned in order to get some details about the man who had died and where the funeral was to take place. That afternoon I left to take a house meeting in Gatooma and then I travelled on to Salisbury. I needed some advice, as this would be the first funeral that I had ever taken. Brother Stegman was very helpful and gave me some excellent advice which enabled me to conduct the funeral a few days later.

This was my very first funeral and I was grateful when it was all over. It was a graveside funeral and I found it difficult to walk at the correct speed, when I was walking ahead of the pall bearers who were carrying the coffin to the graveside. The family were very grateful and shortly afterwards Mrs. Olive Meyer, the wife of the deceased, and her daughter Carrol both came to know The Lord. Mrs. Meyer's grandson also attended the services on many occasions and could quite possibly have made a decision for The Lord at that time. My neighbour and his wife also attended the Assembly on one occasion but that is another story. It is interesting to note, that of all the funerals that I have ever taken this was the only one where I 'know' that people came to know The Lord as a direct result of the service.

Sometime later, after Olive Meyer had become a regular attender at our Sunday morning services, she failed to appear. As a result, on the Monday morning I went around to her house to see how she was. She apologised for not being in the meeting and explained that she had terrible pain in her legs and could hardly walk. The doctor had recommended using a 'heat lamp' on her legs to relieve the pain that she was feeling. In spite of that she was far from well and still could not walk very far and definitely not as far as the Globe and Phoenix Hall.

On that particular morning, I was feeling far from 'spiritual and anointed,' but I spoke to her and her daughter about the willingness of Jesus to heal the sick. I showed a number of verses of Scripture to her and then asked if they had any oil. They replied that all they had in the house was 'cooking oil' but they brought it to me and I anointed her with oil and prayed for her. I cannot really say it was the prayer of faith but I prayed and then went on my way.

The following Sunday, when she failed to appear I must admit I was not surprised as I really had prayed a prayer of 'no faith,' when I visited her home. When I visited her home the following day, you can imagine my surprise when I discovered that she was as right as rain. Not only was she better, but she had given her 'heat lamp,' to a friend as she no longer needed it. In addition, she was now able to walk to and from and the town centre with no problem. Sadly, the reason she had not been at the meeting was that her grandson had fallen off his bicycle on the Saturday and broken his arm, and she had been looking after him. How faithful is our God, despite our lack of faith, He is faithful to His Word! Hallelujah!

In December 1973, shortly before I left QueQue, Olive Meyer wrote her testimony in our newsletter. Apparently in June 1966 she had lost the use of her legs completely. Nevertheless, after some time she was able to walk again but had to take painkillers because of the terrible pain in her legs. When she had been prayed for and anointed with oil in May 1973, The Lord had completely healed her. From that time until she wrote her testimony in December 1973, she had been free from pain. Praise be to The Lord, our Saviour, Healer and King!

The next story is rather sad and involves a

young man that I had met whilst in Gwelo, when I visited as a relief clerk on the Railways. At the time Bill Mews was the minister in Gwelo and we attended all of the meetings with him. I remember travelling to Selukwe with him in a crowded Peugeot 304. They were great times and as we were about the same age, we were a great encouragement to each other. Sadly, the last I had heard of him I was told that he was backslidden.

As a result, I was very encouraged to receive a phone call from him when I was ministering in QueQue. He was not only serving The Lord but he was now an Evangelist. In fact, he was in Gwelo and wanted to know if he could come to QueQue and hold an Evangelistic Crusade with us.

After some conversation I suggested that he take a Sunday evening meeting for us and then we would talk about it some more. That Sunday evening my neighbours the Meyer's came for the first time. To say that it was a good meeting would be very incorrect, and as a result, my neighbours never came again. despite this, because of my previous involvement with this man, I agreed to him returning for a week of special meetings.

It was around half way into the week when I realised that his doctrinal views were very different to mine and from then on, I was on tenterhooks right through every meeting. During that week he preached with varying success every night but succeeded in befriending most of my congregation. However, the last night was something to remember.

Before we continue, it is important that you understand that a terrorist war had begun in Rhodesia and all 'white and coloured' young men were called up for military service to assist the mainly 'black' regular army. There was a regular unit called the Rhodesia Light Infantry (RLI) which was composed entirely of young 'white' men but the Rhodesia African Rifles (RAR) was a 'black' unit who were all volunteers and led by white officers. From the time that I had entered the Ministry I was no longer required to participate in 'training exercises' or 'call ups' which took place on a regular basis throughout the year. However, most of the men in my congregation were required to do their bit.

That night we only had two 'young white men' in the service and at the end of the meeting the preacher said something like the following, **"There is a young man in the meeting this evening, and I could come and put my hand upon your shoulders. You are not right with God and have not asked The Lord Jesus to come into your heart. You will be going into the army in the next few days and you will not be coming back. You must get right with God before it is too late"**

The words may not be entirely correct but that is basically what he said. There were only two young men who could fit the description that he gave and one of them was Rob Cloete whose girlfriend was Mrs. Clark's daughter. According to his own testimony given some months later, Rob was not right with God and when he got up to leave that night his legs were like jelly. As a result, he needed to be supported by his girlfriend in order to get to the door. I am not sure about the other young man but Rob was very frightened by what had been said.

After packing up that night, we returned to

Wayne's flat and no sooner had we arrived when the phone rang. The first call was from Mrs. Clark who said that if her husband Ernie found out what had been said at the meeting that night, she possibly would not be able to attend again. She also told me that Rob did not want to see the visiting preacher at all, but that he would like to see me as soon as possible. As a result, we arranged to meet the following day as he was going into the army that week.

The second call was from Courtney, as the other young man in the meeting that night was a relative of his from Gwelo. As his call was also about what had taken place at the meeting that night, I handed the phone to our guest.

The following day Rob came to see me and he began by explaining why the meeting the night before had made such an impression on him. He explained that he was an instructor in the army, and as a result, he was never called up to go on patrols. But, on this particular 'call up,' he had been assigned to go on patrol for the first time. As a result, he would be exposed to much more danger than usual and that was why his knees had turned to jelly the night before. I explained to Rob that the most important thing was to know Jesus as Lord and Saviour as none of us could know the day of our death. I shared with him the way of salvation and told him that it was the devil who was out to do him in and if he committed his life to Christ who knows what God could do.

After talking for some time, we got on our knees and prayed and he asked The Lord Jesus to save him after which I prayed for him. A little while later I rose from my knees but Rob remained where he was for a long time before he finally got up. He then declared that all the people of QueQue should experience what he had just experienced as he had truly met with The Lord and was now well and truly saved. Hallelujah!

A few days later he reported for duty to do his army call up and an amazing thing happened. They told him that they no longer needed him to go out on patrol duties, and in fact he was not needed at all and could return home. Hallelujah, what a Saviour! He and his girlfriend went on to get married and continued to follow The Lord in another part of the country.

Just before the Sunday evening meeting that I have described, I had been looking forward to saying goodbye to my friend the evangelist; however, there was a problem. He wanted to continue on for another week in QueQue having nightly meetings in the Globe and Phoenix Hall. When I suggested that we would not be too keen to support another week of meetings, he said that if we did not want to do it then he would continue on his own. I was very conscious that my congregation were mostly either new believers or young people and although I was not willing to support another week of meetings in the hall that we used, neither was I keen to see him continue on his own.

As a result of my concerns, I had been to see Courtney and Gail Ferguson and they agreed to host a week of house meetings in their home where our evangelist could preach and where we could keep an eye on him and our congregation. He agreed reluctantly and the week went off with no apparent difficulties. However, sadly, after I left, he returned and caused a few problems for Roland Pletts, who took my place when I left QueQue.

One day I went around to pick up one of the young people for a meeting and his father engaged me in conversation. He was a very successful business man in the town and our conversation went something like this,

The father asked, **"Are you planning to build a church in QueQue?"**

To which I replied, **"Yes in time, although we have only been going a short while, that is definitely our intention."**

"Well do not come to me for a donation, I have already given donations to the building funds of the Baptist's, the Apostolic Faith Mission and the Full Gospel Church and I do not plan to give to anymore," he said.

"Thanks for letting me know, I said, **but that is not the way we operate. We expect our members to contribute, not people who have nothing to do with our movement, so we would have no intention of asking you to contribute to any future building fund."**

I am not sure when we managed to acquire a plot of land in QueQue but it was most likely during the ministry of Roland Pletts, when he arranged for our lovely new church building to be constructed. Having said that, I must admit that I could understand this businessman's point of view if he had been approached by all of these different fellowships. Why should he, a man, who was possibly an unbeliever, or maybe the member of one of the so called 'established churches' support an organisation like ours? I meant every word that I said, and I have never in all of my ministry consciously sort to finance the work of God with money given by the 'unbeliever.'

It was wonderful to have his son attend our meetings, as he gave his life to Christ and also had a mighty baptism in the Holy Spirit. Sadly, I do not know what happened to him after I left QueQue but it would be wonderful to know that he went on to serve The Lord for the rest of his life.

Whilst we are on the subject of 'money', one of the people in my congregation, earned his living as a prospector, and whilst I was in QueQue he sold a valuable claim to a big mining concern. As a result, he was, as it were, 'in the money.' Just after this sale, I happened to meet him while visiting another member of our congregation and he asked me about the financial affairs of the fellowship. At the time our income was very small and we were relying upon the National Development Fund to meet the shortfall in our monthly finances.

After explaining the situation, he suggested that he would make up the difference at the end of each month if I advised him when there was a 'shortfall' in the Assembly finances. He made it clear that he wanted to honour The Lord who had blessed him with such a good sale. Although I really appreciated what he was saying I declined his offer.

At that time, we only took up an offering at the 'Breaking of Bread' service which was held on a Sunday morning. This was the 'believers' meeting and it was the 'believers,' who supported the work of God and not the unsaved. On the Sunday evening when we specifically invited the unbelievers to attend the meeting, we preached the Gospel and never took up an offering but sadly he seldom came to the morning service.

When I declined his offer, he said that if we did not want his money, he would give it to the Baptist Church. I replied that it was not that we did not want his money, but the proper place to give his tithes and offerings was at The Lord's table on a Sunday morning. We would be very grateful for whatever The Lord told him to put in the offering but it was between him and God! It was not long after this that he began to attend the Sunday morning Breaking of Bread service, on a regular basis for which I praised God. What if anything, he put in the offering, was not my business, it was between him and God.

Getting back to talking about the young people in our fellowship I must mention another young person. This was a 13-year-old girl who started attending the services with Wayne and Sylvia. However, despite being only 13, she looked and dressed as if she was going on 18 years old. Wayne and Sylvia were aware that she was mixing with a young man a lot older than herself, and that there were drugs involved, but they were hoping that if she had a real experience with The Lord she would be saved and delivered from the terrible life into which she was heading. When she began to attend our meetings, because of her age, I went around to the home to introduce myself to her parents.

It is important to mention that her parents did not know about their daughter's involvement with this young man and it is also possible that the parents were unaware that she was attending our meetings. As a result, they were not all that keen to have me show up on their doorstep and after a brief conversation they informed me that they had their own church (I think it was the same one that my neighbours father attended as a child, --- closed with no minister), and that their daughter would attend church with them as and when they attended. I was very sad to discover this attitude but had to leave it in their hands.

It may well have been the following week, but it was very soon after I had visited their home, that I was visiting Kingston's (the bookshop) where the mother worked. When she spotted me, she called me over so that she and her husband, who happened to be there at the time, could speak with me. After a brief conversation they said, **"We would like our daughter to attend your church."**

I was pleasantly surprised and naturally agreed right away. Praise God, she was able to attend our services once again. I later discovered that the police had visited shortly after I had been around to their home and warned the parents that their daughter was mixing with a known drug dealer. I am sure this was a real shock to them as they did seem a very nice couple. Perhaps that had a bearing on their change of heart and mind.

Another one of our young people, was a young woman who had a boyfriend who was living and working in South Africa. I have no idea why, but she liked to call me her **'little Pastor,'** or something like that which did not really endear me to her. However, as you know I have been called **'AB Baby'** and **'Abie my boy'** so what's in a name?

Nevertheless, one Sunday evening she returned home from the Assembly to discover that her boyfriend had returned from South Africa. Apparently, it was not long before she realised that something was wrong and suggested that she took him to see me. However, he was not too keen and it was many hours later that he agreed to see me.

That evening, while this was going on, when I went to bed, I felt the need to pray and almost fell asleep on my knees praying in 'tongues.' It was around 2.00am that I heard a loud banging on our front door. Both Wayne and I got up to investigate but when he saw me, he left it to me, and went back to bed, as he had an early start the next morning. I called through the locked door to establish who was knocking at such an unearthly time, and heard this young woman say that she had brought her boyfriend to see me.

As it was such a 'natural' thing to bring your boyfriend to see your Minister at 2.00am in the morning, I opened the door and invited them in. When they were seated, she explained that she had been trying to get him to come and see me since she got back from the meeting early that Sunday evening. Having heard what she had to say, I turned to her boyfriend and said, **"What is the problem?"**

He replied, **"It's the Devil in me!"**

As I looked at the young man who sat on the couch in front of me my first thought was that it was the 'devil,' of drink, or the 'devil,' of drugs, I had no idea that it could be anything else. However, suddenly the Holy Spirit came upon me and I KNEW that it was not drink or drugs, but demons.

Once The Lord had given me that word of knowledge, I was in no doubt what the problem was and so I commanded the evil spirit to leave him. I spoke in a VERY LOUD VOICE and all the time was conscious that we were living in a block of flats and could not help but wonder at my neighbour's response, if they heard me. However, within a few minutes it was all over and he was totally free. In fact, within a very short time, they left and as he went down the stairs, I heard him exclaim, **"Wow, I feel so clean!"**

Before they left, I prayed with them and told them that I wanted to see both of them later that day. When they returned later that day, I explained the Gospel to him and led him to The Lord and he immediately asked to be baptised, which leads to another story.

About that time, I had become increasingly disturbed about the large number of Christian believers who had accepted Jesus as their Lord and Saviour, been through the waters of Baptism, and yet continued to smoke and drink just as they had before. I had also been reading books written by the Puritans who believed in a separated life, something that I also believed! Yet what I was seeing in the lives of so many Christians was making me increasingly disturbed. As a result, I decided that, before I baptised anybody else, I needed to observe a change of behaviour. I came to the conclusion that if people wanted to continue to 'smoke,' they should not ask me to Baptise them!

Sadly, it was at this crucial time that I took this decision. The boyfriend came from a Church of Christ background which believe that you are not saved if you are not baptised. As a result, 'baptism' was very important for him, as he believed that he could not be 'saved' unless he was baptised. I have to confess that this decision of mine made a negative impact upon this young man in spite of the amazing deliverance that he had experienced. When I was not prepared to baptise him, we lost contact with him so I do not know what became of him.

So, before we go any further, let us have a look at what the Scriptures say about 'baptism?' Paul told his jailer, **"Believe on The Lord Jesus Christ, and you will be saved ------. ------. And immediately he and all his family were baptized." Acts 16.31,33**

In fact, instead of putting barriers in the way of this young man, I ought to have considered my own 'baptism.' If you remember, I had told my minister that I wanted to postpone my water baptism. He had taken me to the Scriptures and shown me that as soon as they were 'saved' they got baptised. They did not need to go to 'baptism classes' or 'wait' and see if their decision was genuine when they gave up smoking. Many times, we want to add things but we should not, as we need to leave it to God. Yes 'repentance,' is vital! In fact, 'belief,' 'repentance,' and 'confession,' are all vital if we are to be saved. However, salvation is a work of God, not of man.

Moving on from there, whilst living in the flat in Fitchlea in QueQue, I would 'prayer walk' the area often on a Sunday evening after the meeting. At that time QueQue was growing rapidly and I was really keen to see people come to know The Lord Jesus as their Saviour. There were the Gold Mines in the area, which was the reason that the town was established in the first place. In addition, there was the Rhodesian Iron and Steel Company (RISCO) the iron and steel works in Redcliff. But that was not all, there was also a large fertilizer factory, and the Chrome Mines which were all making an impact upon our town. The 'white' community was growing rapidly and so it was difficult to rent homes, but naturally the 'black' community was also growing and a similar problem was facing them as well, but we will consider that when I return to QueQue.

Because Courtney Ferguson had been in the mining business for many years, he introduced me to a number of very interesting characters. One of these amazing characters was an elderly lady who with her late husband had been in the mining business all her life. When I met her, she was living in a very unusual house as far as I was concerned. The house had been created out of used 44-gallon fuel drums. These had been beaten flat, numbered and secured together to provide a movable home which could be taken down and re-erected whenever the gold ran out and they had to move to a new location. Courtney informed me that what she didn't know about gold mining was not worth knowing.

At the time that I met her, an elderly man was living with her on the mine. He had been the owner of an extremely successful second-hand car business in Salisbury, but one day he had just walked out and never went back. It seems that he had just got tired of the 'rat race' and dropped out, choosing to live in the bush sharing a 'used 44-gallon fuel drum house' with an elderly lady on a gold mine. Years later, I visited her in Salisbury, where she was living in an 'old peoples home.' I suspect that she had moved into town for safety as a result of the ongoing 'bush war' in Rhodesia.

As you have already discovered, I was, **always prepared well in advance,** for the services! Sadly, on many **Sunday afternoons** I would still be at my desk preparing **for that Sunday evening's** service an hour before the meeting! On one of those Sundays, I heard the most wonderful sound. It was one of my neighbours who lived on the ground floor playing with his little daughter in the garden. I was really blessed to hear her squeals of delight as her father played with her on the lawn and when I looked out of the window, I was able to see them both. You need to realise that at this time I was still awaiting God's answer to my third earnest prayer prayed nearly two years before at Lions River!

On another afternoon during the week, something happened that possibly could have brought about the end of my life, or if not the end of my life, possibly the end of my preaching career. I was busy in my room when I overheard a neighbour welcoming his 'girlfriend' who happened to be the 'mother' of one of my congregants, and the 'wife' of her 'father.'

As I sat there, I became increasingly concerned knowing that there was an 'affair' taking place in my building involving the 'mother' of one of my young people. By the way, this had been going on for some time and it was not the first time that she had come visiting, and there was more to the story than I am presenting in this book. As a result, I got on my knees and prayed earnestly about the situation and came to the conclusion that I could not just sit there and do nothing. So, sometime later, after she had gone, I might add, I went downstairs and knocked on my neighbour's door. He was surprised but pleased to see me and welcomed me into his home. However, I was on a mission, and did not beat about the bush but launched in and soon advised him why I had come to visit. After I had explained the reason for my visit, he did not beat about the bush either, and was soon on his feet with the door open, and in as loud a voice as I had used when expelling demons at 2.00am sometime before, he said, **"GET OUT---- OUT--- GET OUT."**

As I was clearly not welcome, I took my leave.

When I reached the safety of my room I fell on my knees and prayed. When I considered what I had done I began to think about the possible outcome of my visit to my neighbour. I saw in my mind's eye, headlines in the local newspaper: -

"LOCAL MINISTER ACCUSES NEIGHBOUR OF ADULTERY!"

Or an even worse headline: -

"LOCAL MINISTER FALSELY ACCUSES NEIGHBOUR OF ADULTERY!"

To be quite frank I had a very bad couple of hours. But as I had another engagement that evening, I was soon on my way out. On my return, I was told that a very angry lady had been to visit, it was the 'mother' of the young woman who was a member of my congregation. It appears that it was a good thing that I was out as I might have been murdered as she was so cross. Sadly, there was no way out, as I now had to visit the lady concerned. This I did, but amazingly, I have no idea how it all ended, yet, one thing is clear, I survived to live another day.

On another occasion whilst visiting a lady who was a

member of my congregation, I invited her husband to come with his wife, as she always attended on her own. I have never forgotten his reply as he said, **"The day I come to church there will be thunder and lightning."**

True enough on the one day that I remember him attending one of our services it was just as he said. I saw him approaching the door of the Globe and Phoenix Hall and there was thunder and lightning all over the place as a big storm was on its way. As he stepped over the threshold he said, **"You see, just as I said, if I come to church there will be thunder and lightning."**

At that time there were two other Pentecostal churches in town, the Apostolic Faith Mission and the Full Gospel Church. In addition, there was the Baptist Church and the Anglican Church, who were ministering mainly to the 'white' community. However, the only Minister that I really had any fellowship with was John Heyns of the Anglican Church. He was a lovely man and became a good friend. On one occasion he said something like this to me, **"I know that we Anglicans can learn a few things from you Pentecostals but you can learn a few things from us as well."**

He was of course correct, and he was the only minister to welcome me back into town when I returned for my second visit to QueQue.

The end of 1973 was fast approaching and the Full Gospel Church arranged a Carol Service and invited the other Churches in town to join them. One of the ministers was asked to share The Word and the other Ministers present were given a portion of Scripture to read, or asked to open or close in prayer. When leaving the church at the end, Richard Morley, who I have mentioned previously came up to me and said, **"You could tell which of the Ministers were filled with the Holy Spirit!"**

I was really amazed at what he said to me that evening. It was apparently obvious to Richard, that some of those present were Holy-Spirit anointed men of God, and others were not. However, most of those present had not been given the opportunity to say much at all, but in spite of that the 'evidence' of being filled with the Holy Spirit was clear for all to see according to this dear brother.

A wedding was in the offing. Wayne and Sylvia were to be married. As a result, Wayne planned to give up the flat as he and Sylvia would find somewhere else to live. When the time came to leave the flat there was a gap of a few days where neither of us had anywhere to stay and we ended up being accommodated briefly by Wayne's brother, Courtney, and his wife, Gail, and their family. They were so very good to me and I praise God for them all.

Praise God for temporary accommodation, but I had to find somewhere to live if I was to stay in QueQue. God was good and I finally managed to rent a house from the Globe and Phoenix Mine, which they were not using at the time. It was a three bedroomed house that had been built many years before and Wayne moved in with me until he and Sylvia were married.

One of the unusual features of the house was the outside bucket toilet. The reason that they had not modernised the house was because the Municipality had plans to build a new road that would take the traffic away from the main street. When the road was eventually built, the house I was renting would have to be knocked down. As a result, the house still had an outside toilet with a bucket, that was removed early every morning, and this was in a town in Rhodesia in 1973!

There were a number of things that I remember about Wayne and Sylvia's wedding which was the very first wedding that I ever took. As an example, at the rehearsal I was not as organised as I should have been, surprise, surprise, and I think Sylvia's mother was more than a little concerned at how things would work out. Another thing that I remember was when the bridal couple were up at the front about to take their vows, I asked them to turn around and face the congregation and give a brief testimony of how they came to know Jesus Christ as their Saviour and Lord. Can you imagine your minister at your wedding doing such a thing? However, amazingly enough, they did it and I am still alive to tell the tale!

The 1973 'Rhodes and Founders' Youth Camp was held that year in Essexvale outside Bulawayo and arranged by Bethshan Assembly. The guest speaker was Henry Duncan who was a very able preacher and brought real blessing to the campers that year. I was not able to be there all the time but I have heard from one who was there, who said that he almost 'froze' to death that weekend. In spite of that it has still been remembered as a great occasion by many of the campers. There were a large number of young people from all over the country and those who organised the camp from Bethshan, did an amazing job.

I had been asked to speak at the Monday morning meeting and so I had to leave very early in the morning to cover the 140 miles to Bulawayo and then travel out to Essexvale, which was some distance out of the city on the Johannesburg Road. That Sunday I was preaching both morning and evening and somehow failed to prepare for this wonderful opportunity. I really did not know what to speak on, but The Lord put one verse on my heart and that was: -

"Open your mouth wide, and I will fill it." Psalm 81.10

Without doubt He did exactly that, as He really did anoint me with the Holy Spirit and 'fill' my mouth that morning.

I arrived at the camp site just minutes before the meeting was due to begin and, praise God, by that time I knew what I was preaching. The Lord placed Genesis 26 upon my heart, the story about how Isaac was required to re-dig, the wells, that his father Abraham had dug many years before. The reason that he was required to re-dig the wells was because they had been filled in by their enemies the Philistines. I spoke about the importance of getting back to doing the things that our 'fathers' in the faith had done which enabled them to witness amazing things. Among the amazing things that they saw were the conversion of large numbers of people, the outpouring of the Holy Spirit, amazing miracles of healing, and the growth of the work of God on every hand.

This had been accomplished because they knew how to pray, which many now fail to do with conviction. They also believed the Bible from Genesis to Revelation and preached it fearlessly. In addition, they spent time together in fellowship and obeyed The Lord by Breaking Bread regularly. These were some of the 'wells' that needed to be dug, if we really want the blessings of God.

After my short visit to the youth camp, I had to return to QueQue and to the responsibilities that God had placed on my shoulders.

Now, believe it or not, there are many things that a Minister is asked to do by members of their congregation over the years, however, this particular 'job,' I volunteered to do. We had an attractive young woman in the fellowship, by the name of Estelle Steyn. She came from a good Christian family in Bulawayo, and was a teacher at the local school, and was also one of our Sunday School teachers. However, Estelle needed to learn to drive, and I volunteered to teach her in my car. Praise God, the pupil was a quick learner and Estelle learned to drive and very soon passed her test. The things we Minister's do!

I have mentioned the visit of my evangelist 'friend' who caused a fair bit of trouble during his visit to QueQue, but as yet I have not mentioned another visitor that we had, who was none other than Paul Lange the minister who had baptised me some years before in Cape Town. He was on a preaching tour of our Rhodesian Assemblies and we were truly blessed to have him visit our new Assembly in QueQue. As usual Paul ministered with authority and blessing, and we were sad to see him go. However, there were two things that I remember in particular from his visit.

The one was that he was not impressed with the Globe and Phoenix Hall that we were meeting in at the time. In fact, he told me that the sooner we found somewhere else to meet the better. However, it was simply not easy to find another venue, but he was correct all the same.

The other, was an incident that happened when he was staying with me. Rhodesia was suffering under economic sanctions at the time and as a result, certain things were not always available to purchase in the shops. So, Paul had come prepared and had packed a number of packets in his case. However, on arriving at my home he discovered that one of the packets had split open and all his clothes etc. were covered in this white powder. (No, it was not drugs--- but for the life of me I cannot remember what it was.) Sadly, to my shame, I confess that, although I offered words of sympathy, I could not but see the funny side. After all they were not MY clothes!

As you are discovering with each page that I write, I am far from perfect, but praise God, He is still working on me!

Sadly, one day I received a phone call from John Stegman which went something like this, **"A.B. I have asked Bill Stevenson to move to Umtali to take charge of the Umtali Assembly, and I would like you to take his place at Hatfield in Salisbury."**

If you remember, Bill had been the Pastor of the Gwelo Assembly when I moved to QueQue, however he had since moved to Hatfield, a new Assembly in Salisbury.

I was shocked, I had been in QueQue for such a short time and so I replied, **"But Brother Stegman, I am just getting going, I have only been here for just over a year."**

John said, **"I know, but we need you in Hatfield. Look, come down for a weekend and see**

what you think, we will provide covering ministry for you in QueQue while you come for a visit!"

As a result, soon after that phone call, I went to Salisbury for a weekend, to preach to the Hatfield Assembly. During my visit, I believe The Lord showed me that they were like 'sheep without a shepherd,' and although I loved the congregation in QueQue with all my heart, I knew that God wanted me in Hatfield. Nevertheless, when I announced that I was leaving, the response of the congregation was much the same as mine had been, when John Stegman had phoned me. One of the congregants in particular, Margie Boshoff, was very clear what she thought when she said something like the following, **"A.B. This is not right, and you are making a mistake, and you are out of God's will by moving."**

It is true that God had been gracious to use me in QueQue but The Lord had someone else lined up to replace me and that was Roland Pletts. In the short time that he was in QueQue, The Lord used him to start a new work in Redcliff which was around 5 miles away, and he was able to plan and erect a new building which was opened before I returned to the town around 16 months later.

Nevertheless, soon after moving back to Salisbury I was walking in town when a friend of mine from another church who knew that I had moved to QueQue called me over and asked me what I was doing in town? He said something like this, **"Hi AB, what are you doing in town?"**

"Hi, ---, I have moved back to Salisbury and am now the Pastor of Hatfield AOG," I replied.

"**Wow, what went wrong?**" He asked.

It was hard for people to understand our

manner of working, and sometimes even harder for us to understand, however, I was at peace with my move to Hatfield as I believed that God was behind it all!

2) HATFIELD ASSEMBLY, SALISBURY. 1974-1975

After I moved to QueQue in 1972 a new Assembly was started in Salisbury, in the suburb of Hatfield, and Bill Stevenson moved from Gwelo to be their Pastor. The building that we occupied had originally been a Dutch Reformed Church, in fact, I believe it was the oldest Dutch Reformed Church building in Salisbury. The address was, 85 St Patrick's Road, and it was right next door to the 'Yellow Orchid' Drive-In Restaurant.

The DRC put the building up for sale, as they had constructed a new church which was a lot bigger and had much better facilities. When he heard that the building was up for sale, John Stegman made an offer for the building on behalf of a new Assembly in Hatfield. However, as the church leaders were not keen to sell to the Assemblies of God, the deal fell through. When this happened, Brother Van den Berg, one of the members of the fledgling Assembly, and a former member of the DRC, took matters into his own hands and purchased the building and then offered it for sale to the AOG. However, when Brother Stegman and the Elders of McChlery Avenue discovered what he had done, they told the dear brother that we could not operate that way. He was told that they would only proceed if the leaders of the DRC were told what was taking place and were willing to give it their blessing.

This was duly done and the Hatfield Assembly was established. However, just before we move on from this subject, I would like to mention one other interesting item about the building. I was later to discover that a clause had been written into the deeds of the building which prohibited the building from ever being used by a 'black' congregation. I am not too sure whether we ever did anything about that 'clause,' however, before I left Zimbabwe, we had a Shona language 'church,' meeting in the building every Sunday afternoon. In addition, their Minister, Philip Chigome, was also caring for the English language congregation which met in the same building.

Moving on from the building that we occupied, to the congregation that I inherited I must say that we were truly blessed at Hatfield. There were some wonderful people in the Assembly including Brother and Sister Van den Berg, Mario and Ros Mariani, Brian (Titch) and Lorraine Holmes, Mrs. June Wilson and her son Roy, Nick and Debbie Marinos, Len Toet and his wife, and others whose names escape me at this moment.

One day when I was visiting Mario and Ros, there was a knock at the door and a friend of theirs called Martin Emmerson arrived with the good news that his wife Margaret had just given birth to a daughter. Their daughter Ashley was born at the Lady Chancellor Maternity Hospital in Salisbury. During the short time that Martin visited I was able to talk with him about the 'miracle' of birth. I mentioned that the birth of a baby was a 'miracle from God' and that we should give thanks to God for a safe delivery. After this short conversation I am sure we prayed for Martin, Margaret and Ashley before he left the house. Our conversation was very short and I did not think much about it at the time.

Years later, sometime after Martin and Margaret had gone into full time Ministry, I visited them at Montgomery Heights, the orphanage that they had established. The acquisition of the building for the Orphanage is a story all by itself as I believe ZanuPF had intended to take it over. However, God had other plans and the orphanage was established providing a Christian education for the children using Accelerated Christian Education, the ACE programme. It was a real privilege to see what this dedicated family had achieved.

In addition, they were taking meetings with farmers and others in the area and a small Assembly was functioning in Concession. Whilst I was visiting, we travelled together to a 'house group' near Concession, and Martin told me what had happened when we first met. He said something like the following, **"After I had met you for the first time at Mario's home, I went to the hospital to see Margaret and our baby Ashley. Whilst there I told her that I had met up with Mario's Minister, and that we had enjoyed a short conversation. I then told her that after that conversation, on my way to the hospital, I felt as if I had been washed or scrubbed inside."**

When he told me what had taken place that day, I was truly amazed at what God had done. I believe that it is important that we recognise that even when we are in ordinary conversation, God can use us if we let Him. Praise God for what He is able to do even when we least expect it! But, although they were members of our congregation for a short time, I did not have the joy of leading them to The Lord. One Sunday evening they went with Mario and Ros to McChlery Avenue where they gave their hearts to Jesus under the anointed ministry of John Stegman.

You can imagine my surprise when not long after they had been saved, Brother Stegman told me, that Martin and Margaret would one day enter the Ministry. What a prophetic word that turned out to be, given just weeks after they became believers. Praise God, many years later they are still ministering the Gospel and serving The Lord.

It was really exciting during my time at Hatfield to see what God was doing. This was demonstrated one evening when we had a baptism in a members swimming pool. I was in the water and looked up at the people and was encouraged by what I saw. First of all, I was thrilled to see Brian and Lorraine Holmes, who had come to know The Lord at McChlery Avenue in 1972. Next to them were Mario and Ros Mariani who had also come to know The Lord at McChlery, with the help of Brian and Lorraine in 1973. In the pool that night in 1974 were Martin and Margaret Emmerson who had also given their lives to The Lord at McChlery, but this time due to the ministry of Mario and Ros. What a joy to have such a proactive congregation who had succeeded in bringing their friends into the Kingdom of God. We all need to be out there sharing our faith as it is a joy to see our family and friends come to Christ!

Talking about having an active congregation, Mario and Ros and Brian and Lorraine were very much involved during those years in an evangelistic music ministry. I was only told recently by Ros that they would often load up a VW Kombi with musical instruments and travel out of town, taking the Gospel to different schools so that young people might hear, believe, and be saved. They were also involved in assisting Neil Gibbs, a very capable evangelist, when he took meetings in places like Kariba. I was largely unaware of these activities at the time and was keen to use the musical talent that was sitting in my congregation, however, they felt called to use their talents elsewhere in taking the Gospel to schools and other places. I will have a bit more to say about the talented musicians we had in Hatfield later.

I must say that I do not remember this incident, but I have been told that it took place whilst I was at Hatfield. Apparently, we hosted an Anglican 'lay preacher' who prayed for the sick that evening. Both Ashley (Martin and Margaret's child) and Brett (Mario and Ros's son) had major physical problems. Ashley had Coeliac disease and Brett was given to having fits. That night both children were taken up for prayer by their mothers and were totally healed. Praise God, we serve a wonderful Saviour, what a testimony!

But, getting back to our normal services, one Sunday I received a number of calls from regulars, explaining that they would not be at the evening meeting. After I had received the third or fourth call, I became quite discouraged. As a result of the absence of these regular members, just before the meeting was due to begin that evening, the Church was almost empty. Having taken note of the situation I went to pray in the 'vestry' and after a short time, a holy boldness gripped my soul and I said, **"Lord, there are only a few people** here tonight but I will preach Your word as usual just as if the Church was packed with people. In fact, if no one is willing to serve You, I am going to serve You, for You are my God. Even if there were not a soul here tonight, I am going to continue to serve You for You are my God! Hallelujah!"

They may not be the exact words that I prayed that night, but having prayed I went back into the main hall and to my surprise we had quite a good turnout. I truly meant what I said, and I believe that God had seen my heart, praise His name!

On another Sunday evening a couple came to the meeting that I had never seen before. As I was saying goodbye to the congregation at the door the man said to me, **"You preach just like Billy Graham!"**

I was very encouraged, as can be expected, to discover that someone had at last noticed! Yet in spite of what he had said, we never saw him again and I must conclude that he must not have enjoyed Billy Graham's preaching!

On another occasion my mother came to the Sunday evening service and after the meeting she said, **"You were preaching so fast, it seemed like you had a train to catch."**

On yet another occasion, while preaching one Sunday evening, I came to the conclusion that what I was saying was not really worth saying at all. I felt that I ought to draw the meeting to a close by saying something like the following, **"Sorry folk, I think we should all go home. I really apologise for this evening and I will try and do better next week."**

But, instead of bringing the meeting to a close, I persevered, and at the end of the message I made an appeal. I never really expected anyone to respond, and

I made the 'appeal' more by habit than anything else. Can you imagine my surprise, when a number of people came to The Lord that evening? Once again it proves that it is: -

"Not by might nor by power, but by My Spirit, says The Lord of hosts." Zechariah 4.6

Despite having been in the building for some time, we still did not have a sign up to say who we were. However, we finally managed to put it up and it was a day of great rejoicing. As it was such an important occasion, I am pleased to say that I have a number of black and white photos which record the event.

HATFIELD ASSEMBLY OF GOD

As a result of our success, a young couple who had often driven past the Assembly, finally knew who we were. That Sunday they came to the meeting for the very first time, and that very same evening they came to know The Lord as their Saviour. This couple turned out to be Chris Scott and his wife who sometime later went into full time ministry in South Africa and at the time of writing, Chris was heading up the Coastal Assemblies in Natal.

Another chap who came to know The Lord in our meetings was a policeman named Mike who had been invited to attend, by one of the congregants. But before coming to the meeting he checked up on a police data base to see who we were. As a result, he discovered that we were what we said we were, an organisation dedicated to preaching the Gospel of The Lord Jesus Christ. As a result, he and his wife came to the meetings and very soon came to know the Saviour.

I remember praying with Mike the night he asked The Lord Jesus to be his Saviour. After the service I went through 'THE WAY OF SALVATION' with him before we prayed together but for some reason, I never suggested that we kneel down. After we had prayed together, I looked at Mike and discovered that he was very relaxed, sitting on his chair with one leg crossed over the other. What it proved to me was that The Lord really does look at the heart of man. When He hears a genuine man or woman pray, He really does respond. Praise His Holy Name!

Many years later, when we were living in England, I discovered that Mike had entered full time ministry in the UK as a Minister of the Elim Pentecostal Church. Sadly, when I spoke to him, I discovered that his first wife had died some years before. He had remarried and he and his wife were serving The Lord in England.

It was in Hatfield, that I first met Chris and Maureen Triegaardt. They had both been members of the Dutch Reformed Church but did not know The Lord Jesus as their Saviour. After they came to know The Lord, they came into fellowship with the Hatfield Assembly. Sadly, Chris was confined to a wheelchair having had a problem with his legs for some time. One day Maureen asked me if the Assembly could pray and fast for a week, and then if we could pray for the healing of her husband at the Sunday evening meeting. I agreed and we spent a week in prayer and fasting asking God to heal Chris when we prayed for him that Sunday evening.

That evening I preached on the power of God to heal the sick in Jesus' name and then asked all those who desired to be prayed for to come to the front of the meeting hall. Despite Chris having been told by the DRC minister a few days before that God does not heal the sick in these days, he came up for prayer in his wheelchair. When I laid my hands on Chris and prayed, he immediately shot up out of his chair and stood on his own two feet. He had not been able to do that for some years, but sadly, he sat down again almost as soon. We were thrilled with what we had just seen but puzzled that he had not continued to stand or even walk around. As a result, we prayed again, but this time we gave him a bit of a hand so that he could stand to his feet. Sadly, he only stood for a few moments before he had to sit down again.

I then prayed for Kirby Cockrell, who had been in an accident some years before and was still having pains in his head. That evening Kirby was completely healed by The Lord and he never had those pains again. Praise God, The Lord is the same yesterday, today and forever, He still heals the sick! Hallelujah!

But what happened to Chris? Why did he stand and then sit down again? Why was he not healed? This was a question that I could not answer!

Well, even now I do not have all the answers, but years later when visiting Middle Sabi where Chris was managing a farm, we learned a little bit more about what happened that evening. He told me that although he was not fully healed, from that day on he was able to do things that he had not been able to do before. As an example, he was able get in and out of the bath on his own and was able to successfully manage a farm. We do not know why he was not fully healed but we praise God for all that He did! A few years ago, Chris went to be with The Lord and you can be sure that he will never have a problem walking again throughout all eternity. Hallelujah!

It was whilst at Hatfield that I prayed for Chris and Maureen and others to be filled with the Holy Spirit. On that night Maureen was baptised in the Holy Spirit in an unmistakable way. As she was filled with the Holy Spirit, Maureen literally erupted, and began speaking in tongues in a very loud voice. When this happened, Chris got such a shock, he nearly left his wheelchair again. He told me afterwards that his wife sounded like a 'fishwife' whatever that means. However, The Lord had really answered His promise by pouring out His Spirit, and in the case on Maureen in a very wonderful way. Remember the Scriptures declare: -

"-----, Repent, and let every one of you be baptised in the name of Jesus Christ for the remission of sins; and you shall receive the gift of the Holy Spirit, ---." Acts 2.38

Now, returning to the subject of healing it was whilst we were at Hatfield that I began to have problems with my knee. It was so bad that it was difficult to climb the stairs to the first floor flat where I lived. One evening we were at a concert given by a Christian singer and it was after the performance that he prayed for my healing. It was near the end of the evening when he informed us that he had promised The Lord that he would pray for the 'sick' every time he had a singing engagement. I felt led of The Lord to go up for prayer that evening, yet, after he had prayed everything seemed to be the same.

That Sunday evening in my own service I asked if there was anyone who wanted prayer for healing. A couple of people came forward and I was joined by two of the senior brethren when we prayed. After we had prayed for the others, I asked them to pray for me. But I instructed them not to 'pray' for my healing as I had already been prayed for a few days before. Instead, I asked them to rebuke this attack upon my body in Jesus' name. It was not immediate, but within a few days I no longer had any problem with my knee and have had no problems to this day. Praise God!

Continuing with the subject of Divine Healing, on one occasion, Brother Van den Berg, was not very well at all, and he had been unable to keep any food down for a number of days. As a result, he and his wife were getting rather worried. Well, that Sunday evening as I was preaching, whilst he was sitting in his seat, God healed him completely. After the meeting he went home and asked his wife to cook him a steak as he was very hungry. He then ate the lot and did not look back. Hallelujah! What a Saviour!

Well, just in case you think that I had forgotten my third prayer, which I prayed in the forest at Lions River, I did not. In fact, it was when I was ministering in Hatfield that The Lord finally answered my prayer. Now, The Lord God clearly told me that He would answer my third prayer, in the same miraculous way that He had answered the other two prayers.

Nevertheless, I had not been idle in trying to bring it to pass, as the following stories, which all took place before I arrived in Hatfield, clearly reveal.

As an example, on one occasion I felt God was leading me in a particular direction because the girl's name was Sarah and my nickname was AB (short for Abraham?) She lived in South Africa and one of my holidays was specifically dedicated to finding out if this was God's will? She was a lovely dedicated Christian and eventually married a lovely Christian man and they have continued to serve God in the town where God placed them. However, when my good friend Alan Keeling found out that I was showing serious interest in her, he went out of his way to speak to her, and said something to this effect, **"Look Sarah, go carefully with my friend AB as he knows nothing about girls!"**

By the way, when Sarah told me, I found it really quite embarrassing. Yet, sadly to say, to some degree of course Alan was right. It is wonderful to have friends who care enough for you to go out of their way to look after your interests. In spite of that, I am not at all sure that I was pleased to hear about Alan's comments at the time!

On one of my trips down to South Africa to the National Youth Camp, Sarah made a point of being there. But, before returning home, she needed to take a trip to see her father. As a result, we left the camp early and I followed her in my own car so that I could meet him. I arranged for the rest of my car load to stay at the camp until I returned the following day. After her mother had died some time before, her father had remarried and Sarah told me how happy they both were. I was made very welcome by her father and stepmother and have never forgotten what she told me about these two, who had remarried after their previous spouses had died.

But, her words about her father's remarriage after her mother died, were completely the opposite to the words of a man that I met in QueQue whilst ministering there. The daughter of this man, attended our meetings when visiting from Salisbury, and asked me to visit her father who lived in the town. He was an elderly man, confined to a wheelchair, who had remarried after his first wife had died. His story was completely different to Sarah's father and when I met him, he said, **"If I had only known, what things would be like, I would never have remarried. I wish I had stayed on my own. It has not worked for me at all. My wife has a number of children and hordes of grandchildren and my home is no longer my own. It was a real mistake to remarry!"**

I have never forgotten meeting both of these people, two men whose stories were so very different.

On one of my trips to see Sarah I came to realise that although she was a wonderful person in every way, it was not the way God wanted me to go. Yet, saying goodbye was very difficult as I had believed that God was leading me. The last night before leaving for home I was quite discouraged and spent some time talking to the chap with whom I was staying. Amazingly, he later went on to marry her, and they have both lived lives that have honoured the name of The Lord. However, that night before I returned home to Rhodesia, we sang a song together which reflected my feeling at the time, as well as the faith that I had in my God. The song that we sang was taken from the

Scriptures and goes like this,

"Though the fig tree shall not blossom, and there be no fruit on the vine,
Though the produce of the olive fail, and the fields yield no food;
Though the flock be cut off from the fold, and there be no herd in the stall;
Yet will I rejoice in The Lord, yet will I rejoice in The Lord,
I will joy in the God of my salvation, God The Lord is my strength! Habakkuk 3.17-19

With that song on my heart, I returned home still without any clear understanding of what God had prepared for me. However, there is a verse in the Scriptures that I took very seriously and it is: -

"He who finds a wife finds a good thing, and obtains favour from The Lord." Proverbs 18 22

The point that I want to make is, that if you do not 'look' you cannot 'find'! So, I continued to look!
There was a lovely girl in Salisbury who was a little younger than myself and we got on very well together. She was a really committed Christian and before I went into the ministry, we would often do contact visitation together as part of a regular visitation programme that we had at the time. On one occasion we visited the home of a young girl who had just been saved. Her father wanted to know who we were and after a while we got into a very serious conversation and he really gave me a hard time. When we left the house, my companion asked me how I was able to

handle the situation so calmly? I replied that I had years of experience in my own home, as my step father had been exactly the same as the new convert's father when we got onto the subject of 'religion,' 'church,' or the 'Bible!'

Whilst ministering in QueQue I came through to see her and as it was a hot day, I felt that I needed to bath and change of clothes before visiting. As a result, fully equipped with a change of clothes and my towel, I went around to see Les and Avril Helen. They were pleased to see me and invited me in for a cup of tea and after a decent interval I said, **"Would you mind if I used your bath? I have come prepared with a towel and a change of clothes!"**

I am sure that they seldom, if ever, had such a request from someone popping in for a visit, yet, without batting an eye they said, **"Sure. Go ahead!"**

Sometime later I invited this young lady down to QueQue for the weekend to stay with one of the congregants. It was a lovely weekend and everything went according to plan, until another guy appeared on the scene out of the blue. He had gone to visit her in Salisbury and when he found out where she had gone, he travelled down to QueQue to see her and arrived at our Sunday morning service. Can you imagine that? What a problem!

Despite my willingness, and in fact my desire, to take the young lady back to Salisbury she ended up travelling back with him and so that was that, I was invited to the wedding!

Yet, all was not lost as God was about to do something amazing, but before we get on to that I have another story to tell. As you can imagine with all the travelling that I was doing, going to youth camps in South Africa, travelling to conventions, ministers' meetings, ministry trips, and the occasional trip, seeking a wife, the mileage gauge on my Mazda had a story to tell. In fact, the gauge was rapidly climbing into larger and larger figures. It was then that two of my good friends Alan Keeling and Malcolm Fraser approached me and said, **"AB we see that you have already done a lot of miles in your car and we have a proposal to put to you. If you are able to find a new car, and are willing to use your Mazda as a trade in, we are prepared to pay the HP on another new car for you."**

I was truly amazed. What a gift to receive, praise God for brothers like that! But there was one slight problem, it was almost impossible to buy a new car in Salisbury or anywhere else in the country. Well, it may have been 'almost impossible,' BUT WITH GOD all things are possible!

Not long afterwards, I was walking through Salisbury one lunch hour, when I walked past a Motor Car Showroom. It was, as usual empty, however, there was one solitary car on display, a Peugeot 304 Station Wagon. Having not seen the car before, I decided to go inside to investigate and make some enquiries about this vehicle. When I asked about the car the salesman replied, **"We did not know anything about these vehicles before they arrived. They came into the country in kit form and are being assembled at the Willowvale Assembly plant. Are you interested?"**

Willovale was the 'Ford' assembly plant but as no 'Ford' motor cars were coming into the country due to 'Sanctions imposed by Britain, the assembly line would take advantage of whatever was available.

In reply to the salesman's question, I indicated that I was definitely interested. He then asked if I had anything to offer as a trade in, on the new car? It appeared that because no one knew that these vehicles were coming there was no 'list' of people wanting the Peugeot 304. All the lists that they had were for the Peugeot 504 and so the salesman could sell the car to me, provided I had a good trade in.

The very next day, I took my Mazda in for them to examine. As it was still a wonderful car, they gave me a good trade in, and within a few days I drove away in a brand new, out of the box, Peugeot 304 station wagon. Because of the faithful contribution of my two friends all I paid after the trade in, was Z$17.00 a month which covered a radio/tape deck which I had installed as an extra. Praise God, The Lord was continuing to answer my prayer. He had not only provided me with one new car, He had now provided me with a second new car! This was truly miraculous, as this had taken place whilst it was almost impossible to purchase a new vehicle in the country! What an amazing God we serve!

When Chris Triegaardt, one of the men in my congregation, saw the car, he said that I must be thinking of getting married as why would I want a Station Wagon as a single man? But the reason I had purchased a Station Wagon, was because that was the only new car available! However, my God was not only in action on the vehicle scene He was about to answer another prayer!

It all began when one of the people in my congregation, decided I needed a little help in finding a wife. A friend of Debbie Marinos, had returned to

Salisbury, after spending some time in England. Sadly, the reason that she returned was because her mother had been diagnosed with cancer. Debbie and her friend had done their nursing training together at Salisbury General Hospital some years before.

After her initial training in Salisbury, her friend had gone to Durban to do her midwifery training. Whilst in South Africa she had miraculously come to know The Lord as her Saviour, but sadly, sometime later had drifted away. She had then moved to the UK to work and whilst there she had come back to The Lord and been baptised at the Elim Pentecostal Church in Plymouth. Debbie was keen for me to meet her, and invited her to the meetings at Hatfield.

And so it was that one Sunday evening she attended the meeting in Hatfield. I was introduced to her after the meeting and so it was that Marion Margaret Hagger, better known as Mally came into my life. I can still remember the dress that she was wearing that Sunday evening as we stood talking in the bright lights outside the church. I really wanted to get to know her, but, I did not want her friend Debbie or anyone else to know that I was interested!

At the time I was attending a Bible Study Course which was being conducted by John Stegman at McChlery Avenue. Debbie spoke to Mally about the Course and told me that Mally was interested in attending, when she was not working. She also suggested that I might like to give her a lift from the nurses' home to the meetings, as she had no transport. Having heard what Debbie had to say I agreed to give her a lift provided I could not arrange another lift for her. However, although I did try and find her a lift, I was really pleased to have the opportunity to get to know her!

Sometime later Roland Pletts accompanied us on a visit to one of the National Parks sites near Salisbury. Whilst there I needed to use the 'facilities' and made my way to one of those PK's that were erected in the National Parks. A PK in English is a 'small house,' or WC! Roland told me later that one should really avoid them because 'wasps' like to make their nests inside. He did not need to mention it as I soon found out and came racing out with at least three angry wasps chasing me and stinging me. Sad to say, Mally and Roland laughed out loud when they saw me running for my life pursued by little wasps.

Sometime after we met, I asked Mally to be my wife and was delighted when she agreed to marry me. But, because we had kept it a little bit of a secret, when I announced my engagement that Sunday to the congregation in Hatfield, (Mally was working) all but a few who were in the know turned to each other and said, **"WHO is he marrying??"**

Just after we got engaged, I was asked to preach at McChlery Avenue. At the end of the service, I was approached by an elderly couple who asked if they could have a word with me. It was Mr. Edmonds and his wife, of Edmonds the Jeweler's in Salisbury. He asked if we had bought an engagement ring yet. I replied that I had not done so and he told me to go into the shop in Salisbury and they would give me a discount on any ring that we chose.

It was a very thoughtful offer; however, he had been retired for some time and was possibly not up to date with the 'price' of rings in his shop. When we visited, we realised that they were all well out of reach of our limited resources. However, praise God, Mally came up with a solution as she had a ring that had belonged to her grandmother which we had reset and met the immediate need.

When we later went to see Mr. and Mrs. Edmonds to explain that we would not be taking up their wonderful offer he took out his cheque book and wrote out a cheque for $200.00 which he gave to us as a gift. It was much appreciated and we were able to use the money to purchase a very good second-hand bedroom suite.

I discovered that Mr. Edmonds had some amazing stories to tell about how he had come to know The Lord as his Saviour! Some years before he and his late wife were living near Johannesburg in South Africa when he invited a very anointed Full Gospel Minister to come and pray for his sick wife. He agreed to come and after he prayed for his wife, he led Mr. Edmonds to The Lord. The hour was late and the distance home was far, so the preacher stayed the night.

When he got up in the morning Mr. Edmonds discovered that his guest's bed had not been slept in and asked him what had happened? He was told that he had spent the night praying that his host would agree to be baptised in water. Before departing for home, he explained the importance of being baptised by full immersion. After being shown the relevant Scriptures, Mr. Edmonds said that he would like to be baptised and as there was a swimming pool outside, he would like to be baptised before his guest left. Sadly, his guest replied, **"I am sorry, we will not be able to do it today as I have not brought my baptism clothes**

with me!

I was amazed when I heard that story; to spend the whole night in prayer, and when God answered his prayer, he put it off for another day, because he did not have the right clothes! However, we need to be careful not to be too critical of this man as God had used him in a mighty way, and as my story reveals quite clearly, we have all made many mistakes and can only trust in God's rich mercy!

Some years after his first wife died Mr. Edmonds married a retired missionary lady who was part of the Assembly in Salisbury who had never married before. During those days there were numerous occasions when large amounts of money were made available for the work of God and I believe some of it at least originated from this generous man. For example, when money was being raised to build a new church building in one of the African Townships, we were told that someone had promised to donate 'x thousand dollars' for the building, provided the rest of the congregation came up with a similar amount he had promised to give $ for $. I believe that the total amount was raised and the church building was erected. Praise God for generous people!

The Hatfield Assembly were very supportive of my engagement and among others things a 'Kitchen Tea' was arranged by Debbie at their home. As there were quite a few people present every seat was taken and three of the ladies sat down on the couch in their living room. Sadly, when they sat down, they got a real surprise and quite a shock as the legs went right through the floor! It was a wooden floor and white ants had eaten away the wood underneath. In spite of this the Kitchen Tea was a great success and Mally was blessed with many useful items for the kitchen of our new home.

One day when I went to meet my 'fiancée' at the hospital after she completed work, I met a young woman that I had known in QueQue. Sometime before, I had encouraged her when her boyfriend of long standing had broken up with her. She was heartbroken and I encouraged her to look to the God who loved her, as He would comfort her and meet her needs. I said things like, **"Trust God and He will bring the right person into your life. He loves you and will not let you down if you trust in Him!"**

However, after I had said these words, she turned around and said, **"Well if that is true, what happened to you?"**

At the time I had assured her that God had not forgotten me and, in His time, the right woman would come into my life. As you can imagine it was a great delight to see her and remind her that God had not forgotten me, as on that day when she asked what I was doing at the hospital, I was able to say, **"I have come to meet my FIANCÉE!"**

Isn't God good!

The venue for the wedding was a problem as it would have been nice to have been married at my own Church, however it was far too small. We did have 85 people one evening for some special meeting, however it was a real squash. As we expected a lot more than 85 at the wedding, we decided to ask John Stegmann to marry us at McChlery Avenue.

The guest list was a real problem as we both had 'family' and friends outside of the Assembly. In addition, I was the Minister of the Hatfield Assembly, and had been the Minister of QueQue Assembly, and in addition I had been a long-time member of McChlery Avenue Assembly. As a result, it was clear that we could not invite everybody to the reception. Sadly, Neil and Marge Gibbs were among those that we were unable to invite but there was no restriction on who came to the actual Wedding service and we were thrilled to see them there.

Now some time before the wedding, Brian came up to me and said that he, Mario, and Martin, had composed a song for our wedding. They had been practising late into the night and would like to sing it for us at the wedding service. I suggested that it may go better at the reception afterwards, but Brian was adamant that it must be sung at the Wedding Ceremony. Having not heard the song and as it was our wedding ceremony, I was a little nervous but at last agreed to include the song.

I should not have been concerned as it was a great song with words of Scripture used throughout. It was a real blessing to have such a unique song sung at our wedding. They also gave us a framed copy of the music and the lyrics as a wedding gift so that we could hang it up on the wall of our home. What a blessing it was to have men like this, and their wives and families, in our fellowship!

The reception was held at the Salisbury Show Grounds and Mally's Aunt, Irma Lucas, did the catering. I was determined that The Lord would be honoured at our wedding, after all we were Christian believers. As an example, I did not want anyone getting drunk at our wedding and so although we had some resistance to the idea, there was no alcohol served at our wedding reception. I was also determined that whoever gave speeches at our wedding, would be a believer.

I had attended a great many weddings over the years, and on many of those occasions, the best man, or someone else, has spoilt the occasion by making inappropriate remarks. They have said things that should never be said at a wedding, and definitely not at the wedding of a man and woman of God. The last thing that I wanted was to have some below the belt jokes, or comments, made at our wedding! As a result, we decided to ask the following to take part: -

Danie Haarhof, an Elder at McChlery to speak for the Groom.
Alan Keeling to be the Master of ceremonies.
Roland Pletts to be best man.
Malcolm Fraser to be the grooms-man.
In addition, my soon to be wife, Mally, asked: -
Debbie Marinos to be the Matron of honour and
Heather Bradbury to be her bridesmaid.

THE WEDDING 2nd November 1974.
Left to right: - Roland Pletts, Heather Bradbury, Fred Tilliduff, Jessie Tilliduff, (my mother) AB and Mally, David & Molly Hagger, (Mally's parents) Malcolm Fraser, & Debbie Marinos

Things did not work out quite as we planned as Mally's parents felt that her brother, Tim, ought to be Master of ceremonies. Tim, who worked in the hospitality industry and was assistant manager at the Jamieson Hotel did a good job, but sadly there were long gaps between the speeches resulting in the reception going on longer than we desired.

When Danie stood up to speak on behalf of the bridegroom he said some very good things about me which I really appreciated such as, **"-------- AB stood head and shoulders above the other young men in the Assembly----."**

Of course, that was stretching it a bit; one of my

congregants in QueQue had called me her 'short Pastor' or words to that effect! He then went on to say something like this, **"He just had to click his fingers and any of the girls would have come running."**

When he said that, which was very nice to be sure, I was truly amazed! As far as I was concerned, I had been clicking my fingers for years with no results! It was only because God had answered my prayer that I was being married that day! It was He who had brought Mally all the way back from the UK to Hatfield to be my wife. However, I was very grateful for his kind words. Thank you, Danie, for all that you said that day!

We went up to Inyanga for our Honeymoon and took the opportunity to spend an extra few days with my sister and her husband before returning home to Salisbury. We then moved into the flat where I was staying not far from the Church which became our first home.

At that time, we used to advertise our services in the Rhodesia Herald every week, and one day I had a phone call from someone who had obviously got my number from the advert. The lady on the other end of the line was one of two people who had attended the Evening Service on Christmas day in QueQue the year before. After a brief conversation where she explained that she needed some help and advice, I invited her to the service that Sunday evening and agreed to visit her home with my new wife after the service.

That Sunday, when we were sitting in her living room, she explained the problem. She told us that she had been sitting in the lounge when there was a knock at the door and when she went to investigate, there was no one there. In addition, she mentioned many other strange goings on, which had all started after she had a friend come to stay, who was involved in Spiritism. As she related her story, I remembered that the last time that she had been in one of my meetings in QueQue she had said that when I was preaching, she had seen something like a 'halo' around my head. At the time I felt that I needed to speak to her as I was concerned that she may have been involved in some way in 'spiritism' however, the opportunity did not arise.

But after she had related to us what was going on in her home, I asked her if she had ever been involved in the Occult? In reply, she said that she had gone to a séance on one occasion but that was all that she could remember. After some discussion I encouraged her to repent of this involvement in the occult and tell Satan that she was a child of God, washed in the blood of Jesus and wanted nothing to do with anything belonging to him. I then prayed for her and we went around the flat and rebuked any satanic or demonic influence in the place. Praise God, she never had any problems after that evening and went on to serve God with all her heart.

Earlier in my story, I mentioned Kirby and Sybil Cockrell. At that time Kirby was an Elder in our Umtali Assembly and his parents lived in Salisbury and attended the Church of Christ. His father had been an Elder in the Church of Christ for many years and so it was a surprise to see them sitting in our services one Sunday. I welcomed them to the services but never enquired any further, but, after they had attended the services for two or three weeks I arranged to go and visit them at their home.

On arrival at their home and after being welcomed by a cup of tea I asked them 'why' they were attending our services as I was aware that he was an elder in the Church of Christ? He then went on to explain that over some years they had come to the conclusion that they could no longer go along with all of the teachings of the Church of Christ. However, as he had been a member of the congregation for so long and an Elder as well, they found it difficult to leave. It was only as a result of 'petrol rationing' that they had at last been able to make the break, as the Church was a long way from where they lived. He had resigned as an Elder and told the congregation that they were leaving. The Elders had then provided them with a letter of commendation to show to the leaders of any other church that they decided to join.

I have often referred to these dear people when ministering. When they came to a different understanding of the Scriptures, they did not destroy the Congregation that they had helped build over many years, they left with a letter of commendation. I honour the memory of these two dear saints of God!

Strange as it must seem to my readers, everyone did not always agree with what I taught, or how I led the Assembly! Sometimes people disagreed with me as I will now explain!

The Breaking of Bread Service was always special, it was where we encouraged all the congregation to participate in what we called Open Ministry. Open ministry was great as it gave everyone in the Congregation the opportunity to be involved. They were able to minister God's Word, share a testimony, read from the Scriptures, sing a song and so on. On this occasion one of the men rose to his feet to share something with the congregation that he believed to be important.

He explained that he had recently seen a film at the Cinema that he felt we should all see. He believed that if we went to see the film it would help us to understand how people were thinking, and therefore enable us to share the Gospel with them in a more meaningful way. He was very sincere in what he had to say, but I had heard about this film and felt that it was the worst advice that I had heard in quite a while and so after he had finished speaking, I stood to my feet and said something like the following, **"I am sorry but I totally disagree with what Brother X has said. This is a terrible film which no believer should go and see!"**

As you can see, I was very careful not to hurt this dear brother's feelings and spoke in a very diplomatic way! But he did not think so and in fact he was very upset with what I said.

However, sometime later he came to see me and this is what he said, **"AB I have seen how The Lord deals with those who oppose you, and I do not want that to happen to me. As a result, I want to ask your forgiveness for opposing you."**

I was puzzled and still am at what he had seen, but quite willingly forgave him and assured him that I had nothing against him as he was after all my dear brother in Christ. Many years later we met up for a coffee when he was visiting friends in Preston in Lancashire in England. Whilst we were together, I reminded him of that incident where he had had something against me. However, he assured me that it wasn't just ONE THING that he had against me at that time, it was MANY!!

You definitely cannot win them all!

Sadly, there was another dear brother who had a problem with me when I was at Hatfield. When I went to see him, I should have asked one of the Elders of the Assembly to go with me. However, on this occasion I went on my own, and in many ways, I am so glad that I was on my own because of what transpired. After we had spoken for some time, he said, **"You are a useless Minister."**

Well, as I have already said, you can't win them all!

Nevertheless, when I was leading the work in Zimbabwe some years later, this dear brother and his wife offered to put me up in their lovely house when I was visiting Hatfield. As I already had somewhere to stay on that occasion, I declined but I was so grateful to know that our God is able to heal even the most difficult situations. Praise His Name!

MEETINGS AT THE NEW SARUM AIR FORCE BASE!

One day I was in conversation with George Bushney and he mentioned that he was doing his military training at New Sarum Air force base outside Salisbury. He then went on to say that he wanted to start a regular weekly meeting at the 'base' for the airmen, and asked whether I would consider coming to preach. The Rhodesian Air-force used the same runway as Salisbury Airport, and I believe this resulted in us having the longest 'civil runway' in the world at that time.

Before writing this book, I sent out a message on Facebook asking any of my friends to contribute stories or incidents that they remember when I was their Minister or when we worked together for The Lord. Sadly, only one responded so I am going to include all that George remembers about that time in his own words: -

"Hi AB just giving you my early recollections of our time in Rhodesia. When I first got saved I had so many questions you invited me to your flat in Hatfield where you cooked me a great steak, egg and chips. Here you started to disciple me, for which I am really indebted, and as a result I started a Tuesday night fellowship at New Sarum and asked you to be the speaker. You jumped at the opportunity and we soon had a vibrant fellowship which grew to over 30 people attending every week. Many people were saved from those meetings and have grown to be great Christians, even one rebel, John Myles who used to wake up at 6.00am and then swore for 10 minutes, without repeating one swear word so great was his swearing vocab. You got him around to Hatfield AOG where you discipled him to the point that he went on to become a full-time worker in the military, as a Chaplain. Those were my early recollections of you. I remember your famous saying. 'We must press on' God bless you, George Bushney.

   As George rightly remembers, he did not have to ask me twice, as I was really keen to get involved. Some years before, when visiting the Assembly in Grahamstown, I had accompanied Noel Cromhout when he visited the nearby South African Army base to minister to some of the soldiers. I do not think that it was a meeting as such, however I had seen the need and when George suggested that I come and speak, I responded right away.

The meetings were arranged in premises belonging to the 'Dog Section,' part of the Security Unit, however the man in charge was away on leave when permission was granted. On the first night, a good number of men had been encouraged by George to attend and I was playing my piano accordion whilst he was leading the singing. While we were singing, two men came in at the back of the hall looking rather mean. They were both rather big fellows and at least one had stripes on his shoulders indicating that he was a man of rank. It turned out that he was in charge of the Dog Section, and we were in his lecture room! When they entered the meeting, they were both smoking, one man was smoking a pipe and the other a cigar.

Now, as you can imagine, I was not impressed, when they both continued to smoke! We were in the 'house of God' and singing praises to The Lord, and I was about to preach the Word of God! But, with some difficulty, I refrained from saying anything and after a while one chap left, later on I discovered that he was Jewish. But the other man continued to stand at the rear of the room, possibly for the whole meeting, though I cannot be sure.

At the end of the meeting, I discovered that one of the men, the chap with the stripes, was really upset. He was really annoyed, as he was in charge of the DOG SECTION, and we had been given permission to hold these meetings in HIS SECTION whist he was away! After this, I heard that on a number of occasions, when he was in the shower, and a little the worse for wear, he would burst out in song and sing at the top of his voice the old children's Sunday School song, **"JESUS WANTS ME FOR A SUNBEAM."**

Although I am sure that he sang the song to mock the rest of us 'believers,' he was quite correct in what he was singing, as Jesus did want him! Not long after that he got saved and after he had given his heart to The Lord, he was serious about serving Him. He went to the officer in charge and requested transport to get to Church on Sundays, as there were no services on the base. This was granted and from then on, he arrived at the Hatfield Assembly in a military land-rover every Sunday morning. His name was John Myles and he later joined the Chaplains Corps and has carried on serving God since moving to Australia many years ago.

Before we leave New Sarum Air force base I need to mention one more incident. One evening I arrived at the Dog Section Lecture Room before anyone else. The doors had not been opened, and as I stood outside, I could hear dogs barking and howling all over the place in the still night air. As I stood there it became increasingly clear to me that we were in a very real 'spiritual' battle. The forces of darkness are very real, but, praise God, we serve a living Saviour and one day soon He is coming again as King of kings and Lord of lords. Praise God, He is The Lord and every knee will one day bow and every tongue will one day confess that Jesus Christ is Lord!

My next story involves another miracle in my life when I ended up,

LEADING A TOUR TO ISRAEL AND MORE BESIDES!

As can be expected whilst I was at Hatfield I met up with John Stegman on a regular basis. For a start, I attended the Bible Course that he was running, and was present at the Ministers' Meetings that he arranged. On one of these occasions, he told me about a trip to Israel that he was organising. He had planned other trips to Israel, but on this occasion one week was to be spent in Israel and a further two weeks would see the group go to Athens, Istanbul, Izmir, Munich, London, and Rome. When he suggested that my wife and I should also go I replied that I would truly love to do so however, there was no way that I would be able to afford it.

It was not long before he approached me a second time and said, AB you must go, it will be such a blessing to you. I had to repeat my previous statement, but that was not the end of it. A few days later he confided in me that he did not want to go as he was exhausted and just wanted to put his feet up and have a good rest whilst on holiday.

He explained that if I could persuade 16 people to go on the trip, I would receive one free ticket from the Travel Agents. As he already had ten people signed up, if I agreed to lead the tour all I needed was another 6 people to receive a free ticket. That sounded good, but I was a newly married man, even if we had one free ticket, I could not possibly afford to pay for the extra ticket so we could both go on the trip! In answer to that problem, he then told me that the existing group had offered to load their tickets so that his wife Yvonne could travel with them and he was confident that they would do the same for Mally!

Having finally been persuaded that it was not going to cost me any money I agreed to take over from him and lead the tour. But it was important for me to discover whether the existing group were happy to sponsor my new wife whom most of them did not know. After doing a bit of investigation, I discovered that the group were quite happy to have me lead them, (someone who had never been in an aircraft before, except once in a military helicopter) but unsurprisingly they were not keen to sponsor my new wife!

But, by this time I was already committed to going on the trip and decided to trust God for the money to pay for the second ticket. Nevertheless, getting a further six people to sign up was not going to be easy as there were a few problems. One of these problems was our Rhodesian passports! Because of international sanctions most of the countries that we would be travelling to would not accept them! That meant that none of the group could travel on a Rhodesian passport.

My wife Mally possessed a British passport as her father was born in England, and I had a South African passport as my father was born in South Africa. During those years it was easier for me to travel backwards and forwards into South Africa with a South African Passport. But many people only had Rhodesian passports and as a result they were unable to make up the numbers that I needed for my FREE ticket.

Another problem was of course money! Although we were going during the 'off season' and in today's terms we had an exceptional deal, it was still a lot of money for people to find. The fact that we were going to be away for three weeks was a further problem as not everyone was able to get leave to be away at that time. Last of all, time was running out, and I am not a good salesman!

As was to be expected one day I received a phone call from the Travel Agent who told me that they needed the remaining names urgently. I promised to get back to them asap and decided to 'put out a fleece' and see what The Lord would do. I prayed something like this, **"Lord if you want us to go on this trip, please show me by providing some more people to join the group or by providing the money that we need by Monday morning!"**

Before the 'deadline' that I had set, I was amazed to get a phone call from my good friend Malcolm Fraser. He asked me how things were going, and I put him in the picture and having heard what I had to say he said, **"AB, the reason I phoned was to let you know that I will pay for Mally to go. If you can, you can pay me back, but there is no pressure, take as long as you like."**

I was amazed at his generosity, and how quickly The Lord had answered my prayer, and knew that without doubt we were 'A' for away, we were going, praise God! I thanked The Lord for answering my prayer and was very grateful for my friend's wonderful generosity!

But things were not quite finalised as I had another call from the Travel Agent as they were desperate to have the rest of the names. We were travelling to so many different destinations and everyone was asking them for final details as to who was travelling. I once again apologised for the delay and asked them for one more week. Having agreed to give me one more week I prayed again for The Lord to provide the people, the money, or else in spite of my friend's generosity I would still have to cancel!

Once more God miraculously intervened, as just after receiving this phone call, I was told that another two people wanted to sign up for the trip. It wasn't just anybody, we were going to be joined by Jim and Mary Mullin! They were such a lovely godly couple, and had been instrumental in establishing the 'work' in Rhodesia, and I was thrilled, but also a little nervous, to have them come with us. Praise God, we were nearly there, we only needed two more and we would be home and dry. It was then that my mother rang to find out how I was, and how plans were going for the trip? After a short conversation she said, **"If you like I can lend you some money, how much do you need to go on this trip?"**

I told her, **"Well $800.00 would be great!"**

She said, **"That's a lot more than I had in mind, but if you need it, I will lend it to you."**

This was not how it was supposed to have been, but there was no mistaking the fact that God had intervened and that He was providing the finance for us to go on this trip.

I had agreed to travel thinking that I would have two free trips but I was now travelling owing R$1,600.00 which was a lot of money to spend on a three-week trip! The difficulty that I was in was highlighted by something that happened as we were about to take off from Salisbury Airport. I was sitting in the middle with Mally on one side and Mrs. Keeling (Alan's mother) on the other. As we were about to take off, I remember her saying, **"The Lord laid it on my** heart before signing up for this trip to 'owe no man anything,' and praise God He provided all that I needed. As I leave on this holiday, I want to praise God that I 'owe no man anything' as it is all paid for."

Having heard what this dear lady had to say the Minister, leading the trip, never said a word in response!

We flew from Salisbury to Jan Smuts airport in Johannesburg in South Africa on my first ever flight. The Airport was enormous compared to our airport in Salisbury but we were only there a short while before we left for Athens in Greece where we spent one and a half wonderful days.

At the airport we were met by our tour guide and the driver of a small tour bus who took us to our hotel. It was a lovely hotel and must have been at least three stars, and amazing for the price. We were visiting in the low season and we enjoyed bed, breakfast and an evening meal. While we were there, we were taken to the sites of Athens which included a visit to the Parthenon. We were all amazed at what we were able to see in such a short time.

But there was a small problem, which took away some of the joy of being in Athens, this great historical city. On our tour we had a Mr. Parkins and a Mrs. Parkins, who were mother and son but at the hotel in Athens, they had been booked into the same room by mistake. As the hotel could offer no other solution except to apologise the tour LEADER which was ME, had to make a plan. Much to my new wife's displeasure I ended up sharing a room with Mike Parkin and my new wife shared a room with Mrs. Parkin.

You need to remember that we had only been married a few months! This was after all a bit like a second honeymoon, except for our time in Athens, where Mally had to share a room with Mrs. Parkins. She was a lovely person, and Mike was a great guy. He later moved to South Africa where he managed to get a job with Cadbury the producers of wonderful chocolate. When we visited Port Elizabeth some years later, we were even able to share in his perks, chocolate!

During the short time that we were left to our own devices, we visited a Greek restaurant and ordered a coffee. We found it difficult to explain that we only wanted an 'ordinary coffee' like we had in Rhodesia. When the 'coffee' arrived, it was so strong that we had to request a lot of extra milk in order to be able to drink it as it was so very strong. We also discovered that it was very expensive compared to Rhodesia!

Having enjoyed our short stay in Athens we were soon jetting off to Ben Gurion Airport in Tel Aviv to enjoy an exciting week in Israel. It was very moving when the El Al plane that we were travelling on played Hatikvah the Israeli national anthem as we were coming in to land. Once again, we were met at the airport by our tour guide and a tour bus and driver and taken to another great hotel for the night. Some of our party were up very early to go for a swim in the Mediterranean; however, we didn't make it. We were then picked up by Amnon the tour guide and Amnon the driver, who both had wives by the name of Sarah, to begin an amazing, unforgettable, week in Israel.

Although all of the places that we visited are worthy of mention we will only consider three. The first one involves one of the best days that we spent in

Israel when we travelled down to the Dead Sea. It was amazing to lie on one's back in the water reading a newspaper or a book and not be in danger of sinking. Sadly, Mally decided not to go in but she took a photo of me lying on my back and waving and most likely saying like others, **"Look at me!"**

On the same day that we visited the Dead Sea, we rode a camel near Jericho and also went up Masada. I would have loved to have walked up, although it was very hot, but we were after all limited by time, and so we ascended by cable car. The fortress of Masada was established by Herod the Great as a place of safety if he needed to escape. It is an incredible place to visit, where you can see his ruined palace on the side of the hill and the fortifications on the top. There are huge water cisterns on Masada, which are filled by an elaborate water system. His engineers dug channels in the side of the mountain which took water UP the mountain and into the cisterns. They used the force of the flood water coming down the hills in the rainy season to force the water up the side of Masada and into the cisterns. A truly amazing achievement.

You can still see the ruins of the Roman wall that encircled Masada and handle the stone missiles that they used to attack the Jewish defenders. You can also see the ramp that the Romans built using Jewish slaves to take their war engines up the mountain.

Our guide Amnon, had assisted in the excavation of Masada some years before and knew the history very well. He told us the very sad story of how during the Bar Kochba rebellion against Roman Rule in 135AD the last place to fall to the Romans was Masada. Sadly, rather than surrendering to the Romans and becoming slaves it is believed that all the defenders, bar a couple of people, committed mass suicide the night before the Romans conquered the fortress. He also informed us that in modern Israel their Commandos have a ceremony on Masada where they vow that Masada will never fall again.

The very next day we attended a service at 'The Garden Tomb' in Jerusalem. In 1883 when he visited Jerusalem, General Charles George Gordon, felt that the empty tomb in this Garden could well have been the tomb where Jesus was laid after He was crucified. Above the garden there is also an open place where the crucifixion could well have taken place, and on the side of the hill, even today, you can clearly see the shape of a skull. There is a bus terminus below the hill of the Skull showing that it is a place where people pass by travelling to and from Jerusalem. The place has been known ever since as Gordon's Calvary and the Garden Tomb is cared for by an evangelical Christian trust. General Gordon who was a committed Christian, sadly died in the Sudan in 1885 defending Khartoum against the Dervishesa, a radical Islamic group.

There can be no doubt that Gordon's Calvary and The Garden Tomb appear to match the description given in the Bible where these events took place: -

"And He, bearing His cross went to a place called the place of a Skull, which is called in Hebrew, Golgotha, where they crucified Him, ---." John 19.17-18

"Now in the place where He was crucified there was a garden, and in the garden a new tomb in which no one had yet been laid. So, there they laid Jesus, because of the Jew's Preparation Day, for the tomb

was nearby." John 19.41-42

On the day that we visited, the preacher spoke about the judgement of Sodom and Gomorrah and how these cities had been destroyed by God. He then said something like the following, *"Many tourists visit Israel and spend time at the Dead Sea. They lie in the water reading a newspaper or similar publication, sunglasses on and possibly wearing a hat or cap and wave their arms in the air and cry out; 'Look at me, take a photo now.' However, they fail to consider that underneath the Dead Sea are the remains of Sodom and Gomorrah, cities destroyed by God because of their sin!"*

As we sat listening to this very anointed message our experiences at the Dead Sea and Masada were still very much at the forefront of our minds. The longer he preached, the further I sank down into my seat as I realised that I had been doing exactly what he was saying on my visit to the Dead Sea the day before. The last thing on my mind as I had been enjoying my 'swim' in the Dead Sea was the destruction of Sodom and Gomorrah! He was a powerful speaker and I have never forgotten that message.

During our week in Israel, we had a number of opportunities to speak with Amnon our guide about the Bible, prophecy, and Israel. When we were at Megedo he explained the prophecies that are in the Bible, The Battle of Armageddon and so on, and after he had finished, I remember saying to him, **"If you know these prophecies so well, and you clearly understand what the Bible has to say about the future, how come you are still in Israel?"**

I think he just shook his head and did not

answer!

    We had had an amazing week, we had been to the Sea of Galilee, visited the old town in Jerusalem, been on the Temple Mount, had a tour of the Dome of the Rock, been to the Holy Sepulchre and of course The Garden Tomb and many other places! We had also been to Hebron, Nazareth, and Bethlehem and even spent a night on a Kibbutz, and were really sad to have to leave. After such a fabulous week, we were sure that one day soon we would return to Israel, the sooner the better! But, sadly, in spite of our desire to return to Israel, we have never been back!

    Our next stop was Istanbul in Turkey where we were accommodated in a lovely hotel overlooking the Bosphorus. It would have been fabulous in the summer but although we were there in the winter it was still amazing! Just the same as our week in Israel, we had a room to ourselves, no sharing, praise God! Our visit was well planned and we were able to visit the Blue Mosque and the Sülemani Mosque which were all huge buildings. We were also taken to the Hagia Sophia Museum which is housed in an amazing building. The Hagia Sophia was built as a Christian Church during the Byzantium era to rival St Peter's in Rome. However, it was converted into a Mosque when Constantinople was conquered by the Moslem's. It later became a museum and sadly I believe it is now once again being made into a Mosque.

    Amongst the 14 people for whom I was responsible on this trip there were two attractive single young women. One had lovely long black hair and the other had lovely long very blonde hair. I knew that there had been cases of young woman being abducted in Moslem countries and was very concerned for them in particular when we visited the markets and bazaars in Istanbul and other places. I asked the whole group to try and stick together as much as was humanly possible in these crowded places.

But, sad to say these two young women did not seem to get the message, and I was constantly looking for them. It was particularly difficult in the Bazaars and markets as they and everyone else for that matter were constantly disappearing. I must have aged many years on that trip, no wonder I am 76 years old today!! However, they were not the only ones to cause me a few problems as there were a few more difficulties to come!

Our time in Istanbul was soon over, and it was time to leave for Izmir a city of over a million people at that time. It had originally been built by the Greeks and called Smyrna in antiquity. As we had a morning flight, and the airport was some considerable distance from the hotel, at around 4.00am that morning we were packed up and on the way. Although we arrived in plenty of time, the flight was delayed, because of bad weather and with little information forthcoming we began a very long wait.

After waiting for some hours, and discovering that other flights were taking off on time, some of our party began to discuss alternatives. It was suggested that instead of waiting to go to Izmir, it would make more sense if we caught the next flight to Munich, which was our next destination. Eventually, because I had become a little frustrated with the discussion, I decided to put it to the vote! I for one could not afford the extra money that would be involved if we cancelled our flight to Izmir. The Lord was merciful and most of the party voted to wait it out, and praise God, although it was late in the afternoon, we were finally able to board our flight to Izmir.

The journey from Istanbul to Izmir was the worst flight of the entire trip! The inside of the plane seemed to be a little run down! As an example, one seat had been taken out and not returned leaving an unsightly gap. However, that was not all, half way into our journey, we hit an air pocket, and the plane seemed to drop out of the sky as we fell hundreds of feet before things got back to normal. It was a really frightening moment but, praise God, it was soon over and we arrived safely.

Once on the ground we were met by our tour guide and taken to the hotel. By now I had developed a routine which was to check all of our cases on and off the tour bus, on arrival at our destination. But on this occasion, I was unable to do what I had intended, as I was asked to go to the desk to assist in checking people into the hotel. As a result, I asked my good friend Roland to make sure that all the cases were taken off the bus, but I neglected to ask him to COUNT the cases as they came off the bus.

We had just arrived in our room, exhausted by a difficult day, when my rest was interrupted. It was bad news; I was told that Bother Jim Mullen's case was missing. I immediately asked my friend if he had COUNTED the cases off the bus? He replied that as far as he understood all the cases had come off the bus but he had not actually counted them! We naturally prayed, and also phoned the airport and did all that we could but no case was discovered for the oldest member of our party. I was really sad but there was nothing that I could do but wait for the morning!

We rose early the next morning as we had a busy day ahead visiting the ruins of ancient Ephesus. This was the sight of one of the Seven Churches spoken of in the Book of Revelation. As soon as the coach arrived, we got on, and praise God, Brother Mullins case was still on board. I was thrilled, and so I am sure was Brother Mullin! What a wonderful answer to prayer!

Our visit to Ephesus was fantastic, and undoubtedly one of the best days of our entire trip. We sang from the top of the Great Theatre which could hold 25,000 spectators and although we did not have such a crowd that day, we sang praises to our King with all our might. We visited the ruins of the Temple of Hadrian and the ruins of St John's Basilica, which had been a large Christian Church. But, the Temple of Artemis, one of the Seven Wonders of the Ancient World, was no longer open for viewing, as it had been destroyed many centuries before. After a lovely stay in Izmir, all too soon we were on the plane and in the air returning to Istanbul from where we flew to Munich in Germany.

We soon discovered that Munich was a lovely city, clean, modern, and well maintained. The hotel was once again excellent, but the restaurant was closed possibly due to it being out of season. We had to eat breakfast at another venue across town involving a ride on an underground train which seemed very strange. Another thing that we found 'strange' was the small baths that we came across in a number of places, you could not lie down and have a soak, it was so small you had to sit up and have a bath. For some of us who had not travelled in Europe before, like myself, the bedding was also different, no blankets, duvets were the order of the day, something I had never come across before.

On one occasion while in the underground station area, we came across a Christian group having an open-air meeting. We were able to join them for a short while as they sang and preached the Good News, although we did not understand the language. It was one of the first times in my life that I had experienced the real hatred that some people have for the Gospel of The Lord Jesus Christ. You could feel the antagonism as people walked on by. Praise God for those who proclaim the Gospel in the open air, it is not always appreciated but people do come to know Jesus as a result!

The reason for our trip to Munich was to visit the Bavarian Castles. The castles were very much like the ones children see in 'fairy stories' but were very real. I remember in particular our visit to Neuschwanstein Castle which was commissioned by Ludwig 2nd of Bavaria in the 19th Century. It was a fantastic day seeing these amazing Castles with all the wonderful scenery as well.

There was a lot of snow around, which made it look even more beautiful. Some of us, like myself, had never handled snow and so a snow ball fight took place among the Rhodesians (travelling I might add on anything but Rhodesian passports!) A lady from Canada, who was on the same coach as us, was really puzzled by our behaviour. Back home where she came from, she had to dig herself out of snow every year and could not understand our enthusiasm for the cold, wet, white stuff.

After a lovely stay we were once again on the move, this time to the UK. No sooner had we boarded the aircraft when we were told that they had one case too many and would we please leave the aircraft and identify our own luggage. As Mally and I rose to leave the plane Cassie Perrioli said, **"AB would you please see that my case is there?"**

Without giving it much thought I said that I would, as we all had a yellow label making it easy to identify, and so it would not be too difficult. We quickly identified the luggage but sadly I failed to count the suitcases and were very soon back on the plane. It was then that Cassie said, **"You did see that my case was put on the plane?"**

I replied that I had, but all the way to London I had a nagging doubt! If her case was not on board I was in trouble!

I was really relieved and praised God that when we landed at Heathrow all of our company, including Cassie, were able to retrieve their baggage. However, after we had picked up our luggage we looked around for our 'guide' but there was no 'guide' to greet us and we did not know what to do. Eventually, I went outside and a short while later discovered a mini bus (God is so good) and asked the driver whether he knew where we would find our transport. Much to my surprise he replied that we were travelling with him. I then asked him why he had not come into the terminal to meet us as how in the world did, he expect us to find him? He replied, **"I did not want to leave my vehicle as we have had a lot of trouble with IRA bombers."**

Coming from Rhodesia where the 'bush war'

was very much in evidence I was amazed! On the entire trip we had been met and looked after except in London and the excuse was 'terrorists!'

We were soon at our hotel which was not much to write home about considering the hotels that we had already visited, but we had a bed and that is what we needed most. We were not sightseeing in London and everyone was free to do their own thing. Most of us were going to spend some of the time at least visiting family and friends, in addition to sightseeing.

Once safely in the hotel we made a few phone calls as we had decided to use our short time in England to visit a few friends and relatives. We decided to try and see my brother Christopher, who lived in Bristol, Aunt Diana, my mother's sister, who lived in Twickenham and friends of Mally who lived in Plymouth. They were all keen to see us although one couple were not keen to put us up. When I replied that we could not visit unless they accommodated us for the night, they agreed to put us up and it was lovely to see them. It seemed we did a lot of travelling during those three days but it was lovely to introduce my new bride to my brother Christopher, his wife Fiona, and my aunt Diana and to meet some of my wife's English friends.

When asked what we saw in England on that trip, I have always replied, **"I saw British rail!"**

In addition to the family members that I have mentioned we very briefly met my uncle Charles Kingston. It is amazing to record that during our short visit to England two of our party, Jim and Mary Mullin actually stayed with my uncle and his family. My Uncle Charles was a cousin of my grandmother and a leading member of the Elim Pentecostal Church in the UK. In fact, just before Jim and Mary Mullen left England for the Belgium Congo, where they laboured as missionaries with the Congo Evangelistic Mission, they stayed with my Uncle Charles. The Mullins later moved to South Africa where they laboured for The Lord in the South African and Rhodesian Assemblies of God.

As we were in England and had never met, was it possible to meet my Uncle Charles whilst we were there? As time was so short and our programme so very full, Brother Mullen graciously arranged to accompany my Uncle Charles to the station in London to meet us. Sadly, we were already on the train when we met for the first and only time. As I looked out of the train window I saw two elderly, but Godly men, waving us goodbye. Everything about the two of them spoke of lives lived in the service of Jesus and my desire was to be like them when I reached their age.

During my childhood, my Uncle Charles and his family sent us Scripture Calendars every year, and I have no doubt that they prayed for our family as well. I only had the privilege of meeting him on that one solitary occasion and it was such a very brief meeting. But, on that brief occasion he gave me the impression of being a wonderful man of God. I used to possess a lovely book that he had written on the Person and work of Holy Spirit, which sadly I no longer have.

Our amazing trip was fast coming to an end and we were soon on our way again. Our next stop was in Rome in Italy where we were met at the airport with a guide and a driver who took us to our hotel. We only had a short stay in Rome but we were able to see a lot in a short time. The ruins of ancient Rome, reveal just how powerful the Roman Empire really was, even after all these years! But, as with all Empires, they come and go, and the only one that will last forever is the one that will come to pass when Jesus rules as King of kings from Jerusalem not too many days from now. Our visit to the Colosseum, which seated 50,000 spectators made the persecution of the Christians in ancient Rome come very much alive. The Arch of Titus which was built in 81-85AD to commemorate the destruction of Jerusalem and the Holy Temple was another one of the sights that we visited.

As can be expected St Peter's Basilica was among the churches that we visited which was quite a sight to see! But we were not impressed by the many signs of idolatry that were all around us. After we visited St Peter's, our guide gave us an option, we could go back to the hotel and have lunch or we could go on to see the Sistine Chapel. Sadly, I have to confess, that by this time at the end of a three-week tour, we had quite enough of famous Church buildings, ancient Mosques, world famous Museums etc. to last us a lifetime, and we ALL chose to skip the Sistine Chapel and go for lunch.

Our flight to Jan Smuts in Johannesburg and then on to Salisbury was mainly uneventful and after an amazing trip we were once again back home. Having never flown before, except for one short flight in a military helicopter, I was now a seasoned traveller having travelled many miles by air with eleven separate flights under my belt. What an amazing trip!

Yet, having arrived safely home there was one small problem, and that was how to pay for our trip? I need not have worried as God had already sorted it out, and within a very short time it was all paid. As an example, my good friend Malcolm told me not to worry about paying back the loan as we could treat it as his wedding gift to us both. The members of the group all chipped in and gave us a 'love gift' to thank us for leading the tour, and in one way or another it was all paid for, within a month or two of our return. Praise God!

Having returned home it was time to get involved once again with the work of God in Hatfield. I have, of course, many memories about those days, such as the time when I was saying good bye to the congregation one Sunday morning. As she was about to leave one of the ladies asked me a question about what I had been preaching on that morning. I answered her to the best of my ability and after speaking to her for some time I said, **"Does that answer your question?"**

Her reply was rather discouraging to say the least. She said, **"No! Would you see if you can answer it the next time, I see you?"**

Moving on to another memory from my time at Hatfield, was an incident involving a journey to a meeting at Lochinvar. We had been running an outreach at the railway housing estate in Lochinvar for some years and I had often preached there, when I was at McChlery. One Sunday evening I was accompanied by an elderly lady who was our pianist for the evening. As we were driving along, I burst into song, which I often did in those years. Now those who know me will understand that I have a loud voice and it must have been somewhat of a shock to my passenger as she reached into her handbag and said, **"Would you like a sweet?"**

I took the hint and stopped singing and enjoyed the sweet. But, talking about singing I was leading the meeting at Lochinvar one Sunday evening when I asked if anyone had a favourite song. No one responded except a boy who was about ten at the time who asked for a song called 'Wasted Years,' which goes like this, **"Wasted years, wasted years, Oh how foolish---.**
Turn around, turn around, The Lord is calling, he's calling you from a life of wasted years!"

As I looked at him, and thought that if at 10 years old he felt that he had wasted a portion of his short life, what about the rest of us? The song has a very important message to convey and that is that we ought to stop wasting our life on things that have no substance and start living with an eye on eternity.

One day the phone rang and I was asked to take the funeral of a 15-year-old girl who had just died. She had been a member of our Sunday School in Lochinvar but I did not know her or her family at all. The funeral turned out to be one of the most difficult that I have ever been asked to take. it was held at the Crematorium and a large congregation were present including Gary Strong a very well-known Methodist Evangelist.

As I began the service it became more and more obvious to me that the family were completely overcome by grief. In fact, they were crying so much that I decided that the only thing that I could do was hurry through the proceedings as rapidly as possible. To be quite honest, I was completely out of my depth, when Gary Strong came to the rescue. I later discovered that he had had some contact with the family and he gently encouraged them to get up from their seats and go to the front of the auditorium and kneel down where he prayed for them. As a result of his actions the family were at last able to gain some sort of control over their emotions.

The Bible speaks of 'death' as being an enemy, but praise God, one day this terrible enemy which sadly affects us all, will at last be no more. We are told the following by Paul the apostle: -

"For He (Jesus) must reign till He has put all enemies under His feet, the last enemy that will be destroyed is death." 1 Corinthians 15.25-26

Although I was only at the Hatfield for 15 months, they were months packed with amazing blessings from God. But this came to an end when John Stegman asked me to move back to QueQue. By the way I must explain, that he was only responding to what John Bond, had asked him to do. Although most of my moves were initiated by myself, and those that were not never caused me much heartache, I know that for many of our ministers the constant moving was a real problem and caused many to leave the movement. However, it was never a serious problem for me!

Less than two years before, when I moved to Hatfield, I was a single man and able to put all my possessions in my car. Now, I was a married man, and when I moved on this occasion, I needed a removals truck to take our furniture and other possessions back to QueQue.

3) QUEQUE ASSEMBLY 1975-1977

We moved in 1975 after a really eventful time in Hatfield. These 'events' of course included getting married, which was the third, amazing and miraculous, answer to specific prayers that I had prayed at Lions River some years before.

The minister who took my place at Hatfield was Ron Davies, who had arrived in the country with his wife Dorothy from the United Kingdom some time before. Their intention was to establish a base to distribute Gospel Tracts across the entire country working with a Mission in Nelspruit in South Africa.

Shortly after getting started, they discovered that they would have to pay import duty on the literature that they were importing from South Africa for 'free' distribution. As a result, they decided to produce their own tracts in Rhodesia and 'Global Literature Lifeline' was established. This became a very effective ministry, distributing literature right across the country. Whilst living in Salisbury and attending McChlery it was not long before Ron was asked to become an Elder, a position that he had occupied in his home church in England. Then he was asked to take my place in Hatfield, when I moved back to QueQue, which proved to be a good decision and the Assembly grew under his and his wife's ministry.

Whilst I had been in Salisbury, and among other things getting married, going on tours to Greece, Israel, Turkey, Germany, the UK and Italy, a lot had been happening in QueQue. While I had been away, a new Church building had been erected, a number of new families had been added to the fellowship, and a new

Assembly had been established in Redcliff.

Just before leaving Hatfield Mally and I, accompanied by Brother and Sister Cockrell, attended the opening of the new Church building in QueQue. The ceremony was attended by ministers from Bulawayo, Salisbury, Gwelo and Umtali and representatives of their congregations. It was a great occasion and an amazing accomplishment for which the minister, Roland Pletts, ought to be congratulated. What he had accomplished in so short a time was truly remarkable. As he explained earlier, he could not have accomplished it without the help of Richard Morley who willingly provided all the expertise at the time. Nevertheless, it was a great achievement by any standards.

QUEQUE ASSEMBLY OPENING. 1974 Mally, Mrs. Cockrell, Bill Plews, Tony Aimer, Mr. Cockrell.

PART OF THE CONGREGATION. 1975 AB & Mally, Danny O,Connor and his two daughters, Brian, Margy and Samantha Boshoff.

Sadly, I have only just discovered that Roland did not even have the privilege of preaching in the new church building before he was asked to move on, and I returned to take his place. Perhaps that was one of the reasons that I do not remember Richard Morley attending the Assembly after I returned. There is no doubt that some of the 'moves' were very puzzling and very difficult for some of our Ministers to handle. However, it really did not affect me in the same way. As I consider these things, I can only say that God could not have given me a better wife. Although Mally was not fond of moving she never complained, for which I was very grateful.

During my absence Danny and Carol O'Connor and their family had become regulars at the meetings. They had both made commitments to Christ, been baptised in water, and their two daughters attended our Sunday School. In addition, like other members of the congregation, Danny and Carol were both very involved in helping to do the outstanding work on the inside of our new building. Yet in spite of this, Danny was still the treasurer of the local Roman Catholic Church, and attended Mass on a regular basis.

In addition to the work that needed doing on the inside of the new building, there was still a lot to be done outside. As an example, we had a real downpour one Sunday before the evening meeting. The driveway in front of the building was just one huge puddle, with mud everywhere. One of our congregants, who had recently moved from Hatfield, was Joan McKenzie, and that night she was dropped off at the meeting by her husband Donald. When he saw the obstacle that his wife had to cross in order to get to the door he said, **"Tell AB to order some gravel for the car park and I will pay for it."**

When Joan gave me the message, I replied, **"Please thank Donald for the offer, but tell him that I will come around and see him."**

Later that week I went around to see Donald and after the usual greetings I said something like the following, **"Thank you for your kind offer, Donald but I cannot accept it! We expect God's people, those who have given their lives to Jesus, to finance the work of God. We are not keen to accept money from those who are unbelievers, as you have indicated that you are. The reason that we do not want to accept** money from 'unbelievers' is because so many people think that they can buy their way into heaven. If I accept this gift from you, I may be stopping you from coming to Christ by encouraging you to believe that you can gain God's favour by the good works that you do. Sadly, it is not possible to gain God's favour that way, as Jesus is the only way!"

I must admit that Donald was truly taken aback by what I had to say and after some discussion in exasperation he finally said, **"My wife is a member of your congregation will you accept the gift from her?"**

Once again, I thanked him for his kind offer and said that I would be happy to accept the gift from his wife and so the gravel was duly ordered and delivered. Later I was to learn that Donald always maintained that the 'Church was only after your money,' however, when he tried to give us some we refused. Praise God, Donald did eventually come to know The Lord as His Saviour and as far as I am aware continued to serve him in the years that lay ahead.

Before we move on, I need to pay tribute to John Heyns, who was the Anglican Minister in QueQue at the time. It is interesting to note that of all the ministers in town he was the only one who came around to welcome me back to QueQue when I returned. No other minister called or phoned and so I want to say thank you to John for being such a good friend!

On a personal level the most exciting event to happen in QueQue was the birth of our son, Mark Broadhurst Robertson, who came into this world on our first wedding anniversary the 2nd November 1975. What an amazing present to receive from my wife on our very first anniversary! However, before saying anything more, there are a number of events that took place at that time that I need to mention.

When we moved to QueQue we ended up living in the old mine house that I had rented before leaving town. Although the house was not perfect, remember it had an outside, bucket toilet, and my wife was pregnant, it was a home for which we were grateful. However, the owners of the house, the 'Globe and Phoenix' gave us notice to vacate the premises by the 31st October which presented us with a real problem. On receiving the news, we searched the town for a suitable property to no avail. There were just no houses available to rent. Some of the congregation, the Boshoff's and the O'Connor's in particular, suggested that we buy a property as there were a number of newly built three bedroomed houses available. In hind sight, I know that we should have listened to them, as it would have saved a lot of problems in the days that lay ahead. However, at the time I felt that the congregation was too small to take on a mortgage for a house, in addition to all our other commitments.

And so, on Monday the 27th October, when my friend Kenneth Mawire came to visit with one of his congregants, we still had not found a place to rent. Kenneth had moved to QueQue and was pioneering a new congregation in one of the townships. That morning Kenneth had come around to ask if I could help one of his congregants who had accompanied him. This man was two months behind on his rent and if he failed to pay within a few days, he would become homeless! I explained that I was very sympathetic, and understood his problem, as I was in a similar situation. On discovering how much the man owed I realised that it was within my means to help and so I gave him the money to pay his rent.

You may not understand the significance of this story, but I believe that as God saw our hearts, as He saw that we were willing to help someone else in trouble, He answered our prayers for our own need. It was late that Monday 27th October that we heard of a house to rent; 76 Hillandale Drive. We viewed the house the following day, Tuesday 28th October and agreed to take the property. To be quite honest we were really desperate and would have taken almost anything at that stage. By the way, it never once crossed my mind to approach the mine authorities and ask for an extension on our lease. They had asked us to leave and we would therefore leave!

Once I had secured the property I phoned George Chesworth, one of the men in my congregation, who was in the removals business, and he agreed to move us late on Friday the 31st of October which was the only time that he was able to do it. As a result, that evening, we started to load the removals van at about 5.30pm and by the time we had unloaded it all at our new home, it was quite late. We were so tired by that time that we just left everything in a heap and fell into bed with exhaustion. It had been a really stressful time for Mally as she was very pregnant, so much so that the very next day she was admitted to QueQue General Hospital as her labour pains had started. But it was only the following evening, on Sunday the 2nd November that our first son was born and sadly I was not present!

As mentioned earlier, whilst I was in Hatfield a new Assembly had opened about eight miles away in Redcliff. This was the Iron and Steel centre in Rhodesia and in the 1970s it was a rapidly expanding town, and so when Roland saw the need, he started a Sunday School. This took place on a Sunday morning before the Sunday Morning service in QueQue and so after Sunday School he would rush back to QueQue for the morning meeting. Later, they also started a Sunday evening service and by the time I arrived back in the area a new minister had been appointed for Redcliff. He was a really lovely man of God by the name of Paddy McCoun.

In order to encourage one another, Paddy and I arranged to swap pulpits now and again. Well, believe it or not we arranged to swap pulpits on the evening of the 2nd November. As a result, while I was ministering the word in Redcliff, my wife was giving birth to our firstborn son! I praise God that Carol O'Connor was by her side as I was not there. In addition, I praise God that we were not homeless as He had provided somewhere for us to live. When I finally arrived at the hospital and was able to see my firstborn son, the nursing sister on duty said that if they were to put a pair of glasses on him, he would be the spitting image of his father. Praise God for the miracle of birth!

As I have already said, what a present to give to your husband on your first wedding anniversary! I was thrilled with my wife and baby son, and we immediately dedicated him to The Lord giving thanks to God for the miracle of birth. Praise His name!

The house was fully furnished, but because all the rooms were so huge, there was plenty of room to accommodate all our furniture as well. It was an old Rhodesian house with a big veranda at the front, and an outside room opposite the kitchen at the back, that I turned into my office. The drive way was at the back of the house between the kitchen and my office.

The house was generally in good order when we moved in, but the kitchen was really dirty. I was very grateful when two people from my congregation, Margy and Carol, offered to help clean the kitchen before Mally came out of hospital. While busy cleaning the kitchen, Margy's daughter Samantha, who was only 3 years old, was playing outside. We were shocked when she suddenly began to scream and we dropped everything and ran outside to investigate. When we saw her, we were horrified to find that she was being attacked by literally hundreds of bees.

To try to protect her from the bees, Margy threw a blanket or something similar over her. As Samantha was allergic to bee stings the ladies then ran for the car to rush her to the QueQue General hospital. However, just before they left, we laid hands upon her and prayed for God to intervene and save her. At the hospital they pulled something like 100 bee stings out of her, and in spite of her being allergic to bee stings, The Lord was gracious and she survived. She not only survived but at the time of writing this story she is married to a minister of the Gospel and serving The Lord in Canada.

We are not sure where the bees came from, but they most likely came from a bee hive that the previous tenants had yet to move from the premises. That ought not to have been a problem as they were on the other side of the building at the end of the lawn. As already mentioned, it was a big building with a very big lawn, and so the bees would have been some distance from where Samantha was playing, so it was a real puzzle.

As we had only just moved into our new house and it was something of a miracle that we had been able to rent it, I had a great idea, or so I thought at the time! I arranged to have a house-warming just as soon as Mally returned from the hospital with our new baby son and invited the whole congregation to our home. Please take note any new fathers, it was a bad idea!

When I phoned Brian to invite him to come to the 'house warming' he said that they would not be coming until the bees were off the property. When I reminded him that it would take place after dark, and bees are not generally known to be around at night, he said that he was taking no chances with his daughter. He also said that now that I was a father I would soon understand. The house-warming went ahead as soon as my family were home, but I am sad to say that my wife was not overjoyed, and I am not too sure what my son thought, as he was not saying a word!

That Christmas we invited all the parents of the Sunday School children to our Carol Service. Among those who attended were Peter and Sally Davis, neighbours of Danny and Carol, whose children were attending the Sunday School. At the end of the Carol Service, I preached a short message and concluded by inviting all in attendance, to the Christmas Day service. I learned later that the message had such an impact upon Sally that her knees felt weak as she got up to leave.

On Christmas day they were again present and I announced that we would have an open house that afternoon at our home to which everyone was invited. Among those who took us up on our offer were Peter and Sally who came with their children. We had a great afternoon and were able to use our large lawn to great advantage and it was not long afterwards that Sally made a decision for Christ.

After the Sunday evening service when she responded to the Gospel, I took her aside and went through a few Scriptures with her, the first one being: -

"For all have sinned and fall short of the glory of God." Romans 3.23

When I showed her the verse in the Bible I said, **"What this verse means is that we are all sinners including you and me."**

To which she replied rather forcefully, **"I am not a sinner!"**

I must admit that I was quite taken aback by her response, however, after a short conversation and going through a few more verses of Scripture we prayed together and, praise God, she asked Jesus to be her personal Lord and Saviour and was born-again. After this I was encouraged to see how quickly she grew in her faith. But sadly, although her husband Peter attended all the services, he had still not made a decision for Christ. However, after one Sunday evening service he approached me, and said, **"AB when I was sixteen, I made a decision for Christ, so where does that place me now?**

I replied, **"Where do you think you are?**

As he knew quite well that he was far from God, after a short conversation I suggested that we start from the beginning. It was clear to me that he had no assurance of salvation and had never really served The Lord. That night Peter asked The Lord to forgive him and receive him into His family. Praise God, that night

Peter received assurance of salvation and went on to be a dedicated follower of The Lord. Both Peter and Sally have continued to serve The Lord to the present day and a short while before beginning to write this book I was in contact with both of them.

Another family in fellowship with us, were the Chesworth's, the chap who worked for the removals firm that I mentioned earlier. He and his wife had a new baby around about that time and asked if I would dedicate their child at one of the Sunday meetings. I agreed and we arranged a date for the service.

That Sunday morning, we had no other musician available, so I ended up playing the piano accordion for the meeting. I was anxious to speak with them before the meeting started as I had a slight problem; I had forgotten the babies name and could not even remember whether it was a boy or a girl. Sadly, that morning they were a little late and I was already leading the first hymn when they arrived.

As I was wondering what to do, playing the piano accordion, and leading the singing at the same time, (who says men cannot do more than one thing at a time) I had a brain-wave and knew what I would do. I would speak to them whilst we were singing what I thought was a well-known dedication hymn which was called: -

'WHEN MOTHERS OF SALEM THEIR CHILDREN BROUGHT TO JESUS'

As the congregation continued to sing the second verse my plan was to stop playing and singing, and step down from the platform, and discover the relevant details. Sadly, when I stopped playing, and singing, the congregation also stopped, as none of them knew the song except me. I am not sure how I managed to get over that one, but the baby, boy or girl, was duly dedicated.

It reminds me of a story John Stegmann told me some time before. As the minister had failed to arrive, he was asked to conduct a funeral service, at a nearby church at the last minute. When he got to the church the congregation were already seated and waiting for him. As he faced them, he realised that he had neglected to ask whether the deceased was a man or a woman, so while they were singing a hymn he stepped down from the pulpit and very quietly asked one of the family members the following question, **"Excuse me, was the deceased a brother or sister?"**

The answer was also quietly given, **"Cousin!"**

Praise God that we can laugh at some of these embarrassing situations.

It was very encouraging to have a number of newly converted couples or families in fellowship with us at that time. One of these was a couple who allowed us to have a house group in their home. One evening the lady of the house said something like this, **"I thought that when I gave my life to Jesus, He would make my life easier, but since I gave my life to Christ, I have had nothing but trouble!"**

You may well laugh, but sadly many people do not understand that we are in a 'spiritual war' and the moment we give our lives to Jesus we become a major target for Satan who is the enemy. Jesus never offered us an easy road, He said 'follow Me' and as we all know the road that Jesus took led to Calvary. We need to remember that any 'dead fish' can swim downstream, but it takes a 'live fish' to swim against the tide of public opinion. It is not always easy to follow Jesus but praise God He is the only one who knows the way to heaven and that is where I want to go and so I will continue to follow Him no matter what comes my way! Sadly, we lost contact with this couple when we left QueQue but I would love to know whether they are still serving The Lord today?

There was another couple who allowed us to have Bible studies in their home but they had still not made a decision for Christ. One day they attended a funeral service and as a result of what they experienced they accepted Christ as their Saviour.

The funeral that they attended took place as a result of a terrible traffic accident just outside Selukwe. There were at least two fatalities, which included a father and his married son. They had only just driven out of their driveway onto the main road, when they were killed in a collision with another car going past at high speed. They and their wives and families were committed Christians and active members of the local Methodist Church. The couple in QueQue attended the funeral and when they saw how the two widows handled themselves in their grief, they realised that their faith was genuine. As a result, they wanted the same faith in God that these two ladies had. Praise God, when we lose a loved one who is a committed Christian, we may grieve, but we do not grieve like those who have no faith. We are only parted for a season; we will meet with our loved ones at Jesus feet. Praise His name!

An interesting fact about these particular

couples was that they had both been approached by the Jehovah Witnesses before they came to us. They could not accept what they were told by the JW's and wanted to know the truth. Praise God, we can all come to know the TRUTH, and HIS name is Jesus, the Saviour of this world.

As a Minister of the Gospel, I have preached on many different Biblical subjects but it was in QueQue that I first prepared a series of Bible Studies on 'THE FAMILY!' At a Conference in South Africa some years before I purchased a book by Larry Christenson called "THE CHRISTIAN FAMILY," however, I had never read it, and it had been sitting in my bookcase for some time.

Then, sometime in 1975-1976 I felt directed by The Lord to read the book on 'THE CHRISTIAN FAMILY.' Having read it I realised it was an exceptional book which Christian couples and parents would do well to read. Although many years have passed since it was first written it is still available and still a good guide to Christian family life. It proved to be a real blessing to me personally, a man who had so recently got married, and even more recently become a father. Once I had read it, I realised that it was a topic that Christians needed to hear as it was not only the 'families' of the unbeliever that were facing difficulties, but also the 'families' of Christians. As a result, I prepared a series of studies on 'THE FAMILY,' based on the Bible, with a lot of help from this book.

Before I continue, I would like to tell you a story about this young single minister who was challenged to write a book on 'The Family' because he saw so many Christian families in trouble. By the time he finished, the book had a great many pages. Some years later, as a young married man, he published an updated version of the book which turned out to be considerably shorter than the first book. Then after he and his wife had produced four young children, he again updated his book. On this occasion when it was reproduced it had even fewer chapters than before and was an even smaller book. Finally, when his children were all teenagers, he produced another update which was now reduced to a tract, with no chapters and only six short pages. This is not a true story I may add, however it could well be, as 'family life' is never easy and we certainly do not have all the answers!

It is interesting to note that although at that time I preached a lot on the family, in recent years I have not been led to do so very often. Yet, a few years before Mally went to be with The Lord, she encouraged me to do so again, but, I have still not done so, perhaps that is something I should consider in the future.

Nevertheless, as a young married minister after I presented this series of studies to my own congregation, I decided that I needed to take it further afield. As a result, over the next few months I arranged to preach on 'THE FAMILY' in a number of different Assemblies around the country.

I was very encouraged when I went to preach in Umtali that Bill Stevenson, the minister at that time, advertised the meetings in the Umtali Post, the local newspaper, and he also produced a number of handbills for his congregation to distribute. When I went to Marandellas, the 'special' meetings were widely advertised and leaflets were distributed all around the town. I was encouraged! They were doing the right thing! When someone as **well-known** as the minister of the **QueQue Assembly** comes to town, it was only right to advertise the fact!!

However, I was about to learn a few lessons, as my next visit was to be to Bethshan in Bulawayo. I had been in touch with Neil Gibbs, the minister, and arranged to share my series of six studies. But, at a ministers meeting in Salisbury, Neil let me know that 'six meetings' would be far too many. He suggested that I cut it down to four, but that I was still welcome. Then around two weeks before I was due to go to Bulawayo, I had a phone call from Neil who said, **"AB, I have been thinking about your upcoming visit and the Sunday evening meeting could be a bit of a problem. The evangelistic meetings are going so well on a Sunday night that I do not want to do anything that might stop what is taking place. As a result, sadly, we will have to cancel the Sunday Evening meeting on THE FAMILY. However, you are still welcome and we look forward to your ministry on Friday and Saturday evenings and on Sunday morning."**

Having heard what he had to say, I was quite discouraged, in fact to be quite honest I was devastated, and nearly cancelled my whole visit. I remember sitting there in my outside study thinking it over and finally deciding that no matter what happened I was going to Bethshan and I would preach as never before. It seemed to me that the enemy was determined to discourage me from preaching what God had given me.

But that was not all that happened to discourage me, as there was more to come. On the Sunday before I was due to preach in Bulawayo one of the Elders from

Bethshan visited our Sunday morning service. I knew him well and after the meeting as he was leaving, I said, **"I am looking forward to seeing you next weekend!"**

He asked, **"Why what's going on next weekend?"**

"I'm preaching at Bethshan." I replied

"Oh, that's new to me, I did not know. What are you speaking on?" He asked.

I was amazed to hear what he had to say! When I had preached in Marandellas, they had given out special leaflets advertising the meetings, when I had preached in Umtali, they had advertised it in the newspaper, however, in Bulawayo it appeared that the meetings had not been advertised at all as even the Elders did not know that I was coming!

If you think that that was bad, there was still more to come. When we went to Bulawayo we were privileged to be staying with Neil and Marge Gibbs, and as we were getting ready for the meeting, I realised that Marge wasn't coming. When I enquired, I was informed that it was only for the youth on that Friday evening! Once again, I was surprised as I had clearly told Neil what I was speaking on and it was not **ONLY FOR THE YOUTH!**

When we arrived at the Youth Meeting, it was encouraging to see how many were present. In addition, there was a special quest singer that evening. After some worship, the singer was introduced and just before he began Neil placed his tape recorder on the pulpit to record the song. He then leaned over to me and said, **"AB, please switch off the tape recorder when you get up there."**

I would not have minded had there been no tape

recorder, but to be told to switch it off, when I got up to speak, that was too much! As a result, by the time I arrived at the pulpit, to switch off the recorder, I was determined to 'sock it' to all who were there that evening! I was determined to preach God's Word as never before and proclaim with power what He had laid on my heart. Praise God, The Lord was good to me that night, and at the end of the meeting Neil said, **"We should have recorded that!"**

After he said that I said in my heart in reply, *"Too true Neil, too true!"*

As I have already said, The Lord was good to me that weekend, and after the Sunday morning meeting Neil said to me, **"We could have had that message at the evening meeting!"**

Once again, I said in my heart, *"It would have been great if that had of happened!"*

I have included the above in my story because as preachers we are God's servants not man's, and our reward comes from The Lord. I do believe that the devil wanted to stop me preaching in Bulawayo but I also know that God used this incident to change me, and I am so grateful that He did. My dear friend, Neil, had no idea of what was happening in my heart and unless he reads this book he will never know. He did a tremendous work in Rhodesia/Zimbabwe and I am indebted to him in many ways and have nothing but admiration for him. Thank you, Neil, for inviting me to Bethshan!

While in QueQue we were blessed with the company of Paddy McCoun who often came to spend time with us. It could well have been something to do with the fact that my wife Mally was a good cook and he was a bachelor! We also continued to swap pulpits and on occasion, I was able to sit under his anointed ministry. I will never forget a message he preached on the **"THREE RIGHTEOUS MEN"** taken from **Ezekiel 14.** Over the years I have often spoken about these three men and thank God for Paddy who pointed them out to me!

In the book of Ezekiel, we learn that the people of Judah, and in particular their leaders, refused to listen to the many warnings that God sent to them though His spokesmen, the prophets. As a result, He finally sent this message to the people of Jerusalem: -

'"Even if these three men, Noah, Daniel, and Job, were in it, (Jerusalem) **they would deliver only themselves by their righteousness," says The Lord God.' Ezekiel 14.14**

If you study the stories of Noah, Daniel, and Job, you will discover that their 'faith' and 'righteous' living resulted in other's being delivered from death. In the case of Noah, because of his 'righteousness,' his family were delivered from the Worldwide Flood that took place in his day. The 'righteousness,' of Daniel resulted in God revealing Nebuchadnezzar's dream to him. As a result, Daniel, his three friends Shadrack, Meshack, and Abednego, and the rest of the wise men of Babylon were saved from the wrath of Nebuchadnezzar. Finally, after a terrible time of trial God restored Job, and when he prayed for his 'friends' God healed them.

Nevertheless, the sins of Jerusalem were so great that the patience of God had finally run out. He said that even if these three righteous men were in Jerusalem, they would not be able to save the city from God's judgement. In fact, they would not be able to save anyone, family or friends, other than themselves, when God poured out His judgement upon the city. In spite of being three of the most righteous men to have ever lived their own righteousness could help no one but themselves, as God had made up His mind to destroy the city of Jerusalem.

I have preached on these "**THREE RIGHTEOUS MEN"** on many occasions since then, emphasising that salvation is an individual thing. It is vital that we realise that we cannot take anyone to heaven with us, neither can we trust in the righteousness of a family member, friend or religious leader to save us. Salvation is an individual thing between us and The Lord.

One day when Paddy was visiting, we discussed the possibility of having an Evangelistic Crusade in the town. We felt that we could count on our two Assemblies, QueQue and Redcliff, that were within eight miles of each other, and in addition there was the Apostolic Faith Mission, and the Full Gospel Church. These were all Pentecostal Churches, but there was also the Baptist Church who we felt would support the Crusade provided we had a preacher that was acceptable to all. After some discussion we decided to go ahead and present the idea to the other ministers in town.

Not long afterwards we met together and agreed to have a Crusade, which we would hold in the school hall. The guest speaker would be Gary Strong, a well-known Methodist Evangelist, who you will remember assisted me at that difficult funeral in Harare. This plan was duly set in motion and from then on until the

Crusade we met each week, for a combined prayer meeting in our different Church buildings. The prayer meetings were successful with a good number attending each week but, some of our people felt a little restricted, because of a desire not to offend the non-Pentecostals among us. However, we were eventually ready for the Crusade with counsellors, musicians, and stewards, as well as Gary Strong our guest evangelist.

Before the Crusade I was informed by certain long-term residents of the town that QueQue had never had such an event where the different churches had joined together to proclaim the Gospel. Our evangelist, Gary Strong, was the right man for the job, and a great preacher. Sadly, we did not see many 'new converts' at the Crusade, but the Christian community of the town were truly encouraged by the meetings and enriched by working together.

Out of the many people who attended the meetings, John McKenzie, the brother of Donald, who I have already mentioned, was one of the only people that I know who gave his heart to The Lord at that time. He was living in QueQue but working at Thornhill Air force Base in Gwelo.

He continued to work at Thornhill after the change of government when Rhodesia became Zimbabwe. As a result, he was working there when a number of aircraft were destroyed by unknown assailants, generally believed to have been from South Africa. After this took place all members of staff at the base were called in for questioning. However, when John was taken into the interview room he turned to his interrogators and said, **"I know that you have a very important job to do so could I please pray for you** before you begin? I want to ask God to guide you today."

When John said this, his interrogators were taken completely by surprise and as a result gave him permission to pray. Nevertheless, after he had prayed, they still gave him a very tough grilling, but John had called upon The Lord and He was present in that room. Praise His name!

While Gary Strong was staying with Mally and I in QueQue we had some interesting conversations. Unsurprisingly, because of all that was going on in the country at the time, one of those conversations concerned the political situation in the country. I remember him saying on one occasion that the government of Ian Smith could take a little bit of the wind out of the sails of the Nationalist forces by changing the name of Rhodesia to Zimbabwe. I was a patriotic Rhodesian, as I am sure he was, but the thought of my country being called Zimbabwe was 'a bridge too far' at that time in my life, but maybe Gary was right, in any case right or wrong it is now Zimbabwe whether we like it or not!

Moving on to another subject, one of the things that we were very grateful for in Rhodesia was something called 'right of entry.' Ever since the founding of the country, ministers of religion had been given the right to address their own young people once a week, in the public schools. This was called 'right of entry,' however, it was not always successful as on many occasions the person responsible for a particular class sadly failed to show up. As a result, every week the school had to provide a teacher or teachers to look after those whose staff were absent. Near the end of

1975 the Deputy Headmaster asked the Ministers of all the Churches in the town to attend a meeting at QueQue High School.

It is quite possible that we in the Assembly of God may have been passed over, had it not been for John Heyns, the Anglican Vicar, who made sure that I was included. We were relatively new in town and had only a few students at the High School. In spite of that, praise God, I was present at the meeting where the deputy head presented a new plan for 'right of entry' at QueQue High. He wanted it to be put into effect the following year and suggested that instead of the existing system, which was not perfect by any means, we support the following: -

1) The morning school assembly would be taken twice a week by one of the ministers in town.
2) The assembly would include two hymns, one at the beginning and one at the end.
3) In between the hymns the minister would have around 5-10 minutes to address the entire school of around 700 students.
4) The roster would be prepared by the minister who had the most students at the school which turned out to be my friend John Heyns from the Anglican Church.

Although all of those present had some misgivings about this 'radical' new idea we agreed to give it a try and so from the beginning of 1976 the plan was put into operation. As the minister who at the time, possibly had the smallest number of students at the school, I was grateful to have a couple of opportunities during the year to address the entire school assembly and considered it a great privilege!

At the end of the following year, we had another meeting with the deputy headmaster and were informed that since the start of the new proposals his punishment book had dropped by 50%. He attributed this result to the school assemblies being conducted by the ministers of the town. Praise God that through this new programme God's Word was proclaimed to the entire school with wonderful results.

As I have already mentioned, because we had so few children in the school, I did not get many opportunities, however, I do remember one assembly in particular. On that morning as I stood before the 700 students of QueQue High School I declared with great authority, **"I went to PLUMTREE SCHOOL, the best school in the country!"**

There was a momentary hush, before they all began to boo me or something similar. I then said, **"You are quite right to do what you have just done, and I did not expect any other reaction! But why do I say that? The reason you should object when I say PLUMTREE is the best school in Rhodesia, is because YOU are at QUEQUE HIGH SCHOOL! If you are a student here and it is not the BEST SCHOOL IN THE COUNTRY, YOU ought to make it YOUR business to make it THE BEST SCHOOL IN THE COUNTRY! Why would you want to attend the WORST SCHOOL in the country? You should make up your mind that as long as YOU are at QUEQUE HIGH SCHOOL it will be the BEST SCHOOL IN THE COUNTRY!"**

I then went on to say that God always expects us to do our best whether we are at school or elsewhere and most likely referred to the following Scripture: -

"And whatever you do, do it heartily, as to The Lord and not to men, -." Colossians 3.23

Sometime later, I was informed that my short message that day had been discussed by the schoolchildren long after that morning. It appeared that it had made a big impact upon them, which was very encouraging.

On one occasion Des and Kathy Nish were on holiday in Rhodesia from their Assembly in Bethlehem in the Orange Free State. They visited QueQue and stayed with Brian and Margy Boshoff. I asked Des if he would share the Word at the weekly house meeting which was being held in their home. The subject that he chose was **'WHAT HAPPENS WHEN WE DIE?'** It was an excellent study and I will always remember how well he spoke. I was amazed as he took us from scripture to scripture and longed to have a command of the Scriptures that he evidently had.

While speaking about the house meetings at the home of the Boshoffs I want to relate another incident that took place. Margy's grandmother came to visit and stayed some time with them, and naturally attended the meetings. She was a lovely old lady and a blessing to all, however, one evening we had a load of young people in attendance and they were very lively to say the least. In any case at the end of the meeting when most of the congregation had left, I said something like the following as a bit of a joke to her gran, **"You really made a lot of noise this evening. Hopefully next week you will be quieter?"**

It was supposed to be a joke, but must have come out wrong. As already mentioned, it had been the young people who had made a racket. In any case the damage was done as she took it personally and told me she would not be attending the services again. I felt awful, but what I said I was not able to take back. Sadly, we all say things that we wish that we had never said, may God help us with our unruly tongues!

On one occasion, and only once, Kenneth Mawire asked me to preach to the congregation that he had established in one of the townships. It was a real privilege, to be the preacher at a Gospel Crusade over several nights. But after preaching at a number of evening meetings, and then taking the Sunday morning service at my own Assembly, and finally the Crusade meeting on the Sunday afternoon, I was really exhausted. That Sunday evening when I arrived for my own meeting, I was so tired that I had to sit down to play the piano accordion before preaching. Who said Ministers only work on Sundays?

My dear friend Kenneth, was always keen for us to be part of what he was doing as a preacher of the Gospel. On a number of occasions Roland and I travelled to places around the country where he was preaching. On one occasion I managed to borrow a lovely tent from Peter and Sally Davis and we travelled in my Peugeot down a very corrugated road to the town of Gokwe. We then travelled on what was more like a track, than a road, way out into the bush to a place called Goredema.

As we were travelling between Gokwe and Goredema a police landrover passed us carrying a number of fully armed police reservists going the other way. As it happened, one of the men was a member of my congregation and when he saw me, he nearly fell out of the vehicle with surprise. I imagined him saying to himself, **"What on earth is my Pastor doing way out here. Has he not heard that there have been terrorist incidents not too far from here?"**

In any case when we arrived at Goredema we were met by Kenneth who as always was pleased to see us. We immediately set about pitching the tent, as it was already quite late in the day. Very foolishly, my fault, we pitched the tent on the brow of a hill, and as a result it could be seen for many miles by friend and foe. Once we were sorted, Kenneth asked me to accompany him to visit the leaders of the community. After I had been introduced, I remember saying something like the following, **"We are here because we believe in Jesus and have come to share his love with you. We know that there are dangers around but we are not scared, and if it is our time to die, we will die, but if not, someone could point a gun and shoot me and I would not die!"**

Having met with the village leaders and said such brave words Roland approached me and said, **"AB we are foolish to spend the night here, and we are doubly foolish to spend two nights here. We need to pack up and go tomorrow!"**

I was shocked and replied, **"Roland if you think I have travelled down some of the worst roads in Africa and then leave before the main congregation arrive tomorrow night then you are mistaken."**

I knew that once the word got out, many more people would attend the meeting the following evening and so I was not at all keen to pack up and go home before then. However, Roland was persistent, and eventually I agreed to have a word with Kenneth to ask his advice. Once we had talked to Kenneth and heard what he had to say, I agreed that we would leave after the morning meeting. And so, it was after a couple of good meetings in Goredema we set off for home early the following afternoon.

I must at this stage include my friend Roland's recollections about this trip as he says, **"I actually thought we had an uneventful first day with Kenneth and it was only the second day that I felt The Lord speak to me about the need to leave. I think I can also recall that on the first night I saw a couple of men sitting right at the back of the meeting and felt unsettled by them."**

Nevertheless, as it turned out, it was a good thing that we left when we did, and I may well owe my life to my friend Roland as we were told by Kenneth some months later that at the evening meeting, after we had returned home, some strangers arrived asking where the 'white' men were?

Now, before we leave Goredema, I have a couple of stories to tell as we visited a number of times over the years. On one occasion when we arrived, we discovered that Geoffrey Mkwanazi had just finished a week of meetings and was about to return to Bulawayo. We arrived in Roland's VW Kombi sweating and rather dusty from the journey, wearing shorts and open necked shirts. Both Kenneth and Geoffrey arrived to greet us and we were amazed to see Geoffrey holding an umbrella in his hand to shield himself from the sun, and dressed in a suit and tie looking very smart out in the African bush. I cannot remember how Kenneth was dressed!

As we prepared for the evening meeting, I discovered that Roland hadn't brought his 'tie' and so it was decided that whoever was preaching would wear the 'tie,' as having witnessed Geoffrey wearing a 'suit and tie,' we did not want to let the side down!

One evening while we were there, I was preaching (and wearing the tie) when a cry went up from the congregation, **"Nyoka, nyoka!"**

They were all sitting on the veranda of an African trading 'store' and I was standing a little distance away, in the cool night air facing the congregation. Someone was holding a Tilley lamp so that I could read my Bible and notes, but when the cry went up Roland quickly took hold of the lamp and advanced to where the commotion was taking place. He found the snake and captured it, and went out into the darkness where he released it into the bush. He later told me that it was a perfect example of a particular type of snake which was harmless and he would have loved to have kept it and placed it for safety inside his shirt. However, he knew that if he did that, the meeting would have been over, as the people would not have settled down. My friend Roland was very talented and had worked for the Rhodesian Museums and was an expert in the wild life of the country and a great painter as well.

On another occasion, I had a letter from Kenneth where he invited me to come down to Goredema and **'end the revival,'** however, I think what he really meant, was that I should come and preach at the final meetings of a series. Hopefully, when I went on that occasion I never actually **'ended the revival!'** On another occasion we travelled there in Roland's VW Kombi and the people were so grateful that they gave us a 'live goat' to take home. When we arrived in QueQue, the goat was donated to the Robertson family as Roland did not want it. It met its end at the local abattoir and we discovered that goat is actually very tasty and was enjoyed by all the family.

THE CONGREGATION AT GOREDEMA.
This was Mally's first visit to Goredema. Kenneth is in the front row on the far right with his wife Grace in the front the third from the right.

One Sunday morning back in QueQue, Kenneth Mawire decided to pay our Assembly a visit. Our Assemblies were always open to everyone but because of the racially divided residential areas and racially divided schools, ours was a 'White' congregation and the one Kenneth pastored across town was a 'Black' congregation. Because the presence of Kenneth, a 'black' man, at our Breaking of Bread service that morning was so unusual it caused a fair bit of tension.

As a result, at a later meeting, I made it clear that 'anyone' black or white was welcome to come to our meetings and if I heard any complaints, they would have to deal with me! At the time of writing this book this lovely man of God, Kenneth Mawire, is over 98 years old and still preaching the gospel in Zimbabwe and even travelling down to Mozambique.

In those years we were always keen to extend the work of God wherever The Lord opened the doors. As a result, when John Taylor asked if we could hold some meetings in the small mining community where he was working, I was keen to go. I had got to know John the last time I ministered in QueQue and one week night we arranged for a couple of car loads to travel to the Empress Nickel Mine for a meeting. It turned out to be a great meeting and we repeated the exercise a number of times at his request. Sadly, sometime later the mine closed down and the whole community moved away.

It seems amazing that with all this taking place I offered to travel down to Wankie to look after that Assembly, while Richard and Leslie Nash went away on holiday. I volunteered because Wankie is over 200 miles from Bulawayo where our nearest Assembly was located and it was easier to provide covering ministry for QueQue than for Wankie.

Our son, Mark, was just ten months old at the time we went to Wankie. In spite of that we took our little son to the Victoria Falls which is one of the wonders of the world! However, do you know what he did? He was more interested in having a sleep than having a look at these mighty falls! Nevertheless, Mally and I enjoyed the wonderful views of the mighty

Victoria Falls whilst our baby boy slept. To remind us of our stay in Wankie, we had a visit from a photographer who took some lovely pictures of the three of us!

THE ROBERTSON'S IN WANKIE. 1976

For those who are not familiar with Rhodesia, Wankie was a coal mining town situated in an extremely hot area of the country. In order to try to keep the temperature down inside the houses a lot of the more modern houses were built with an extra wall on the outside with a gap in between.

In the coal mines, the coal seams were so large, that in order to bring the coal out of the mine they drove huge trucks, and I really mean huge, down into the mine. With all that coal it was strange that the Rhodesian government allowed the railways to phase out the steam locomotives and replace them with oil? We could produce coal in abundance, but all the diesel had to be imported and international sanctions made it increasingly difficult to acquire the fuel.

Like most of our Assemblies, the Wankie

Assembly was quite small, but it catered for a real need in what was quite an isolated community. I remember Paul Brown, one of our young men who went into the ministry and moved to South Africa, saying to me one day that he had prayed something like this, **"Lord I surrender my life to you, use me as you will, but do not send me to Wankie PLEASE!"**

That might not be quite the way he prayed but it was something like that. Wankie was a small town with a population of miners. They were not really settled, as people would come and go all the time and so it was very difficult to establish a viable congregation. As already mentioned, it was very hot pretty much all of the time. Just before we leave Paul, in case I fail to mention it, he did a wonderful work at McChlery when he led the junior youth, and he had a lovely singing voice. On one occasion we had an outreach in the Central Park in Salisbury and Paul sang a wonderful song about: -

"BLIND BARTIMAEUS."

It was a great song but I have never heard it sung since, and have not been able to find it on the internet. Paul's parents had been missionaries in the Belgium Congo and his mom who was known as Aunty Mary was a real faithful member of our congregation when I was a young Christian.

Among the people we met in Wankie were Tommy and Terry Archibald. Tommy was working on the mines in Wankie at that time. They later went to South Africa where they entered the ministry and became part of the Coastal Assemblies under Mike

Attlee. At the time of writing, they are living in Scotland and continuing to serve The Lord. We had some great experiences in Wankie, but it was soon time for us to pack our bags and return home to QueQue.

One Sunday morning when we were back in QueQue, we had a visit from a young man by the name of Tim King who was visiting from Bulawayo. He was around 17 at the time and when he arrived at the door of the Church, he said something like this, **"Good morning AB, you can sit and relax this morning as I am happy to preach!"**

I thanked Tim for his offer but said he could leave it to me as I had it under control. He had come to visit one of the young women in the Assembly having met her at one of our youth camps. It was wonderful to have people visiting from other Assemblies around the country and to know that we were part of such a lovely growing family.

On a couple of occasions Mally and the ladies in the congregation organised a midweek outing for some of the older people. We travelled out of town to one of the beauty spots in the area, where a picnic lunch was enjoyed by all, helping to make each one of those outings a great success.

One of the things that I remember about QueQue was the large number of 'hard up white men' that came to my door. Eventually I was convinced that they were passing my name and address around as it seemed that there was always someone new coming to the door. Finally, I made up my mind that that was that, no more 'handouts!'

It must have been less than a week later when there was a knock at the door and it was a 'hard up white woman.' She had a 'story' to tell, as I had learned to expect! They always have a 'story', to tell! The story that she told was that her car had broken down, and she had to get to Salisbury on the night train and so would I please provide her with the money for the ticket?

I explained that I was no longer able to do that, as too many others had taken advantage of my generosity, and I had a wife and family to support. Nevertheless, she wore me down, and eventually I agreed to go down to the station with her and buy her a ticket for the night train to Salisbury. I was definitely not going to give her any money!

When we arrived at the ticket office, we were informed that it was too late to 'buy' a ticket for the train that evening. If she wanted to travel on the night train she would have to speak to the Conductor when the train arrived at around 10.00pm and if they had room on the train, she would be able to buy a ticket.

I had no desire to be there at 10.00pm and so I asked what the price was, and gave her the money for her journey to Salisbury. When I did so and parted with the money, I was sure that I saw a gleam of victory in her eyes as she took my cash!

Later on, that evening I decided to put my theory to the test and find out whether my name was being passed around as an 'easy touch' to all the 'needy' in the town? As a result, I phoned Seymour Edwards one of my congregants and the conversation began like this, **"Good evening, Seymour, would you be willing to go on a 'pub crawl' with me this evening?"**

There was silence at the end of the line and so I

explained what I had in mind and he agreed to accompany me. That evening we visited every drinking hole that we could find and to be quite honest I was amazed at how many there were. Although we did not come across the lady concerned, we did find a number of people that we did not expect to see! Having completed our 'pub crawl,' I dropped Seymour off and returned home.

When I returned home, I decided that I would have to go to the Station if only to satisfy myself. I had to find out whether this woman would be there to catch the train. When I arrived at the station, she was nowhere to be seen! I was about to go home, when I saw her emerge from the waiting room and when she saw me, she said, **"I see that you are checking up on me!"**

I mumbled something in reply but just then the train arrived and as a result I was with her when she spoke to the Conductor. Having established that she could board the train she purchased a ticket and was asked if she required a bed for the night? She looked in my direction and as a result I was required to put my hand in my pocket once again, and pay for a bed. I should have stayed at home!

Sadly, many people who want nothing to do with Jesus, or what He stands for, are quite willing to come with outstretched hands expecting God's people to provide for their needs. Not only that but the money is often spent on drink and drugs. In addition to that, many Christians are being persecuted for their faith, marginalised from society, and no one is helping them. It is true that we cannot help everyone however, we need to assist our 'brethren,' our Christian brothers and sisters who often have no one else to meet their needs. Needy Christians need to be our first priority after our own family!

Moving away from that subject, on a regular basis, we used to get together for 'Ministers' meetings' at different venues around the country. These were great occasions where we were able to pray and minister God's Word together and discuss what was happening around the nation. On one occasion we met up at our home in QueQue and my wife arranged a lovely meal which we all enjoyed.

As we were taking our seats, the two seats at either end of the table remained un-occupied. As a result, I indicated to the last person to come to the table, that he should take the one seat as I was preparing to sit at the other end of the table and without thinking I said something like, **"There's a seat for you at the bottom of the table."**

As a result, these very 'spiritual' men all turned to me and said, **"So YOU are at the TOP of the table?"**

As mentioned earlier I was always having my leg pulled. Around the table that lunchtime we had Bill Mundell, John Stegmann, and Neil Gibbs who all possessed a wonderful sense of humour. As can be expected we had a lovely meal, thanks to my wife, and many, many laughs before we finally left the table. Although we usually had a fair distance to travel to those 'meetings,' they were a tremendous blessing in so many different ways and I am deeply indebted to my 'brethren' for what each of them contributed to my life.

There is one more story that possibly should have been included during my time at Hatfield but as it involves QueQue I will relate it here. McChlery Avenue, my 'home' Assembly, as I have already mentioned was a very generous fellowship. They had donated a piano to the new Church in QueQue but it needed to be transported to QueQue. As we had an old VW Kombi in Hatfield which was used for transporting Sunday School children, I offered to deliver the piano.

The journey down to QueQue was uneventful, however, the steering was quite difficult and I had to concentrate all the time keeping both hands on the steering wheel. After delivering the piano I set off on my journey back to Salisbury and sadly ran out of petrol some distance from Hartley. I think the petrol gauge was faulty. I ought to have checked the fuel before setting off back home. While I was considering what to do an almost new car pulled up and the driver who was a little bit inebriated offered to help. As it would soon be dark, after some discussion, he came up with a plan. As we were only a few miles from Hartley, where I ought to be able to get some fuel, he suggested that he would 'push' me to the petrol station.

He got into his car and drove it up close until his 'bumper' connected with the 'bumper' of the Kombi. He told me that if for any reason I needed to slow down, I should indicate, and then off we went. It was fine to begin with but as we went faster, I was keen to tell him to slow down; however, I dare not take my hands off the wheel. It was a hair-raising drive and I was so pleased when it was over. Praise God, that no damage was done to his car and that we arrived safely at the garage in Hartley where I was able to get some fuel and was soon back home. However, if anyone offers to 'push' your car with another vehicle it may be better to say that you would rather walk!

One of the ladies attending the meetings always came on her own, in spite of her husband apparently being a believer, he never came with her. One day I made a point of going to see him and discovered that the reason he never attended our meetings was that he was a strong believer in British Israel-ism. They believe that the people of the British Isles are 'genetically, racially, and linguistically the direct descendants' of the Ten Lost Tribes of ancient Israel. We do not have time to go into this in this book, however, it is a teaching that I do not accept. Nevertheless, with a lot of persuasion he at last began to attend our services and I was hoping that over time we would be able to deal with this false teaching as we studied the word together.

An election took place on the 31st August 1977 and the Rhodesian Front, the party led by Ian Smith, the Prime Minister, was expected to win once again. However, a new political party called the Rhodesian Action Party, had been established, and this party was supported by our British Israel friend. The party had been formed in opposition to the negotiations that the Prime Minister had begun with some of the more moderate black political leaders. Although they were hard line in defending the status quo, many of the policies they stood for were decidedly Christian principles.

The election took place and once again the Rhodesian Front was overwhelmingly voted into power. On the day that the results were announced we had a prayer meeting at the Church and I heard one of the members of the congregation pray, **"Thank you Lord for allowing the 'Rhodesian Front' to win the election and for the overwhelming defeat of the**

'Rhodesian Action Party.'

It was a difficult moment, as my friend, who was a keen supporter of the party that had been very convincingly defeated, was present that night. As a result, I made sure that I followed up on his prayer with a prayer of thanksgiving, thanking God that He alone is in control and we submit to His perfect will.

Somewhere around this time John Stegmann who had done such a great work in our country, advised us that he felt it was time to return to his homeland of South Africa. At a Ministers' and Elders' meeting at McChlery in Salisbury on the 4th August 1977 He read the following verse from the book of Jeremiah before telling us of his decision: -

"If you have run with the footmen, and they have wearied you, then how can you contend with horses? And if the land of peace, in which you trusted, they wearied you, then how will you do in the floodplain of the Jordan? Jeremiah 12.5

There was no doubt that things were changing in Rhodesia and John and his lovely wife Yvonne were returning home. We would surely miss them as during their time in Rhodesia, John had accomplished an enormous amount, and I and so many others, owed him and Yvonne so much!

John & Yvonne Stegmann & Mark in South Africa 1979
Our Peugeot 304 Station Wagon in the background.

There could be no doubt that there was no one who would be able to fill his shoes as he was a unique individual! Nevertheless, praise God, there was a man, very different from John, who was able to take on the job of leadership in the country under John Bond. His name was Neil Gibbs and during his leadership of just over 6 years he did an amazing amount to proclaim the Gospel right across the land. During those years we were truly blessed to work with Neil and his lovely wife Marge.

In spite of my love for all my congregation and all the great things that had been happening in QueQue I felt that it was time to move on. As a result, I phoned

Neil to let him know what I felt and he replied by saying something like the following, **"AB, the only thing that I have available is Umtali. It is not an easy situation but we need someone there as soon as possible."**

In reply, I said, that I was willing to go to Umtali just as soon as it could be arranged. We then fixed a date which was immediately after the 'Family Camp' where I was the main speaker. The Camp had been arranged by Danie Haarhof one of the elders at McChlery, and was being held at Lake McIlwane. Like most congregations, QueQue had its own problems and while in conversation with Neil Gibbs I asked if someone with a little experience could to be sent to QueQue when I moved on.

When I announced that we were moving to Umtali many in the Congregation expressed their disappointment as Mally, Mark, and I had made a lot of good friends. At my last Sunday evening service, I called all of the men up to the front and challenged them to support my successor with all that they had. I was amazed to discover that more than a dozen good men came to the front that evening. Among those men was Alison and Penny Hardwick's father, who was a school teacher at QueQue High School. When his daughters first started attending the meetings and he heard **what I was preaching** he very nearly banned them from attending. Praise God, he subsequently came to know Jesus as his Saviour and Lord. I was amazed to discover that in that small fellowship there were five teachers at the time we moved on to Umtali.

The congregation laid on a farewell 'braai' at someone's house, where we were able to enjoy good food and some good conversations. I took the opportunity to ask Danny O'Connor how things were going being part of two separate congregations? The last time we had discussed his situation he said that he was trying to establish a Catholic Charismatic group in QueQue and so I asked him how it was going. He replied that nothing had happened and so I said, **"Danny, it is time to leave the Roman Catholic Church and put your weight behind the local Assembly."**

We left a few days later to go to the Family Camp, and then on to Umtali. Praise God I can report that Danny took my advice and left the Roman Catholic Church and committed himself and his family wholly to the local Assembly. Sometime later they moved down to South Africa where he became an elder in the Alberton Assembly. We were privileged to stay with them on a number of occasions when travelling down to Cape Town and have many happy memories of those times.

Before we move on, I would like to share a story that Danny and Carol told us when we visited them in Alberton some years later which is quite revealing. Their Minister at the time was Lawrence Wilson and his wife Margaret, who had come out of our Assembly in Salisbury. One day Danny and Carol felt that they ought to arrange to visit them, basically to show them how much they valued them as a couple. I believe the conversation went something like this.

Danny greeted Lawrence, **"Good evening, Lawrence, would it be possible for us to come around and see you this week?"**

Lawrence replied, **"Yes, that would be possible, how about Thursday evening?"**

"That sounds great, we will see you on Thursday at about 7.30pm." Danny replied.

On the evening in question, they had been at the Wilson's home for about ten minutes when Lawrence said, **"Well, what's the problem?"**

Danny asked, **"What do you mean, what's the problem? we have no problem!"**

Lawrence asked, **"Well why have you come? No one ever visits us unless they have a problem!"**

Danny said, **"We just wanted to come around and tell you how much we appreciate you both."**

I understand that Lawrence and Margaret were quite shocked, to discover that they had just wanted to spend some time visiting them, in order to show them how much they appreciated them both. The words may not be exact but that is basically the story that Danny and Carol told us. I do trust that all those reading my story will take note that many Ministers and their wives need to be encouraged as they are continuously giving out and on occasion, just like anyone else, they also need encouragement!

Well, initially my replacement was going to be Ron Davis and his wife Dorothy and when I shared this good news with the QueQue Assembly they were very excited. Ron and Dorothy had a lot of experience and would without doubt do a great work in QueQue. However, this was not to be as the Elders of the Assembly in Hatfield persuaded Neil Gibbs that Ron and Dorothy should continue on at Hatfield. As a result, my replacement turned out to be a new man by the name of Gerry Swart who had moved down from Zambia to Rhodesia with his wife and family. Although Gerry was new in the Ministry, I encouraged the

Assembly to support him in the same way as they had supported Mally and myself.

The Family Camp at Lake McIlwaine was a blessing to all who came. One of those was my British Israel believing friend, who while at Lake McIlwaine took some lovely photographs of Mark, Mally and myself. I also remember standing under a tree in the hot sun having a long conversation with someone and getting badly sunburnt. I was wearing 'slops' and my feet really were burnt in the sun and ever since that day I have made sure I do not repeat that mistake.

The only time that I was able to meet Gerry was when he visited me at Lake McIlwaine. I gave him a list of regular members and said that he did not need to worry about any of them as they would stand behind him when he went to QueQue. However, there was one man that he needed to treat with a little caution and that was my British Israel friend. I encouraged Gerry to give him time, avoid a discussion on the subject until he had gained his confidence and just show him love and God willing, in time, hopefully, he would change his opinions.

Sadly, within a few minutes of our conversation my BI friend engaged Gerry in conversation and that was the end of that! I do not share this to point the finger at anyone, as if that conversation had not taken place at Lake McIlwane, it would have taken place not many days later in QueQue. But I was just so sad that it had to take place when it did, which resulted in this man not attending the Assembly again. I was sad that having spent so long working with this man it ended the way it did! Once again, I stress, this is not to point the finger at Gerry who was a lovely man of God, it is only to explain what happened.

Well, after a successful Family Camp, we set off for Umtali, but, before we left for the City of Umtali we were given some 'encouraging' words by certain people in Salisbury like, **"Hi AB, I believe that you are moving to Umtali? Listen, do not be discouraged if you fail, as others have gone before you and did not succeed!"**

Another one was, **"Hi AB, I believe it's your turn in the wilderness?"**

Well, despite the words of 'encouragement' like that, we set out for Umtali.

4) UMTALI ASSEMBLY. 1977-1978

UMTALI ASSEMBLY.

The City of Umtali was established on the border of

Mozambique in the beautiful Eastern Districts, which is a very lovely part of Rhodesia. It did not have a large population and although it was a border town, the border was closed when we lived in Umtali, and the tourist traffic that used to flow through the town to Beira, no longer came. We were living very close to Rhodesia's premier coastal holiday resort and yet we were unable to visit. My wife, and most of the 'white' population of Rhodesia, had often travelled to Beira before the border was closed, but in spite of living so close, whilst pastoring the Assembly in Umtali, I still have never been to Beira.

Although I was not particularly conscious of it at the time, Umtali had been very badly affected by the economic sanctions that the British Government had persuaded the United Nations to place upon our country. The port of Beira was closed to Rhodesian imports and exports and the rail traffic that used to come through the town had ceased. In addition, the Feruka Oil Refinery built just out of town, had been closed down in 1966 due to the British blockade on oil imports coming into Beira. Previously the crude oil had been pumped through a pipeline from the docks at Beira to the refinery. In addition, we now had a hostile government on the other side of the border, as the Portuguese had left on the 25th June 1975 and the country was now ruled by Frelemo, a Marxist Government, committed to the downfall of Rhodesia.

When Bill Stevenson left Hatfield to go to Umtali in 1974 he took on more than the local Assembly. In addition to caring for the local fellowship he was involved in an outreach at Inyazura, a small town some 20 miles from the city where former members of the

Assembly were working. If that was not enough, there was also an outreach to Rusape, a town some 60 miles from Umtali. As a result of this workload, sometime before I arrived in Umtali, John Stegman asked Roland Pletts to move from Marandellas to Umtali to assist Bill in building up the work.

Some years before this, when Bill was in secular work in Umtali he was involved in a motor accident with a young man. At the time of the accident his whole family were in the car but God was gracious, only the cars were damaged, and none of passengers or drivers were injured. The young man was Roland Pletts. As a result of the way the Stevenson's handled the whole affair they were able to invite him to the Assembly. It was there that Roland came to know The Lord under the ministry of Bill Mundell. This naturally resulted in the Stevenson's and Roland having a very special relationship.

When Bill arrived back in Umtali, he discovered that the mortgage on the Assembly building, had been arranged in a way that ownership of the building would never be transferred to the local fellowship. Because of his understanding of these things, he was able to resolve the issue while he was there. Although there was a flat attached to the building it was rather small for a family, and it appeared that shortly before Bill arrived back in Umtali a manse had been purchased.

However, the house, which was in a good part of town, at 141 Upper 3rd Street was a rather run down, 'double story.' While Bill was there, he arranged for the roof to be repaired, which was quite an expensive undertaking and the most important issue. Sadly, although the main work was completed, certain things were not done properly and some of the money had been retained until the contractor completed the work satisfactorily. But, for whatever reason, the contractor never returned to finish the job and therefore he never received the final payment, but praise God the roof never leaked.

Before we left QueQue we advised my sister Avril and her husband Patrick of our new address. One day when they were visiting Umtali on a shopping trip they decided to see if we had arrived, but when they arrived at the address, they came to the conclusion that they had the wrong house as surely, we were not going to be living there! The outside of the house was badly in need of a paint job, the garden was very overgrown as no one had been living in the house for possibly as long as a year, and it really looked in a bad way.

But they did have the right address and we moved in a few days later. Once again, I want to praise my wife Mally for being so willing to move, even though she never found it easy. She was willing to live in some 'interesting' properties, as she shared my life and ministry (remember QueQue with the 'bucket' toilet in the garden outside the house?) However, I have to say that it was by far the happiest home that we ever lived in, and when we moved on, we really missed our 'double story' home, in Umtali!

So, what had happened to Bill and Roland who had been working together in Umtali and districts before I arrived? Well, Roland returned to the Midlands and became the Pastor of the Redcliff Assembly. As far as Bill is concerned, he returned to secular work for a season in Salisbury. In addition, he was involved in a work in Bindura with Dave Stevenson who was a District Commissioner with the Ministry of Internal Affairs. Sadly, when they both left Umtali there was no one available to replace them. As a result, when I made myself available, sometime later, it must have been as a result of someone's prayers.

We arrived in Umtali in the middle of the week and my good friend Rob Day, who was now working in the city, came around to visit with his wife Cathy. They presented us with the keys to the Assembly and advised us that most of the rather small congregation would be away that weekend. As they would be out of town, they gave us the rundown on the weekend meetings which included, where the 'unleavened bread and non-alcoholic wine' for the Saturday night Breaking of Bread were stored. Praise God, in spite of being told that most of the regulars would not be there that Saturday evening, one thing we did know, was where the Assembly was located!

That Saturday evening, we arrived early to open up and prepare for the meeting. However, in spite of searching high and low we could not find the items needed for the Breaking of Bread. We finally gave up looking and I set out to look for a shop that was open. After a while I returned with a bottle of Coca-Cola and some bread, as that was the closest that I could get to the 'unleavened bread and non-alcoholic wine' that I wanted. In spite of our efforts, the only person to arrive for the meeting was a young policeman who had just been transferred to Umtali. As a result, Mally, Mark, the young policeman and myself 'broke bread' together in the presence of God. Numerically, this was an even worse welcome than I had had in QueQue in 1972, but praise God, The Lord was there!

The next morning, we had REVIVAL as including us, there were about SIX people present. One of the congregants was Mrs. Friend a lovely dedicated lady. While we were in conversation after the service, she asked whether we had a lounge suite? She told us that she had just had her house done up and was getting a new suite, but her old suite was almost new and if we would like it, we were welcome to have it. As it turned out, we did not have a lounge suite, and planned to purchase one in Umtali and so we readily agreed to have it.

The suite was delivered a few days later and just like we had been told, it looked as if it had never been used. However, it was 'yellow' and my wife did not really appreciate 'yellow,' but it was also 'free,' and 'yellow' or not, we really did appreciate the gift, and it remained in the family for some years. If you remember with just a handful of people in my first meeting in QueQue, Wayne Ferguson offered me somewhere to stay. Now on our arrival in Umtali with only around six people in the meeting, Mrs. Friend provided us with a lounge suite which we really needed! God was continuing to look after us!

That Sunday evening, our congregation was around six, and it never grew for almost twelve months. It was really difficult for me as a preacher to see no growth for so long! But when the same people faithfully attend, I believe we need to continue to faithfully minister to them.

I have already mentioned in some detail my experiences with the 'contacts' that I was given in QueQue when I first arrived in that town. I would now like to mention what happened when I went to visit some of the 'contacts' that I followed up in Umtali. Remember the Assembly had not had a full-time minister for possibly a year and on some weekends, there was no one available to travel to Umtali to take the meetings, however, I am sure that one of the locals would have taken the services when that happened.

One of the 'contacts' that I went to visit was a man that I only ever knew as Brother Gee. When I introduced myself and invited him to the meetings, he had the following to say, **"If the Assembly of God were not willing to look after the few sheep that they had, they do not deserve to have any at all."**

I think that this was in reference to the fact that on some weekends after Bill and Roland left there had been no covering ministry available. He then said, **"The Good Shepherd gave His life for His sheep, He did not run when He saw the wolf coming!"**

I believe that this was in connection with the 'terrorist war' being waged in the country. It was definitely more real and dangerous in the Eastern Districts than it was in Salisbury. However, I must stress that he wrongly concluded that my fellow ministers had moved away because of the war. Sadly, Brother Gee did not return to the fellowship but he did continue to serve The Lord. Amongst other things after the war ended, I heard that in spite of being almost blind and of an advanced age he travelled into Mozambique giving out Christian tracts and encouraging people to turn to Christ.

Another 'contact' that I visited was a man who told me that the most important thing for him was his family. He did not have time to come to church, as he was busy all week providing for his family and at the weekends, he needed to spend time with them. Sadly, by not taking care of his own spiritual life there is no doubt that he would fail to teach his family about the God who created him. In addition, if he considered God to be so unimportant that he could not spare the time to worship Him with other believers, his family would also think that God was unimportant. This was a dangerous path to take, as The Lord Jesus made it very clear that when He returns, if we have not acknowledged Him in this life, He will not acknowledge us in the future!

"Therefore, whoever confesses Me before men, him I will also confess before My Father who is in heaven." Matthew 10.32

Despite failing to encourage these two men to return to fellowship, I praise God for the faithful people who made our stay in Umtali such a joy. As already mentioned among them were Mrs. Friend, Rob and Cathy Day, but there was also Mrs. Amm and her son Howard, and Dave and Wendy Rennick and many others. Praise God for faithful people!

It was not long before I realised that the Sunday afternoon meetings in Rusape were just too much for me to handle. Saturday evening and Sunday morning in Umtali, then an afternoon meeting in Rusape, followed by an evening meeting in Umtali was a bit too much to handle, in particular with the distances involved. There were four or five families involved with the work in Rusape plus a few individuals, but because of Army and Police Reserve 'call ups,' on most

Sunday afternoons at least half of the men were always missing. Because of the distance from Umtali and my responsibilities there, it was not possible for me to "grow" the Assembly and provide the 'pastoral care' that the congregation needed.

After the service one Sunday afternoon a member of the congregation asked if he could have a word with me. He told me that unless the Assemblies of God were able to provide a full-time minister for the fellowship in Rusape it would be better to close the whole thing down. If we closed the work down, the small congregation could link up with the Apostolic Faith Mission who had a functioning Assembly in the town. I agreed to discuss the issue with Neil Gibbs but knew that there was just no one available at the time! In addition, the small local fellowship could not possibly support a full-time minister.

After discussing it with Neil Gibbs, I advised him that it was not possible to provide a full time Minister for this pioneer work in Rusape. I also said that if he felt that he would be better off in the AFM then that is where he should go, and sadly, that is what he did! As a result of his decision, I spoke to the rest of the congregation and we agreed that the whole thing was no longer viable and sadly we closed the Assembly in Rusape. I say sadly, as it is never a good thing to 'close' a preaching point, however, I must admit that I was pleased, as it was too much for me to continue to do on my own.

One of the families in Rusape were the Letley's who lived in Inyazura where we continued to hold a midweek meeting. This was so much easier for me to arrange, and so they continued to be part of the Umtali

Assembly. The meeting was held in the afternoon and was a blessing to all who attended. Some of them lived in the village and some were farmers from the surrounding area.

Although we closed the Rusape work I was still keen to develop the wider work wherever I could. As a result, we arranged a few evening meetings in Inyazura. As it was unwise to travel between the two towns after dark, this meant staying overnight. On one occasion, I had retired for the night and was in bed at one end of the house in an outside room, when something disturbed me. It sounded like 'gunfire,' and I was sure that the village was under attack! The 'gunfire' continued for some time, and then stopped just as suddenly as it had started and all was quiet. What puzzled me, was that there was no response from the village in any way, which I just could not understand?

As I just could not work it out, it took me sometime to return to sleep. It was a real puzzle, until the next morning when much to my relief, I discovered that the village had not been under attack. What I had heard in the middle of the night were noises emanating from the hot water system! You can laugh but it was serious at the time!

Back in Umtali, one Sunday morning a young school girl by the name of Charmaine Lobb arrived for the morning meeting. She was a boarder at Umtali Girls High School and her family were living in Middle Sabi. When her father, filled in the school application form, he answered the question about 'religion,' with Assembly of God! As a result, every Sunday morning Charmaine walked from the boarding hostel to the meeting, in the company of other school girls who were going to the Presbyterian Church. Their Church was just up the road from us, and when they walked past our building, she would leave the group to attend our meetings.

Her father Errol's involvement with the AOG had begun, when he was working with the CMED (Central Mechanical Equipment Department) near Wankie, the other end of the country some years before. One day he decided to go across the border to Livingstone, for a night out, in what was then Northern Rhodesia. It appears that after drinking too much, he was arrested by the police and locked up. I am not sure how long he was in custody but while he was there, he was visited by Bill Mew who was ministering at that time in the Wankie Assembly. It was as a result of this visit that this dedicated man of God, led Errol to The Lord. It is possible that as a result of living out in the bush with little fellowship or teaching, he subsequently drifted from The Lord. Yet, when his daughter went to boarding school in Umtali he knew that he ought to send his daughter, to the same people who had led him to The Lord.

I am not sure when or if the Assembly would have turned the corner and begun to grow, but things definitely began to change when Mike Howard was posted as a teacher to Umtali Boys High School. Shortly after he began to attend the Assembly, he was able to bring a number of the students with him to the meetings. Some of these boys came to know Jesus as their Saviour and as time went on as many as twenty or thirty boys were attending the services from the High School.

One Sunday morning I suggested that while we sang a particular song, we do a 'Jericho march' around the inside of the building. This was greatly appreciated by the students and they wanted to do it every meeting. However, on the following Sunday I felt that we ought not to make it a regular thing and didn't do it again, much to their disappointment. It is possible that when the girls saw so many boys attending our meetings, that they started to attend. As they walked past the Assembly, heading for the Presbyterian Church some of them began to follow Charmaine into the meetings, which increased our congregation substantially.

I am not sure what I would have done about this situation if it had continued. But it was taken out of my hands when the Headmistress put her foot down and told the girls that they were to attend the Church that their parents had specified. In spite of the girls no longer being able to attend, Charmaine continued to attend the meetings faithfully and she became a part of our family, as Mally made her very welcome at our home on Sundays after the meetings.

One Sunday evening I advised the congregation that we were going to do something different the following week. After our time of praise and worship we were going to have an evening of testimonies, I was not going to preach, I wanted to hear from them. I encouraged them to come prepared and assured them that we would all be blessed as we listened to testimonies of what God had done in their lives. The following Sunday I was not disappointed as things turned out exactly as I expected. However, the only testimony that I remember went something like this,

"Some time ago I was going through a very difficult time in my life. So much so, I was even tempted to end my own life. One night the temptation was so great that before I went to bed, I felt that I needed to take some precautions to stop anything happening in the dark hours of the night. As a result, I went and got my .22 rifle from the cupboard and broke it up. I took out the cartridges and hid them in one part of the house, the bolt I put in another part of the house and finally the rifle itself was locked away somewhere else. That night was one of the darkest in my entire life, but praise God, The Lord watched over me and I eventually came out of that dark depression."

As I sat there and listened, I realised that had I not given this dear brother the opportunity, we would never have heard this testimony. Sadly, this dear brother has had to face a number of serious challenges during his life, but in spite of that he has continued to remain faithful to the God who called him.

As already mentioned, our house was a 'double story,' and there was no carpet on the stairs and Mark was under a year old when we arrived. We did not have any of those fancy 'stair gates' that are so common today and one day Mark was upstairs and wanted to come downstairs and before we could stop him, he slid down on his tummy. In spite of the fact that we brought them up tough in Rhodesia, we were still quite concerned when we first saw him do it, however, Mark loved it!

It was in Umtali that Mark first began to walk and I can see him in my mind's eye taking his first steps. We laughed and he laughed when he managed a few steps and then fell down. Praise God for children, they are truly a blessing from God! It was also in Umtali that I remember getting up in the middle of the night to attend to Mark in order to give Mally a break. He usually needed a nappy changing and then wanted another bottle of juice which he called 'kim' and was not satisfied until he had his 'kim.' He suffered a lot from colic as a baby and I would often walk backwards and forwards patting him on his back and encouraging him with the following words.

"We must through many tribulations, enter the kingdom of God." Acts 14.22

Although it is very true, I am not sure that I would recommend what I did, however, this is my story.

While in Umtali, we had a small dog who we called Fred after Fred Basset. This was a little difficult when my mother and Uncle Fred came to stay. I had to do some fast talking when introducing our mutt! Sadly, whenever we went away, as an example, every month down to Middle Sabi, Fred would also take off. This was despite the fact that he was never left on his own, as our servant, whose name was Ground, lived on the site in the 'kaya' at the back of the house. Sadly, although there was a hedge around the property, there was no fence and no gate.

On the first occasion Fred went missing, we spent a lot of time looking for him. We finally discovered him at the home for unmarried mothers not far from where we lived. From then on whenever he went missing that is where we could find him. When we left Umtali and moved to Chipinga our neighbour was thrilled to take Fred off our hands as her little dog had just died. The next time we saw him he was a 'fat' little dog completely spoilt by our neighbour. She, by the way had both a fence and a gate, and so Fred could not take his own exercise anymore! When we saw him, he was thrilled to see us all and we were also thrilled to see him. It was great to see him looking so well, although he definitely was over fed!

Before we proceed, just a word about our servant whose name was Ground. He was an excellent worker and although we only were able to pay him a very small wage, he never complained. He was just grateful to have a job. One day I was surprised when he took delivery of some furniture. When it was delivered, I must have assisted him in getting it into his quarters and discovered how many dresses his wife possessed. I was truly amazed to find that she had more dresses than my wife! I asked him how he did it and he replied that he had bought them on credit from Zimbabwe Furnishers, whose slogan was:

"Njore Njore Zimbabwe Furnishers!"

Prior to 1965, it was not possible for 'Africans' in Rhodesia to get 'credit' but in that year a Mr. Cohen opened his first shop in Umtali which was willing to provide 'credit' to 'African' customers and later, because of the success of the project, many shops were established. Their slogan, **'Njore Njore Zimbabwe Furnishers,'** became very well-known right across the country. It was as a result of the 'credit' provided by this business, that my good servant Ground was able to purchase furniture and a large number of dresses for his wife.

At our farewell in QueQue, before moving to Umtali, the congregation had given us a parting gift in appreciation of our labours among them. When we arrived in Umtali, we purchased a new lawn mower with the money. There was a fair bit of grass around the property and we needed to have it looking nice. The lawn mower was not a motor mower, or an electric mower, but a simple Rhodesian made, push mower. This type of lawn mower worked very well on bowling greens with short grass, but was not really suitable for long grass which was what we had when we first arrived in Umtali.

However, soon after we arrived, we met up with Luke Pambangomba one of the Pastors working with Nicholas Bhengu and the Back to God, Crusade. In order to assist him, as he was struggling financially, I asked him if he would like to do some gardening for us? He readily agreed, and I gave him our new lawn mower, and asked him to cut the grass. He was a very strong man and he made sure that the grass was cut, but I am not sure that I was ever able to use the lawn mower again. I am at fault, the lawn was very overgrown and we ought to have cut the grass down, before using our new lawn mower!!

In spite of that, our 'pastor-gardener' had a real heart for God and was a real blessing to us. One of his desires was to provide for the many orphans that were the outcome of the terrorist war, however, I am not sure that he was ever able to do what was on his heart.

Getting back to our family story, The Lord blessed us in Umtali, the same way that He had blessed us in QueQue when Matthew David Robertson was born in Umtali General Hospital.

Sometime before this major event, we met up with a group of believers from different congregations around the city. Among them were Billy and Glenda Nel who attended another Pentecostal Church in the city. We became good friends and when the time came for Mally to go into Hospital, we were able to drop off our son Mark with the Nels and their family.

Once Mally was booked in, the sister on duty advised me to go on home and have a good night's sleep as it would be a long time before our baby was born. I ought to have stayed right there and not listened to her, as later that night, Monday the 27th July 1977, our second son Matthew was born. When I arrived in the morning it was all over and we were the proud parents of another lovely boy. If you remember, I was preaching in Redcliff when our first child was born, and when our second son was born, I was in bed sleeping. But you will be pleased to know that on this occasion, I never arranged a 'house warming' or 'welcome home party' when Mally came out of hospital! I was learning slowly!

My sister Avril and her husband Patrick came through to Umtali and took Mark back to their farm in Inyanga for a few days to give Mally a little time to adjust to our new baby. About a week later we went up to the farm, stayed a couple of days, and brought Mark home. Praise God for giving me a wonderful wife who had, up to now, presented me with two lovely sons!

During our time in Umtali, a number of people came around to the Church and also to our house asking for help in one way or another. One of these men was a middle aged 'white man' whom we did our best to help. As mentioned earlier there was a lot of work needed to be done on the house, and so I agreed to help him, if he was willing to do some work for us. This, he was pleased to do, and as he had nowhere to stay, for a short while we let him sleep in the Church apartment. This was possibly not a wise thing to have done, but we were trying our best to assist him both physically and spiritually.

While he was with us, he attended the midweek Bible study, and one evening he was accompanied by a couple of friends. They turned out to be 'ladies of the night,' but naturally they were as welcome as anyone else at our meetings. Sadly, I ought to have preached a simple Gospel Message but instead, I just carried on with the Bible Study that I had planned. The congregation included our homeless man, his two friends, the 'ladies' that I have mentioned and another visitor, a man doing his Army 'call up' in Umtali. In addition, there was Mally and Mark in his 'carry cot,' and Howard Amm, who was the only other member of our congregation present that evening. Quite an interesting turn out for a mid-week meeting!

We only saw the 'ladies of the night' on that occasion and the homeless man left soon afterwards. Sadly, the man on 'call up' died in a contact with terrorists, not long after he was in Umtali. I suppose the lesson that we can learn from this, is that we never know who will be in the meetings and how soon they will be called to stand before God, so may The Lord help us to be sensitive to His leading at all times.

One day an 'African' painter came around to the house. Somewhere along the way we had stopped speaking of the 'black people' as 'natives' and began to refer to them as 'Africans.' In addition, we did not generally refer to the 'white' people as 'white' but rather as 'Europeans' which is really quite strange, as I was born in Africa and so was my father!

In any case this man came around and offered to paint the outside of our house! It was not really strange that he felt that we needed a painter, as the house was looking really shabby! As he promised to do the job for a very reasonable price, we took him on and what a difference it made. When he had finished painting, it looked like a new house! If the painting had been done before we moved in, my sister would never have driven by, thinking that we could not possibly be staying in such a house. It really did look great, and in time we were also able to do the inside of the house. As I have already said, it was the happiest house that we ever lived in, possibly during our entire marriage. We loved it praise God!

Now, because the Assembly was near the centre of town, we did from time to time have visitors who wanted a 'hand out.' The first one that I want to speak about was a well-dressed 'black man.' To be quite honest I do not recall him ever asking for any help, it appeared that he just came along for a chat. He was "living off' a relative in Umtali whilst looking for work. But there were no jobs to be had and so every now and then he would come and see me for a chat, and complain about his personal situation.

Usually, he would arrive just as I was about to head off home at lunch time, which was always a bit annoying. One day true to form, he arrived, just as I was about to return home for a bite to eat before travelling to Inyazura for the afternoon meeting. Because of his bad timing, I was not too keen to listen to his complaints about not being able to secure a job, whilst living off his relatives, and doing nothing in return. As a result, I said, **"You are a Shona and as a result you have land in the tribal areas, is that so?"**

He replied, **"Yes, that is so, my wife is at home with our children."**

I replied, **"I have no land, but you have land and so you are very blessed! But the question is, what are you doing with the land that you have? Another question that I would like to ask you, is where does your wife get water?"**

"My wife has to walk a long way to get water." He replied.

So, I said, **"Instead of wasting your time walking up and down in Umtali, why do you not go home and dig a well so that you can have water nearby. Plant a garden and grow some vegetables for your family to eat and sell the rest to your neighbours. You are wasting your life here, go home and do something with the land that you have and stop wasting your time"**

You may well think that I was rather harsh in the words that I used, however, after further conversation I had to go and said goodbye and went on my way. Many months later the same man came around to the Assembly. As I had not seen him for such a long time, I asked him where he had been? He told me that he had been at home cultivating his land. I was thrilled to hear what he had to say! Possibly my words had made a difference and had an impact upon his life! Praise God!

Sometimes people forget what they have, and are always complaining about what they do not have!

On another occasion it was a 'white' man who arrived at the assembly, shortly before I was due to leave to go home. His request was for a clean shirt as he said that he was due to attend an interview in Salisbury. I was suspicious as he looked like a 'drinker!' They are so easy to spot, but when I questioned him, he maintained that he had quit drinking some time before. When I confronted him with the Gospel, he made a profession of faith in Christ on his knees as we prayed together. I then agreed to take him home so that I could provide him with a clean shirt.

I phoned home and asked Mally if he could join us for lunch. When we arrived at home, I ran a hot bath for him so that he could have a wash and brush up. His clothes ended up being burnt as they were so dirty and I had to look in my wardrobe to see what I could give him. I had a lovely suit which was a mustard colour but I never wore it as Mally did not like it, (remember she did not like 'yellow') and as he was going to an interview, I thought he may as well have it. I gave him a complete set of clothes from top to bottom, shoes included I am sure, and when he came down for lunch, he was looking pretty good.

But, although he was living on the street, when we sat down to eat, he just pecked at his food. This was another indication that he was still on the bottle! Nevertheless, I once again gave him the benefit of the doubt, and after lunch, I took him out of town and put him on the Salisbury Road to help him on his way to his upcoming interview. But, just a matter of days later I saw him dressed in rags sitting on the side of the road in Umtali! He had sold all the clothes that I had given him to buy cheap booze. I was really disappointed, but, my involvement with this particular man was far from over.

Some months later he paid us a visit at our home and this is what he said, **"I am now in the army working as a cook, and I am short of cash and pay day is not till next week. I wondered if you could advance me a few dollars which I will pay back as soon as I get paid?"**

As you can imagine I was not impressed when this man asked me to lend him some money. I replied with some force, **"You must be joking! The last time I saw you, I allowed you to have a bath in my home, gave you a complete set of clothes, put a meal before you, and took you out of town so that you could hitch a lift to Salisbury. However, you sold my clothes, bought alcohol with the proceeds, and a day or so later I saw you out of your mind sitting on the side of the road dressed in rags. After all that, you have the cheek to come back to my house and you want me to provide you with cash for more booze? You have to be out of your mind! No, I will not!"**

Once again, you may feel that I was a little harsh with my words, however, that is what happened. Having heard what I had to say he went on his way but, that was not the end of the story, the saga continued. It was some months later that Mike Howard, one of my congregants, returned from a stint in the bush with the army. After the service one Sunday evening he asked me if I knew this particular man as he had spoken to him about The Lord whilst in the army. However, when this man asked what church Mike attended and discovered that he attended the Umtali Assembly of God he said, **"I am not interested! Sometime ago I went to your minister and he refused to help when I was in need. No, I do not want to go to your church."**

As you can imagine, I was rather annoyed, and

explained to Mike exactly what had taken place on the two occasions that we had come into contact with this particular man.

But the story continues. There was yet another occasion when our paths crossed. In fact, it must have been only a few days later that I came across our 'friend' 'thumbing' a lift when I was driving down one of the main streets in Umtali heading out of town. I pulled over and he got in the car and after he was seated, and we were driving down the road, I addressed him. I told him that I was not happy with what he had said to Mike Howard. I told him that he had lied about what had taken place between us and that it was high time he got right with God as he could not continue to live his life the way it was going. Once we had gone a few blocks I dropped him off and to my knowledge I have not seen him again.

His story is a very sad story, which is repeated again and again in every town and city across the land. Men and woman become hooked on alcohol and from then on, their lives just spiral downwards. Praise God, it does not have to be the end of the story as The Lord Jesus is willing to forgive the sin and restore fallen mankind. It would be wonderful to hear one day that this man came to know the joy of forgiven sin, and the freedom from his bondage to alcohol. What a thrill that would be to be able to truly call him 'brother!' That would really be a cause for praising God!

Now, my next story is almost unbelievable, however, it really happened. It was a Sunday afternoon not long before we were due to leave for the evening meeting. The phone rang and it was a man asking for help. He was phoning from a local hotel and after a short conversation I said that I was unable to do anything for him at that time, but, if he came to the evening meeting we could talk later. We picked him up on the way to the Assembly and he told us this remarkable story.

According to him, he, his wife, and little daughter had been living and working in the Congo when the Simba rebellion took place. Sadly, during the violence his wife and baby daughter had been killed but he had managed to escape. His journey had taken him out of the Congo and through Tanzania and Mozambique and finally across the border into Rhodesia.

If you do a little research, you will discover that the Simba Rebellion took place between 1963-1965 but pockets of resistance continued until the 1990s. During this period there were large civilian casualties and a minimum of 200 foreigners and 20,000 Congolese were executed by the rebels and that is only part of this terrible story. In putting down the rebellion, the Congolese Army was also responsible for terrible atrocities and thousands of deaths.

His story was frankly unbelievable. For one thing, the distance from the Congo the way he claimed to have travelled, was well over a thousand miles. In addition, because of the danger of terrorist incursions, the border with Mozambique around Umtali was protected by landmines. Yet, in spite of this, he won us over because of the terrible story about the 'murder' of his family. That evening a policeman who was a member of 'Special Branch' and a very new believer was in the service. Even he was taken in and his heart was touched by this poor man's plight. We took him home after the service and gave him a bed for the night, although we stressed that he would have to report to the Police Station in the morning.

Just after I got up the following morning, I was surprised to see him burning some papers on the open fire that our servant had outside his 'kaya.' When I asked him what he was burning he told me with tears in his eyes that they were photos of his wife and family. He said that they brought back too many memories and he was unable to handle them, but his story made us very suspicious.

Not long afterwards, we dropped him off at the Police Station and the Member in Charge wisely made sure that he was interviewed by another officer and not the man that he had met the night before. We were leaving town that morning to travel to Middle Sabi (more about that later) and we asked Mike Howard to look after him in our absence. The police discovered that he was an escaped convict from South Africa who had crossed the border somewhere near Beit Bridge.

Despite the fact that none of his story was true, and that we had all been totally deceived by this 'escaped convict,' some good did come out of this incident. I am not sure whether Mike Howard led him to The Lord before he went back to South Africa but he did commit his life to Christ. Mike remained in contact with him and as far as we are aware, he continued to serve The Lord. Praise God, The Lord truly works in mysterious ways.

We had a very good Ministers' Fraternal in Umtali and we had some inspiring times together. When I arrived in the city, I was made very welcome and discovered to my surprise that at the Ministers'

Fraternal the Dutch Reformed Minister was leading a study on the Baptism and Gifts of the Holy Spirit. He was a lovely born-again believer who was also filled with the Holy Spirit.

One day I met him outside Umtali Boys High and he asked me how things were going at the Assembly. My reply went something like this, **"I have a very small congregation in Umtali, only about a dozen regulars, however, praise God they are all 'born-again believers.'**

He replied, **"Sadly, I have a congregation of around three hundred and most of them are not 'born-again' and so my 'evangelistic field' is my own congregation."**

What a sad situation to know that out of a Church Congregation of around three hundred people this man of God knew of only a few who were truly Born-Again Believers! Sadly, this is not a unique situation and many congregations need a 'revival.' You do not become a 'Christian' by attending a Church, you become a Christian when you repent of your sins and ask The Lord Jesus to be your own personal Saviour and Lord! Once you have done that, it is vitally important to become part of a Bible-believing fellowship, so that you can grow in your new faith.

It was at the Fraternal in Umtali that I came across the Methodist Minister of my childhood. He was a truly lovely man, but when I met him as a fellow Minister, I was really saddened to discover that he, unlike many of the other ministers in the fraternal in Umtali, was not a 'born-again' man. Sadly, my recollection is that he only came on one or at the most, two occasions to the Fraternal!

The senior Anglican minister in Umtali was John

Knight and he had only recently become a 'born-again' believer. Before coming to Umtali to lead St. John's Anglican Church he had been in the Anglican 'ministry' for around 11 years. When he arrived in the city, his 'born-again' parishioners soon realised that he was not a 'born-again' believer and were anxious to see him 'saved.' As a result, they began leaving relevant material in places where he would very likely see them and hopefully read them. Not long after he arrived in Umtali and most likely to some degree, because of their faithful prayers, he came to know The Lord as his personal Saviour. In 1987 his story was published by Hodder Christian Paperbacks in a remarkable book called "**RAIN IN A DRY LAND.**" It is a story well worth reading and when it was published it soon became a best seller.

Once John Knight had committed his life to Christ there was no stopping him. Whilst we were in Umtali they had what was known as a "LAY WITNESS MISSION" at his Church. As far as I know a 'LAY WITNESS MISSION' was a concept established by Gary Strong the Methodist Evangelist, whom we had invited to QueQue some time before.

The plan of a **LAY WITNESS MISSION** was to invite your 'unsaved' friends, family, business associates, and neighbours to as many different 'events' that you were able to host. At these 'events' one of the visiting **'LAY WITNESSES'** would be invited to give their testimony of how they came to know Jesus as their Lord and Saviour. The host Church would put on 'events' like Men's Breakfasts, Coffee Mornings, Fellowship Lunches, etc. which concluded with one of the visiting 'LAY' people presenting his or her testimony. Ordinary people would explain to ordinary people how they had come to believe in The Lord Jesus Christ. The climax of the weekend would be the Sunday morning service where people would be asked to publicly commit their lives to The Lord.

On the Monday morning after the Mission at Saint John's Church, we were hosting the Ministers Fraternal meeting at our home but John Knight was unable to attend. However, Chris Sewell who was working at the Church with John Knight, came in his place. He was so excited that he could hardly contain himself, and as soon as he had the opportunity, he said something like this, **"We had an amazing weekend at Saint John's for which we praise God! At our Sunday morning service yesterday, more than one hundred people made a commitment to Christ. It was an extraordinary weekend and we give God all the praise!"**

I may have underestimated, or overestimated the numbers who came to Christ that weekend but it was a lot of people and it was an incredible success. Like all the ministers, present that day, I should have been rejoicing as great things had been accomplished that weekend in Umtali. However, sad to say, that day I found that I was struggling to rejoice. To my shame I was thinking, *"How could this be happening at Saint John's Church of England? Have I not been faithful to the dozen or so people that you have given to me Lord? Why have YOU not done something like this at the Umtali Assembly of God? How come that you have chosen to do this at St. John's?"*

Yes, I know that it was shameful, however I am telling the story of my life and sadly that is how I felt that day! I have asked God to forgive me and I really do praise God for what was accomplished that weekend for His Kingdom. Chris Sewell, a former policeman, who gave the report that day, was a truly lovely man of God, and he went on to serve God with Africa Enterprise a very good Evangelistic organisation.

Getting back to John Knight, Mally and I got on very well with him and his wife Jill, and on one occasion, I even suggested that we have a joint Crusade together, however, that is as far as it went. He and faithful members of his congregation went on to establish the 'ONE WAY CENTRE,' a Christian Worship Centre in a disused factory in the industrial sites that was to be used by the entire Christian Community in the City.

It must have been over the Whitsun Weekend in 1978 or 1979 that John Knight organised a special event at the 'ONE WAY CENTRE' and invited the ministers and their congregations to come and enjoy fellowship together. After a good time of enthusiastic worship, I was asked to preach for about ten minutes on **John 17. 1-26** with special emphasis on the words that I have highlighted in the following passage: -

"I do not pray for these alone, but also for those who will believe in Me through their word; THAT THEY MAY BE ONE, as You, Father, are in Me, and I in You; THAT THEY ALSO MAY BE ONE IN US, that the world may believe that You sent Me." John 17. 20-21

After I had spoken briefly on the above portion of Scripture, the whole assembly were divided into groups, with the Ministers present being in a group by themselves. In spite of my congregation being so small,

I learned later, that one of my congregants had been chosen to lead every single group and as the speaker for the day I was asked to lead the group of ministers.

Among the Ministers present were two Baptist Missionaries who we will hear about later in my story and they kept on challenging me about what I had said in my ten-minute message. I had emphasised that The Lord Jesus was only able to accomplish what He did in the power of the Holy Spirit and true UNITY is only really possible when we are all filled with the Holy Spirit. True unity can only be achieved when we are operating in the power of the Holy Spirit when preaching the Gospel. Later on, I apologised to John Knight because we spent so much time discussing this issue that I was unable to deal with the questions that John had set for our group. However, all said and done, it was a great weekend and I was really encouraged by the achievement of my congregation no matter how small it was.

You may recall that we had Chris and Maureen Trigaardt and their family in our congregation in Hatfield. When they moved away from Hatfield, they moved to Middle Sabi, where in spite of his disabilities Chris was the manager of a farm. Soon after we moved to Umtali they visited us on one of their shopping trips, and invited us to their farm. After some discussion we decided to travel down on a Monday and return on the Friday. This became a monthly trip and whilst there we would have four meetings; a Gospel meeting, Bible Study, Breaking of Bread and a Ladies' Meeting. This monthly routine was to lead to some amazing results as many people came to Christ.

The Middle Sabi Irrigation Scheme was one of a

number of incredibly successful projects initiated by the Rhodesian Government. It began with the construction of a large dam on the Sabi River, a river that is not much to write home about in the dry season but is quite significant during the rainy weather. Once the dam was constructed the river water was pumped into a canal and from there pumped onto large farms established alongside the canal. Interested farmers were invited to apply for a farm and those who were successful were able to purchase 500 acres of farmland. This land was able to produce two irrigated crops every year. In spite of this, the farmers who were not used to irrigated lands complained that 500 acres was too small and so in addition the government allowed them to lease a further 500 acres of land as well.

Right from the start these farms proved very productive to the farmers who had successfully applied for the land. The main crops that were produced were winter wheat, and cotton. The production of wheat was essential as this was one crop that we were unable to produce in sufficient quantities for the nation. When we first went to Middle Sabi many of the farmers used aircraft to sow their wheat fields and crop spraying was often done from the air. It was an amazing sight to see, although as time went on it proved to be too expensive for most of the farmers and alternative methods were employed.

The wheat was harvested by mechanical harvesters and had to be done before it was damaged by rain. It was wonderful to see how quickly a large field could be reaped. When it came to the cotton crop if enough labour could be recruited it was picked by hand as it always brought a better price when put up for sale. However, cotton picking is really hard work and in spite of being able to earn a better than average wage there were often not enough cotton pickers available. As a result, a mechanical cotton harvester was called in to bring in the harvest. I was always fascinated to see huge piles of freshly picked cotton, stacked alongside the road waiting to be taken to market.

When the fields had been freshly ploughed, awaiting the sowing of a new crop, you could see the huge Baobab trees clearly. They had been left in the land when it was initially cleared. The other trees were chopped down and cleared away, but there was some superstition surrounding the baobab and so they were left in the land. If you have never seen a baobab tree, imagine a tree with a large trunk and its roots in the air and you may have some idea what it looked like. On one of our trips, we came across an enormous baobab that had come down in a storm and I have a picture of my sons climbing on top of the fallen trunk. It was a very big tree!

All the farm houses were surrounded by high fences because of the security situation. Inside the fence there was usually a large house, sheds, lovely gardens, and more often than not, a swimming pool as it got very hot in that area. The 'compound' where the farm workers lived was much more modest, in fact sometimes it was much like a run-down rural African village. But, most of the farmers were in the process of building proper brick houses for all their workers. Due to the number of farm workers involved this was being done over a number of years.

There was a police reserve unit in Middle Sabi,

but it was considered to be a 'safe' area. When we visited, we travelled up and down the canal at night to the meetings. In spite of this, I am aware of a number of 'incidents' in the area. Sadly, the first one involved a farmer by the name of Peter, who was tragically shot and killed one night. The second was when the police reserve headquarters in the area was attacked and destroyed. However, praise God, when it was attacked, all the reservists were out on patrol and no one was injured. The last one took place right at the end of the war, in fact possibly when the war was over. The owner of the property we used to visit, was shot up and badly injured, in the outside room that we had previously used every time we visited.

It was in Middle Sabi that we got to know Errol and Davril Lobb who were both restored to the faith and became very committed members of the fellowship. They had four lovely daughters, named Charmaine, Melanie, Eleanor, and Deadrie. They were both serious about their faith in The Lord and later entered full-time Christian Service and, as of the time of writing this story, they are continuing to preach the Gospel.

Every month before our visit, Maureen would phone each and every farmer and let them know that we were coming. As a result, we always had a good turnout at our meetings. Mally and I would sleep in the outside room and usually Mark slept inside with the other children depending on who was home, as the older children were at boarding school. So much happened during these visits to Middle Sabi that I cannot comment on them all, but I will try to present some of them.

On one of our visits, the home where we were having our meeting was completely packed, which was not unusual. As I looked around at the people who were there, I was aware that there were a number that I had not seen before. As I was preaching my eyes were drawn to one of the farmers who had a good growth of beard and looked quite angry. In addition, every now and then he would leave his seat and go outside and return a short while later. I could not make it out, but suspected that he was going out for a smoke, even though he was not out of the room for long.

This man's wife was listening very closely to what I was saying and when I made the appeal at the end of the message, she responded immediately by raising her hand. After a final hymn or song, we closed the meeting in prayer just as her husband re-entered the room. When I discovered that he also wanted to commit his life to Christ we went into another room and after I had shared a few scriptures with them we prayed together. That night Rod Hein who came from a Church of Christ background and his wife Ellie who came from a Dutch Reformed Church background came to know Jesus as their Saviour. I later discovered that the reason Rod went in and out of the meeting was because he was checking on their two children who were asleep in their car just outside the window where we were meeting.

Sometime later we were having a Breaking of Bread service and less than a dozen people were present. As we met around the table of The Lord, I felt that we ought to join hands and pray together while standing up. We had only been praying for a short while when Ellie fell to her knees because the presence of the Holy Spirit was so real. One by one we all joined her on our knees as we were all very conscious of the presence of God!

Since that eventful evening, when they both trusted The Lord Jesus as their Saviour, Rod and Ellie have gone on to do great things for God in full time ministry. They became Missionaries in Mozambique ministering to the poorest of the poor. The area they operated in, was controlled by RENAMO who for many years waged war against FRELIMO who took over from the Portuguese when they left Mozambique.

Some years ago, my eldest son Mark met up with a man from Mozambique, and when he discovered that Mark was born in Zimbabwe, he asked him if he knew Rod Hein. He said that he was quite famous in Mozambique because he had assisted in bringing peace to the country. It appears that the leader of RENAMO was not prepared to attend the peace talks with FRELIMO unless Rod was the pilot of the plane that took him there. I was able to tell Mark that not only did I know him, but I had had the pleasure of leading both Rod and his wife Ellie to The Lord in Middle Sabi.

The Royal Navy patrolled the ocean off Beira and no more tankers were docking with fuel for the pipeline to the refinery in Umtali. As a result, our fuel supply was dependent upon the good will of South Africa. On one occasion individual South Africans had donated very generously to purchase tanker loads of fuel to keep our motorcars running.

With all the travelling that we were doing it was impossible to get a big enough allocation of petrol coupons from the Government. As a result of our involvement in Middle Sabi and all the rest of the travelling that we were doing, our need for 'petrol coupons' was constantly increasing. In fact, it increased each time The Lord opened another door for our ministry. The cost was also a problem, as I could not expect our small fellowship in Umtali to pay for all the travelling that we were doing. Neither did I feel that I should appeal to the National Development Fund of the AOG to pay for our needs.

Each time we travelled to Middle Sabi a round trip of 180 miles or more, we had to trust God for our needs. Every month when we set out on our journey, we either had no money to pay for our return, or no petrol coupons to purchase the petrol, or neither money nor coupons! Let me make it quite clear, we never asked anyone for help in this area and yet God always supplied. I praise God that our main human benefactors were Chris and Maureen Trigaardt. It was amazing how almost always it was Chris who provided for our needs, not only accommodating us each month for four days but also providing the wherewithal for us to return month after month. We were always very grateful for their support, in fact without them, there would never have been a successful outreach into Middle Sabi or the establishment of the Chipinga Assembly.

Long before we began to go to Middle Sabi, the two Baptist Missionaries, that I mentioned earlier, had been ministering to the farmers. Both of them conducted a Sunday service in the valley every month, which was well supported and very much appreciated. As it happened both these Missionaries were on furlough in the USA when I began travelling to Middle Sabi.

Soon after he returned from furlough, I had a conversation with one of these Missionaries. As we talked, I realised that he was speaking about my 'evangelistic ministry!' I was quite surprised as I have never considered myself to be an 'evangelist!' I have always felt that my ministry was more of a 'teaching' ministry. However, since returning from furlough he had discovered that a number of people had come to Christ in Middle Sabi during his absence. Knowing that this had taken place as a result of my ministry in the area he considered me to be an 'evangelist!'

I later discovered that both of these men presented the Gospel very clearly when they visited Middle Sabi. Yet, neither of these men ever challenged people to make a decision for Christ, they never made an 'appeal.' As a result, it appears that they had 'sown' the seed in Middle Sabi and I had come along and had the privilege of reaping the harvest. I always made an appeal after I preached the Gospel as I expected a harvest, and praise God, The Lord was gracious as most months we returned having led one or more people to Christ.

The City of Umtali was right on the border with Mozambique and once the Portuguese had handed over political control of the country to the Marxist Frelimo leadership in 1975, we were faced with hostile neighbours. Our neighbours, were totally committed to supporting the terrorists who were dedicated to the removal of the Rhodesian Government. In addition, the new rulers were Communist and anti-God.

As explained earlier in my first book, the Portuguese Assembly that we visited in Lourenço Marques in 1969 had experienced a major move of God.

A new building was constructed for a very large congregation and two flats were included in the plans to accommodate the ministers. The new building was confiscated by Frelimo just after it had been completed. Years later the believers were finally allowed to use the building again but they had to 'buy' it back from the government.

One night whilst we were living in Umtali the City came under Mortar attack. We got the children out of bed and squeezed into the cupboard under the stairs which was the safest place in the house. The mortar attack came at a very inconvenient time for one of our congregants, as she was busy giving birth in the Maternity ward of Umtali General Hospital at the time. But praise God, the attack did little damage as the following day we discovered that most of the mortars had landed on the golf course, and no one was injured or killed. The story went around that perhaps The Lord did not like golf, however, there can be no doubt that The Lord had watched over the city as His angels diverted all the mortars onto the golf course!!!

One day after visiting Middle Sabi we travelled up to Mel setter to see Maureen Triegaardt's brother and his wife in spite of the war that was raging all around us. They had attended our meetings in Middle Sabi and wanted us to visit. Pete Bredekamp and his wife Audrey and their two little boys were living on the Gwendingwe Forestry Estate where he was working.

There was a good tarmac road from Chipinga to Melsetter however it was a winding mountainous road and would have been an ideal place to set up an ambush as you were unable to put your foot down and get a move on. We travelled, the whole family, on that windy, mountainous road to visit and minister to the Bredenkamps. While we were there Pete showed us around the forestry estate and it was amazing to see how much they were doing. The one thing that stands out in particular was where they dumped the sawdust from the sawmills. Pete pointed out the smoke that was rising from the base of the mountain of sawdust. He explained that it burned day after day 365 days a year and was largely caused by the heat generated by pressure that this mountain of sawdust was under.

Sometime later, we heard an amazing story of The Lord's protection upon Audrey. She had just had her car washed and was driving down the dirt roads of the estate when she came upon a large puddle. Not wanting to dirty her clean car she avoided the puddle and drove on. A short while later an army truck came down the same road, but the driver did not bother to avoid the puddle, he just drove straight through. A landmine was hidden in the puddle and immediately blew up when it was driven over by the truck. Praise God, no one was seriously injured but the vehicle was badly damaged. However, had Audrey driven through the puddle in the car that she was driving she could very easily have been killed. Praise God for His protection!

It was great visiting Pete and Audrey as they were so open to the Word of God and just drank in everything that I taught them. In addition, Pete and Audrey's two boys must have been quite taken with my 'preaching style' as I heard that they loved to take it in turns standing behind a box and pretending to be me and preaching to one another. When I heard what they were doing all that I could say was, Hallelujah, preach it boys!

On one occasion, I was on my own, on one of my trips to visit the Bredenkamps and I travelled with an armed escort in a convoy of vehicles out from Umtali. Whilst waiting for the convoy to start I was approached by one of the convoy leaders and asked if I could give a lady a lift. When I said that I was not going all the way to Melsetter but to Gwendingwe they contacted her husband and arranged for him to meet her at the turn-off to the Estate. The journey seemed to take no time at all as I had a wonderful opportunity to explain the Gospel to my passenger. When she left my car and I was travelling the last leg of the journey to the estate, I remember praying something like this,

"Lord, I am so thrilled with the opportunities that you are giving me, thank you for such a wonderful conversation with this lady. I know it is dangerous driving on these roads but I really believe that you will protect me from being blown up by landmines, as there is so much work yet to do. Hallelujah!"

Praise God, He must have heard my prayer or I would not be writing this book. God has been so good to me! Praise His name!

Before we move on from Gwendingwe I have one more story to tell. It may well have happened on that same visit. Nevertheless, while I was waiting with a few others for the convoy to arrive from Melsetter to take us back to Umtali, a lady approached me and said, **"Good morning. I am ------, who are you?"**

I replied, **"Good morning! My name is AB Robertson."**

She said, **"I have not seen you in these parts

before. Who are you with?"

To which I replied, **"I am a Minister, I have just been to visit the Bredenkamps."**

"I do not recognise that name, what branch of government are you with?" She asked.

"Oh no, I am not a Minister in the Government, I have a much more important job than that! I am a Minister of the Assemblies of God, a preacher of the Gospel of Jesus Christ." I replied.

At that, I think she was about to lose interest, but the convoy arrived, and we were on our way. I may have been a bit cheeky in what I said, yet, I do represent The Lord Jesus Christ, a King who has an ETERNAL KINGDOM! Hallelujah!

One of the men who attended our services in Rusape actually came to the meetings from Inyanga, some distance away. I believe that it was through his efforts that I was given opportunities to minister the Word of God in Inyanga and Juliesdale, which was near where my sister and her husband were farming.

The Church of the Good Samaritan in Juliesdale was a beautiful building with a wonderful view of the fantastic Inyanga scenery. The window behind the pulpit gave a view that was really breathtaking. I had the opportunity to preach there on a number of occasions as the building had been erected in order that preachers from a variety of backgrounds could take services in the area.

Sadly, not all preachers preach the unadulterated Word of God and some make some amazing statements. I was told that one of the ministers who preached in this lovely building had the following to say to his congregation, **"Never bother The Lord with trivial things like, 'Lord I have lost my keys,** please help me find them.' Remember The Lord has much more important things to take care of than your lost keys!"**

I have used this story on many occasions as it shows just how far people can be from God. Of course, The Lord wants to hear about your 'lost keys,' and anything else that troubles you. If you know Him as The Lord of your life, He is FATHER GOD to you. He loves all of His CHILDREN and is only too pleased to help us find our keys if we are willing to ask Him!

In addition to this lovely Church building, there was also a lovely little Church in the Inyanga village some miles away. I preached there on one occasion and possibly more, and again it was a real privilege. On the one occasion I spoke about the healing power of God and possibly prayed for a few people after the service. After the service as people were leaving, I was talking to a couple of ladies when one of them said, **"I believe that The Lord is going to use you in the days ahead to pray for the healing of many people."**

At the time it was like a 'prophetic word,' yet, in spite of seeing a number of people healed over the years it has not been a major part of my ministry. Maybe it should have been, but up to this time in my life it has not been a major part of the ministry that God has given to me.

Although during this time I had the support of Mike Howard in Umtali and others who could assist me with the ministry, it was obvious that I needed some assistance, as opportunities were all around us. As a result, I ought to have been very pleased when Neil Gibbs phoned me and made me an offer of an assistant.

It appears that Idris Davies who had previously

been an Elder in the Umtali Assembly had made himself available to minister full time after his retirement. As Idris and his wife had lived for much of their lives in Umtali, Neil wanted to know if I would like him to come and give me a hand. In hind sight Idris would have been ideal, however, I was still a young man and I think that I was a little fearful that we would not get on too well and so turned down his offer. Looking back on it many years later I do believe that I really missed God's provision at that time.

Somewhere along the line we took a short break as a family. We went to stay a few nights at a Motel which was considered to be quite safe not far from Umtali. While we were staying there the proprietor of the Motel asked me what I did for a living. I explained who I was and what I did and stressed the fact that we travelled to places like Inyazura, Middle Sabi, Melsetter and Chipinga. We then had the following conversation.

He asked, **"Do you carry a weapon?"**

"No, I am not armed." I replied.

Quite angry, he said, **"So you won't carry a weapon! Well, one day in the future I will open the newspaper and read the headlines: -**

'MISSIONARY, HIS WIFE AND CHILDREN MURDERED ON THE ROAD TO UMTALI.'

When everyone reads the article, they will say, 'How terribly sad that these things keep happening!'
However, I will say to myself; 'WHAT A FOOL- HE NEVER PROTECTED HIS WIFE AND FAMILY.'"

Well, that guy really got to me, and as a result of that conversation, I decided that it was time I purchased a weapon in order to protect my wife and family. There could be no doubt that the places that I was travelling to, were dangerous and anything could happen. If I owned a weapon and we were attacked, at least if I fired back, we may well survive. But, if I failed to return fire, we would most likely all be killed if we were attacked.

However, purchasing a weapon is not easy if you are short of cash.

That week Malcolm Fraser was called up and was sent to Umtali to audit the army books. He was unfit for active service but was well qualified to audit the accounts of the army. Whilst in town he came to visit and I told him what had been happening to me and in particular what the Motel proprietor had said. Malcolm was quick to say, **"AB, buy the gun! Send me the bill and I will pay for the weapon."**

Let me once again make it quite clear, I had not told him the story in order to have him pay for the weapon, however, The Lord had it all sorted. He let an unsaved man convince me of the need to travel with a weapon and then sent along a friend to visit and provide the wherewithal to purchase the weapon. A few days later I purchased an LPD (light machine gun) and a gun cabinet to keep it safe when we were not travelling.

The Lord was truly watching over me as the only time I fired my weapon was at a rifle range to try it out. Sadly, I am not sure how it happened, but when firing the gun, I managed to break my glasses and had to visit the opticians to get new glasses. Nevertheless, from then on it went with us every time we travelled out of town. Our sons were advised that if we were attacked, they were immediately to lie flat on the floor at the back of the car. Praise God, we were never attacked and I never had to fire my weapon to protect my family.

Whilst we were living in Umtali two events took place that really rocked the nation. One took place on our doorstep and the other took place at the other side of the country.

It must have been the weekend of the 17-18th June 1978 that Ron Davies came to preach at our Assembly in Umtali. He ministered the word of God at our Sunday services and promoted the work of 'Global Lifeline Literature' at the same time. But before that, on the Saturday morning, we went to visit the Elim Missionaries, many of whom were known personally by Ron and his wife Dorothy. They were now living in the Vumba, just 15 miles outside Umtali.

From the beginning of their work in Rhodesia the Umtali Assembly had been very closely associated with the Elim mission. Yet, whilst I was in Umtali we had no personal contact with the missionaries. Idris Davies, who I mentioned previously, once told me that he had accompanied the Elim Missionaries when they were first allocated land by the tribal Chief in Inyanga, around 1948. The mission station at Katerere was very successful and by the time they moved to the Vumba, in addition to ministering the Good News of The Lord Jesus Christ to all the surrounding area, they had a successful hospital and school complex as well. The security situation had made it impossible to continue resulting in the move to the Vumba!

Although the facilities at the old 'Eagle School' in the Vumba had only accommodated 150 'white boys' in the past, there were twice that number who had transferred from the Mission school at Katerere. In spite of the fact that many of them had to sleep on the floor, they were thrilled that they could continue their education. When Ron and I visited the missionaries, he particularly wanted to meet up with Peter and Sandra McCann and their two children, and Roy and Joyce Lynn and their new born baby. I did not know any of the missionaries, but was glad to accompany Ron on the visit.

I quote from an Elim Church article called, **"VUMBA – A summary of the tragic events**.

"Friday 23 June 1978 is remembered as being the darkest day in Elim history. On that day, twelve people were slaughtered at the Elim Mission station in the Vumba Mountains, Northern Zimbabwe. Another would die a week later. The sheer brutality of this massacre shocked the world."

The thirteen people included 3 men, 6 women, and 4 children, one being a three-week-old girl.
As I look back on this terrible time, I remember it as by far the darkest day of the terrorist war. It just seemed that a cloud of despair descended upon the City of Umtali. I attended the funerals in Umtali as did many others, believers, and unbelievers, as the nation was shocked.

This of course was not the first time that the 'terrorists' had targeted missionaries in Rhodesia as Roman Catholic, Dutch Reformed, Salvation Army and American Baptist workers had also been murdered, however this was the worst, in the numbers involved, and the sheer brutality. If this tragedy was not enough, we were to experience another tragedy which took place on the other side of the nation not long afterwards.

On the 3rd of September 1978, Rhodesians were shocked to discover that the terrorists of Joshua Nkomo's ZIPRA had shot down an Air Rhodesia Vicount called the Hunyani with a Soviet made Sam-7 missile. The aircraft which was carrying 52 passengers and 4 crew, was shot down 5 minutes after taking off from Kariba. We later discovered that due to the amazing skill of the pilot 18 people survived the crash and of those, all but 5 decided to stay next to the aircraft and wait to be rescued. Sometime later, after the five survivors left the sight of the wreck, a group of fully armed terrorists arrived and opened fire on the survivors with a view to killing them all. However, 3 people were able to survive and were later rescued but the other ten were shot dead in cold blood. The 5 who had abandoned the wreckage were all later found and rescued.

There are two reasons why I am telling this story. The first one is to reveal that we were living in very dangerous times. The second involves a young woman called Mitzi Rees, who after we left Hatfield had become a very faithful Sunday School teacher at the Assembly. Sadly, Mitzi Rees was on that plane that day, and never came home. Mario Mariani and Brian Holmes (two of the talented musicians that were in the Hatfield Assembly) composed and recorded a song in her memory. They included the song on a record that they produced as a tribute to this faithful young girl.

As we consider how this young girl's life was so tragically brought to a close, we need to consider our own lives, as who knows how long we still have to live, before we too come to the end of our lives? We need to keep close to Jesus as we never know when our last day may be, there is no doubt that Mitzi, who I must say I never met, would have been surprised to have known in advance that her life would be over so soon.

However, moving away from these very sad stories, we were able to praise God that the Assembly began to grow. One day I had a phone call from a Mr. Le Grange who had, I believe been an Elder in the Presbyterian Church. He asked if he could come and see me. Apparently, his son Rob and his wife Leslie had come to know The Lord in Bulawayo, and then his other son and his wife had also been saved and he wanted to know what it was all about. Within a short time of coming to see me, he and his 'wife' had given their lives to The Lord and wanted to be baptised. We had arranged a date for the baptism, when someone informed me that he and his 'wife' were not actually married.

On discussing this with them, I discovered that he had been widowed sometime before, and so had she, and they had come to know one another when their children had married each other. They had not legally tied the knot because it would have made a big impact on their joint income. Mr. Le Grange had a small farm outside Umtali, but they felt that they could not really survive if she lost her widows pension, and so they just moved in together.

On discussing the situation with them I was very conscious of the verse that says that we ought to,

"Abstain from all appearance of evil." 1 Thessalonians 5.22 (KJV)

They were a mature couple who had married children with grandchildren and they were setting a bad example for their own family to follow. I told them that I was happy to baptise them but only after they were married legally. They accepted what I said and a date was set for the wedding, after which I was only too happy to baptise them both. They were a lovely couple and a great asset to the local fellowship.

It was not long after they were baptized, that Mr. Le Grange was telling me about a wonderful gift that 'God' had given to him. He explained to me that the gift was being able to 'divine' water. He told me that he had a very developed gift and was able to discover water underground, where many others were unable to do so. I listened carefully to what he had to say and then we had the following conversation.

"Do you think that this is a gift from God? I asked.
"Yes, most definitely." He replied.
I asked, **"When did you acquire this wonderful gift? Was it before you came to know Jesus as your Lord and Saviour, or afterwards?"**

He then told me that he had been able to 'divine' water, pretty well all his adult life. I then asked him to go and pray about it as I did not believe that it was a gift from God as The Lord has made it very clear that He condemns **'divination.'**

"There shall not be found among you anyone-----that useth divination -----------." Deuteronomy 18.10 (KJV)

It was only a few days later, possibly the following weekend, when an excited Mr. Le Grange shared the following testimony. He said something like this,

"After our conversation I asked The Lord to reveal whether it was correct to practice 'water divining' or not, and left it in His hands. The other night I had a very strange sensation, it seemed that something good was coming upon me working its way down my body from my head to my feet. As this was happening something evil was being forced out of my body and leaving via my feet.
When I got up in the morning, I distinctly felt The Lord tell me to go and 'divine' for water. He seemed to be leading me to a very big tree on the farm where 'water divining' had revealed a large underground stream. I selected a suitable 'water divining' rod and walked to the correct place but nothing whatsoever took place.

I believe that The Lord has shown me that it was not a gift from Him by removing it altogether from my life."

What a story, praise God, he was now as convinced as I was that all 'divination' is unacceptable to the Holy God that we serve and is a part of the kingdom of darkness. Yet, not everyone will agree with what I have just said, in fact when I told the DRC minister in Chipinga this story, sometime later, he was really upset with me. He believed that the ability to 'divine' water was a gift from God. Sadly, we had to agree to disagree!

While we are speaking about the Le Grange family, I have one more story to share which involves Mr. Le Grange's daughter and her husband, who also came to know The Lord as their Saviour and started to fellowship with us. In fact, it was his son in law, who was the Policeman in the story about the escaped South African prisoner, that I shared earlier.

In conversation with them shortly after they came to know Jesus as their Lord and Saviour, I encouraged them to get 'baptised.' However, they were not convinced that it was necessary and were not willing to go through the waters of baptism at that time. Yet, it was not long afterwards that they came to see me and said that in their daily Bible Readings, The Lord had made it clear that they ought to be baptised. Having heard what they had to say, I explained that the verse that they had shown me did not in fact deal with water baptism. Nevertheless, I was pleased that The Lord had impressed upon them their need to be baptised, and not long afterwards they went through the waters of baptism witnessed by members of their entire family.

In those days it was a little unusual for one of our 'African' ministers to preach to one of our 'European' Assemblies. In spite of this, I had asked Jeremiah Kianga a well-known preacher from Harare to come and minister at the Assembly in Umtali. His visit was much appreciated and I expected him to stay with us in our home, another rather 'unusual' thing in Rhodesia at the time. However, Jeremiah had a brother who lived in Umtali and he had arranged to stay with him.

While we were living in Umtali, my sister and her husband had arranged for their son Stuart to be 'christened' by the local Anglican Minister in Juliesdale. We were invited to attend and arranged to be there on the day. I was rather taken aback when my young nephew had a little water poured on his head and was 'welcomed into the Church of England.' It is so sad that people do not read the Scriptures, as baptism can only follow, repentance, belief, and your own personal statement of faith in The Lord Jesus Christ. None of these things are able to be done by a little child. We need to get back to the Bible, and do what the early Church did in the book of Acts!

Staying with the Church of England, I think it was the Vicar of Rusape who made a visit to my sister's father-in-law one day. After he had introduced himself and had been welcomed into their home, he said to this elderly gentleman, **"I thought I had better get to meet you before someone asked me to conduct your burial service!!"**

There is no doubt that the Vicar of Rusape called a spade a spade! As this man was on his church register and as he had never seen him in any of the Church services, he felt that it was time to meet him. If I remember correctly, he was a lovely man of God.

Not many months before we left Umtali, we had a family join us from the other side of the country. The husband was an electrician and he had been transferred to Umtali by the railways and they were a lovely addition to the fellowship. It was some time after they moved into town that he came to me with a 'vision,' that The Lord had laid upon his heart.

The war was affecting many families in the country and he felt that The Lord wanted him to establish a 'home' where people who were 'shell shocked' or needed a bit of tender, loving, care, could come and stay, for a little respite. I must add that when he presented this 'vision,' it was presented very dogmatically by saying; **'THE LORD HAS SHOWN ME.'**

Now let us be quite clear, if **'THE LORD HAS SHOWN YOU'** there can be no discussion! If **'THE LORD HAS SHOWN YOU,'** who am I to argue with you or indeed try to guide you. Who can argue with what The Lord has said! Nevertheless, I did not argue with the general concept as we could all see that many people were being affected by the ongoing war, in particular those who lived in isolated areas like the farming population.

As a result, when I shared the 'vision' with my friend Malcolm Fraser he agreed to contribute R$1000 to the project and proceeded to send me a cheque. One day our friend took me to see a house that he felt would serve the needs of the people that he was hoping to assist. Due to its poor condition, it was available for a very modest price, but it would need a lot of work before being used. It was located in a fantastic area just outside a game reserve not far from town. The house was very run down and needed a lot of work before it could become a viable project, but it was such a lovely peaceful area that once it was renovated it would be ideal for the job.

Sadly, because he was so sure that this was a 'vision' from The Lord, he handed in his notice with the railways in order to do this 'full time.' He then tried to get a mortgage to purchase the property which was declined because he was not working. When he told me what the problem was, I very nearly agreed to put my name on the mortgage application. Had he remained an electrician on the railways he could have purchased the house and in time he could have done it up. Only when the 'vision' was up and running should he have considered giving up his job. The house was soon snapped up by the National Parks and the opportunity was lost. (I will speak about the gift of R$1000 later)

The 'outreach' to Middle Sabi had resulted in a number of people coming to know The Lord as their Saviour, however, just like any other community, people move and one of the families decided to move out of the Valley and return to Chipinga. Rod and Ellie Hein left the relative safety of Middle Sabi and moved onto a coffee farm some distance outside Chipinga. Once they had moved, they encouraged me to start a Church in the village of Chipinga.

When I enquired, I discovered that, the Anglican Church was not having any services in the town. The missionaries, that I have previously mentioned, each conducted a monthly Sunday service in the Anglican Church. As a result, of Rod and Ellie Hein's encouragement, I arranged to take a monthly service on one of the remaining free Sundays, to determine what the response would be.

On the first Sunday that I preached in Chipinga, a couple who worked on Ratolshoek Tea Estate were in the meeting. They had business in Chipinga on Monday morning and had stayed overnight at the Chipinga Hotel and were thus able to attend the Sunday morning service. When I made the appeal, at the close of the service, they both committed their lives to Christ. It was a real confirmation to me that God was leading us to move to Chipinga.

Shortly after this, I decided to visit this couple on the estate. They advised me to arrive at a certain time so that they could escort me in an armoured vehicle the last few miles of the journey. They said that the most dangerous section of my journey would be travelling through the Mount Selinda Mission. I was really saddened to hear what they were telling me. The Mount Selinda Mission was a medical and teaching mission run by the United Methodist Church but over the years it had become a hotbed of political activism.

I reached the border of the estate before I encountered my escort and soon afterwards arrived safely at their home. It was good to meet with these new Christians and we had a great evening together. They were right on the border of Mozambique and would often hear gunfire from their home, as the security forces made contact with terrorists. Sadly, the terrorists hid anti-personal mines where the tea pickers worked, which caused a number of terrible casualties. The roads of the estate were also often mined, which made it a dangerous area to live and work.

During the evening, my hosts told me of an incident that took place shortly after they arrived on the estate. It had been far from funny at the time, but in hindsight they were able to laugh. They were in bed one night when they heard what sounded like a series of explosions which seemed to be taking place very close to their home. It was not unusual to hear gunfire as I have already explained, but this seemed to be very close and made them quite concerned, to say the least.

Every now and then they would hear another explosion and then a period of quiet followed by another explosion. They had a very disturbed night and it was only in the morning that they discovered the cause of the "explosions." There was an avocado pear tree that had branches which overhung the house. In the middle of the night a number of avocados had fallen off the tree and made an awful noise when hitting the galvanised iron roof. You may have laughed when something similar happened to me one night in Inyazura and you may laugh at this story, yet, at the time it was far from funny! But after a great visit it was time to return to Umtali.

In any old building there is always a need for repairs and improvements and the Umtali Assembly was in need of some improvements. I heard a story of an incident that happened before my arrival which highlights the importance of maintaining old buildings. Apparently whilst waiting in the foyer of the building, one of the members was leaning against the wall when it collapsed and he fell through the wall into the room on the other side. Sadly, white ants, which are a real problem for any wooden structure in Rhodesia, had succeeded in eating all the wood, of which the wall was made, all that remained was a number of coats of paint!

Despite much maintenance having been undertaken during the tenure of previous Ministers there was one job that needed doing. We were blessed to have Dave and Wendy Rennick in the Assembly at the time and Dave agreed to do this particular job. He did an excellent job, however, just before he completed the job he was transferred back to Salisbury. As he was not going to have time to complete the job before he left, he handed it over to me. It needed an electric drill, able to drill through some serious concrete, but I agreed to complete the job.

At this juncture I feel that it is important that I mention the name that I have called my ministry for many years! I have called it **'THE UNFINISHED TASK,'** as until The Lord calls me home there is still a lot of work to be done. **S**adly, that little job in Umtali is also on the list, it is one of the UNFINISHED TASKS in my life!!

Before we moved on to new pastures Mike Howard made himself available to enter full time ministry. It was arranged that Neil Gibbs would come down to Umtali and 'lay hands' on Mike in much the same way that had happened to me some years before. Yet, this was very different to my entry into full time ministry. Mike invited a number of people to witness his 'Ordination Service' and looking back on it, I do not think that I 'invited' anyone to my 'laying on of hands!' Nevertheless, it all took place at a special service after which Mike initially went to Inyazura. He continued the outreach that I had been involved in and had some measure of success with the farming community.

Meanwhile I asked Neil Gibbs to provide a replacement for me in Umtali, as I really felt the call of God upon my life to move to Chipinga. When I spoke to John Bond about a move he said, **"You have my blessing to move to Chipinga, however, you will never be able to establish a self-supporting Assembly in Chipinga as it is just too small."**

I thanked John Bond for his backing and began to make plans to move to Chipinga.

As the work was continuing to expand it was difficult to provide ministers for the national work however Neil did send a young couple to visit. They stayed the weekend and the husband ministered at the meetings. I must admit that although they were a lovely young couple and his preaching was acceptable,

I was not convinced that they would make the grade in Umtali. Sadly, I am sorry to say, I never passed on my fears to Neil Gibbs at the time.

Having spent less than two years in Umtali, the day arrived for us to leave. They had been very blessed and eventful years. While in Umtali Chris Triegaardt made us a house sign out of an old plough disk which said, "**EBENEZER**" meaning "**Thus far The Lord has helped us.**" I was very impressed with it, and was keen to take it with us to Chipinga, but, Mally was not keen, and so it remained in Umtali. Once again, my wife and our two young sons were having to pack up and leave their much-loved home. Uncle Fred, my step father, made it quite clear what he thought. He said that I was mad to take my wife and two young sons into such a dangerous area.

As I write this story I must once again honour my wife who was prepared to follow me into what was an increasingly dangerous area. But I really felt the call of God to move to Chipinga.

The Assembly was left in the hands of this young couple from Bulawayo with Mike Howard keeping an eye on things from Inyazura.

5) CHIPINGA ASSEMBLY 1978-1980

I have always considered that the most fruitful time of my entire ministry in Rhodesia/Zimbabwe was our two years in the little border town of Chipinga. In some ways it was the most difficult period of my ministry, but without doubt it was the most productive. There are so many things that I remember about those two years, as if they were yesterday, and hopefully I will be able to put at least some of what I remember on paper.

When we moved into town Rod and Ellie Hein had done everything possible to welcome us. They could not have done more to make us feel at home. Among other things, they acquired a very nice house, 156 Moodie Street, for us to rent, which had a view of the countryside out the back. The house was newly painted and was looking spruced up and clean with some lovely 'yellow' curtains in the living room.

Sadly, the inside of the house had been painted with a light-yellow paint which was just tooooo much for Mally to handle. As mentioned earlier, 'yellow' was not my wife's favourite colour, and now in addition to having a 'yellow' lounge suite, we had 'yellow' curtains, and 'yellow' walls! It was just a little too much! We thanked Rod and Ellie for all that they had done but requested that the inside walls be repainted in white paint, which was soon arranged.

You may remember that Malcolm Fraser had given me R$1,000.00 to invest in the project in Umtali that had now been abandoned. I held on to the cheque until I was satisfied that the project was viable, and when the project failed to get off the ground, I phoned Malcolm. I asked him what he wanted me to do with the money and after some discussion he agreed to invest it in the new work in Chipinga.

As a result, I was able to open a bank account, and start a set of books for the new fellowship as soon as I arrived. I was also able to pay the rent for the house. Having this money in the bank starting from scratch in a new town was an amazing blessing to me.

As can be expected, because it was a pioneer work, until I was able to persuade someone else to take on the job, I was also the treasurer.

You may be interested to learn what it was like going to the bank in Chipinga at that time. It was like being in the American 'wild west' and quite an experience. I would be one of very few customers that were not 'armed' with some kind of weapon on almost every occasion. Many of the customers were farmers, who came into town fully armed, in mine and bullet-proofed vehicles to draw money to pay their labourers.

Another amazing thing about Chipinga was the 'financial' commitment of the congregation to our new fellowship. Instead of never becoming self-supporting, I believe that we were pretty well 'self-supporting' from the word go. Not only did we have that initial R$ 1,000.00 to start us off, but God was faithful in providing us with a group of very committed believers who made sure that the fellowship was financially viable right from the start.

Yet, despite our warm welcome, before we had fully unpacked, I felt that The Lord gave me a glimpse of the future. He showed me clearly that in the years ahead I would return to my home Church, McChlery Avenue in Salisbury, as the Pastor. It was so clear that I phoned Neil Gibbs to tell him what I believed The Lord had shown me. The conversation went something like this, **"Hi Neil, I felt that it was important to let you know what The Lord has shown me. I believe that The Lord wants me to move to McChley Avenue as the Pastor!"**

Neil answered saying, **"Well AB, just in case you did not know I have only just moved to McChlery Avenue myself as their Pastor and have** barely unpacked!"

I replied, **"Sorry Neil, I did not mean NOW as we have also not finished unpacking in Chipinga. I just wanted you to know that I believe that The Lord wants me to return to McChley Avenue sometime in the future."**

I would not normally have phoned Neil with such a statement, but it was so clear that I felt that he had to know. However, Chipinga was my first priority!

As explained previously, a few months before moving into town, I began to take a monthly Sunday morning service in the same way that my two Baptist Missionaries friends had been doing. But once I moved to Chipinga I made sure that I conducted services on the other free Sundays as well. Initially, I continued to work with the 'INTERDENOMINATIONAL FELLOWSHIP' in the town. But it was not long before I realised that this arrangement was not sufficient! We had to provide a full range of services or else it was no point being there at all!

Now, in order to cater for the farmers and others who worked on the Tea Estates, the Sunday services had to be held in daylight hours. It was too dangerous for anyone to travel after dark. As a result, we ended up with two services every Sunday morning. The first meeting was an evangelistic service held in the Anglican Church whenever it was free and the other was a Breaking of Bread service held in our own home. We always had tea/coffee and snacks between the services at our home. Everybody was welcome and many in the congregation helped by providing refreshments.

It is important to mention that we were welcomed by the other residents when we arrived in town. They assisted us in many ways as we settled among them. For example, the local butcher, who was a believer and part of the 'Interdenominational Fellowship,' informed me that I would receive a 10% reduction on the price of any meat that I purchased in his butchery. This was a real blessing as I am sure that his was the only butchery in town. We naturally were very happy to take advantage of his very generous offer and praised God for His provision. The Butchery also sold locally produced honey which was the best that I have ever tasted, however the 10% reduction was only on the meat!

    The same man also offered to pay the wages of a 'nanny' to help look after our two sons. I believe that his offer was designed to assist her, as well as us. She had looked after his own children when they were babies and she was now unemployed. As we had two little boys under four years old Mally was thrilled to accept his offer. The woman concerned was a lovely person and a real blessing to us whilst we were in Chipinga.

    Before we move on from the 'butcher,' I must share something of his story. He lived just out of town with his wife and family on the road that led to Birchenough Bridge and on to Umtali. Their house could be seen from the road and surprisingly for Rhodesia the building was constructed out of wood. One night they came under attack and this is the story as I remember it.

    During the attack three 'rockets' were fired at the house and many rounds of ammunition. The first rocket exploded without hitting the house, and killed the man who had fired it. The second rocket hit the house and went right through the wooden walls and exploded outside the building. The third and final rocket went right through the wooden walls and then somehow managed to get entangled in the curtains above the window on the other side of the building and failed to go off.

Although many rounds of ammunition were fired during the attack, praise God, those inside were unharmed. At the time of the attack, a baby had been asleep in a cot in a bedroom, and one bullet lodged in the wooden wall but failed to penetrate. The baby had been on the other side of the 'wooden wall' and the bullet ought to have penetrated and killed the child. The only thing that the occupants of the house could say was that God had sent His angels to protect them that night. This was one of many miracles of deliverance recorded during this time for which we all praised God.

In spite of our warm welcome it was clear that not everybody was excited by our arrival. In fact, even my butcher friend made that very clear to me. Yet before he left town, sometime before we moved on, he told me that in spite of his original opposition to our coming to Chipinga, he was really pleased that we came and acknowledged that it had been of God.

I am quite sure that the majority of 'Christians' were not happy that we had moved into Chipinga. Most of them were quite happy with the Sunday services being held two or three times a month and did not really want anything more. In addition, if that were not enough, it was clear that the 'unbelievers' did not welcome our arrival either, and we already knew that Satan was not keen that the Gospel would be preached with authority and anointing in the town. Because we were not really 'welcome' in town, we appreciated the wonderful 'welcome' we received from Rod and Ellie and a few others.

That first year in Chipinga was a real struggle and but for the encouragement of my wife and the support of Rod and Ellie who were new believers, I could easily have given up. During that year it seemed that every advance we made in the work in Chipinga was met with opposition and a lot of it sadly came from other Christians in the town. Yet, in spite of the opposition, praise God, the Gospel was being preached and people were saved.

It was not long after we arrived in town that I started a midweek, evening, Bible Study at our home. Sadly, we seldom had any men attending, it was usually only women. But, one Sunday morning something took place which changed everything, but before I tell the story from my perspective, I will let Simon Rhodes explain what happened in his own words. At the time, he was second in command of BSAP (CID) Special Branch in Chipinga.

TESTIMONY TO THE LORD BY SIMON & RINA RHODES.
CHIPINGA ASSEMBLY OF GOD (1979) WITH AB ROBERTSON

"And The Lord God took the man whom He had (newly) formed, and placed him ..." Genesis 2:15

As forty years have passed since 1979, both Rina and I can now look back with hearts of praise and deep gratitude, as we see how our Heavenly Father sovereignly placed us as young born-again newly formed Christians, into what was just the right garden seedbed, that being the little Chipinga Assembly of God church in Rhodesia. God in His great foreknowledge knew that a good foundation needed to be laid and Chipinga would be just the right place at the right time, so that we could be taught and cared for by His servant AB Robertson, and in so doing, we were being prepared for a lifetime of Christian ministry and service in God.

It was soon after receiving Jesus Christ as our Saviour, that the BSAP transferred me to CID Special Branch in Chipinga in 1979. My sister Ann (now Fourie) was born-again before us and she and Ray were fellowshipping at McChlery Avenue Assembly of God in Salisbury. Unknowing to us, Ann had contacted Abe Robertson as the AOG Pastor in Chipinga and informed him of our recent transfer.

Abe soon followed-up on us. Visiting our home on three occasions he successfully encouraged us to attend fellowship with him and Mally and the few faithful believers meeting with them. They were surprisingly comprised of mostly committed women at that time. However, not many weeks later, Abe ministered the word in season and a loving rebuke and heartfelt exhortation was felt by several men present, including myself, as Abe asked, "where are the men in this church?" It was at that Sunday morning meeting that I was convicted to rededicate my life to God and volunteer to become more committed by getting involved in practical ways to serve the local church. I was one, among several men who had responded under the conviction of the Holy Spirit. We had gone forward and stood together for prayer at that unforgettable meeting. Amazingly, during our three years in Chipinga, we witnessed how God used that relatively small local district church to equip and send seven of its men, including myself, into His service and ministry in and through the Assemblies of God in Zimbabwe.

I started serving in the church by handing out the hymn and chorus books at the door before meetings. Then later having been trained by Abe, kept the accounts for the offerings and church finances. Abe encouraged us to attend Bible study groups at Middle Sabi and Melsetter, travelling with him in the evenings after work. Something unique to the Assemblies of God, was the fact that room was made for people to grow in ministry of the Word at open-ministry sessions, at the Breaking of Bread meetings. From those open-ministry times the sharing of the scriptures grew into more opportunities for younger Christians to share in the Sunday services, preaching as well.

In Chipinga, due to the bush war at that time, we avoided additional travel risks by holding a Breaking of Bread service immediately after the Sunday morning Gospel service. At the open ministry times around the table of our Lord the different ministry gifts became more apparent in those who shared the Word. Gradually Abe would let us take Bible studies on our own and he encouraged us into more and more preaching opportunities. In 1981 Abe took us to our first regional Assemblies of God conference held at CYARA in South Africa. Rina and I attended and had to leave Adam as a new baby, with Don and Lorraine Odendaal. Sovereignly, God was preparing us for His wider service among the churches in new horizons.

By the time we returned from The Bible College of Wales, Abe Robertson had moved to Bulawayo and was the Pastor of Bethshan Assembly in Famona. Abe opened the way for me to start full-time ministry there as his assistant Pastor, first at Bethshan and later I was ordained and appointed as the Pastor of my first church, which I led at the Bulawayo North Assembly.

In 1986 there was a need of a minister in Shurugwe (Selukwe) and after prayer we accepted the call. Then in 1989 we moved to more closely serve the Gweru (Gwelo) Assembly by living there until 1991 when we emigrated to South Africa to join Lawrence Wilson and the pastoral team at the Church on The Rock in Edenvale, and later led the Faith Fellowship Centre in Dundee, two former assemblies that had been a part of the South Africa Assemblies of God under the national leadership of John Bond.

Now in 2019, as Rina and I write, we can testify to forty years in ministry together as a couple. A new chapter is being written of the acts of the Holy Spirit in continuation. In eternity we will share together in and marvel at all that our Heavenly Father has done through us to glorify His Son Jesus Christ here on earth. Dear Mally has gone before us and is already in heaven.

Rina and I had a very good foundation, and we will always love and respect Abe and his late wife Mally for the God-given role they played in laying that foundation in our lives and our walk thus far with The Lord Jesus. Abe has been a spiritual father and valuable mentor, and to this day he remains a precious older brother in Christ and a very dear friend of ours.

"Let us go on .... Receiving the end of our faith, even the salvation of our souls".

"He shall see His seed".
"Thou shalt bring them in and plant them in the mountain of Zion Thy Sanctuary as Thy inheritance"

To God be the glory in everything always. Amen.

His servants and your brethren in Christ Jesus,

Simon, Rina & Adam Rhodes
(Alberton North, Johannesburg, South Africa 2019.)

I have included the testimony of Simon and Rina Rhodes as an example of what God was doing in that little Church. I am thrilled to hear how much they benefited and how it has sustained them over the years. We can praise God, that theirs is only one of the testimonies of people who either came to know The Lord or else were stirred up to serve Him. It is wonderful to record as Simon has already mentioned, that in a congregation which never numbered more than 30 people, a number of people subsequently entered full time ministry and are still faithfully serving The Lord mostly in Africa.

 Now, back to my story, the mid-week Bible study was attended mainly by women and the men were sadly absent. But on Sundays, things were a little different as Rod Hein was always present if at all possible. There was also Don Odendaal who with his wife Lorraine had a farm some distance from Chipinga. They became faithful members of the fellowship and in time there were others. Don and Lorraine, I believe, were led to The Lord by Mike Howard when he took one of the Sunday services in Chipinga, before we moved into town.

On that Sunday morning that was to have such an impact upon Simon and Rina Rhodes, I had only just begun to minister on **Isaiah Chapter 6.1-8** when I believe the Holy Spirit took over in a very powerful way. As I was preaching, I found myself saying things like, **"I am sick and tired of preaching to a group of women at the midweek Bible studies. Where are the men?"**

It was a very strong message and a man who had never attended our meetings before, sadly never came again. When I enquired about him some time later, I was told that he was still running! That was a shame to say the least, but as it has been said, **"You can't win them all!"**

At the end of the meeting, I closed in prayer and said, **"I will be in the Vestry (it was an Anglican Church) and if anyone wants to talk to me, that is where I will be."**

I went into the 'vestry' and put my feet up on the desk and felt quite sure that I had really 'blown it' that morning. Nevertheless, shortly afterwards I was encouraged by a knock on the door, and after taking my feet off the desk, I invited whoever was 'knocking' to come in. I was disappointed to discover that it was one of the elderly ladies and not one of the men. We spoke for a few minutes and I prayed for her and then she left and closed the door. Immediately afterwards there was another knock on the door and it was another lady, and by that time I was convinced that my words which I believed had been really anointed by the Holy Spirit, had fallen on barren ground. After a short conversation we prayed and then she also left the vestry.

It was only then that Simon and Rina came through the door and we prayed together. After we had prayed, Simon assured me that he would be present at the midweek Bible Study from then onwards. Yet, in spite of having promised, he never made it to the meeting that week. He phoned me from out of town to say that he was delayed and sadly would not be present that evening, but from then onwards he was a regular. The next person to come in was Jim Nissan the local baker, followed by the Post Master and possibly one or two more.

God had begun a major work in the hearts of the 'men' of Chipinga and from that week onwards, praise God, the midweek Bible Studies were composed of men and women.

It was a great place to be, as the people were hungry for God's word. Two of those people were Steve Bowen and his wife Linda. They were both teaching at the junior school where Steve was the deputy headmaster, however, for the whole time that we were in Chipinga they never appointed a Headmaster! They were so keen to discuss things, that every week after the Bible study, they were the last to leave. I can remember Mally and I standing at the gate talking to them until long after the others had gone home. Praise God, some years later, they also went into the ministry and are still living in Zimbabwe and currently Steve is the Pastor of the Assembly in Marondera.

One of the ladies attending our services was Badsie Snyders who was the mother of Ellie and

Lorraine. She had been a Church goer most of her life but we all knew that she had yet to be saved. She and her late husband had worked on the Cashel Valley Estate. This was where the Cashel Valley frozen peas and other frozen vegetables were grown and prepared for market. Sadly, he had been killed some time before when the Estate had come under attack and she had subsequently moved into town.

One Sunday, I cannot remember why, we ended up having two Gospel meetings one after the other in the Anglican Church, instead of having a Breaking of bread service at our home for the second service. Rod and Ellie and Don and Lorraine were unable to attend the second service and it was at that service that Badsie committed her life to Jesus. I believe that it was in God's plan that her family were away that morning in order to give her the room that she needed to make her own personal commitment to Christ. From that day she never looked back but served The Lord with all her heart.

Before we move on from this lovely family, I would like to relate a story that I was told by Don and Lorraine. One day, before we moved to Chipinga, they were just about to drive into town from their farm when Lorraine changed her mind and decided to stay home. Don had just passed through the gates when he came under attack and one of the bullets went right through the seat where Lorraine would have been sitting had she not changed her mind and stayed at home. When Lorraine heard the shooting, she immediately grabbed a weapon and ran down to the gate to assist her husband as he fought off the attack. Praise God, they both survived.

As I understand it, not long afterwards whilst they were away from the farm, as a result of another attack, the house was burnt to the ground. In the house was furniture that had been brought with their grandparents from South Africa, when they came to Rhodesia with the Moodie Trek many years before. The furniture was priceless with great sentimental value but it perished in the fire. They naturally were devastated, and never rebuilt the house. Instead, after making some repairs, they moved into the original house that had been built on the farm. This house was situated right next to the main road to Chipinga and as such was perhaps a little safer.

Sometime during our first year in Chipinga, I had a phone call from Mike Howard. He asked if he could send a converted terrorist recruiter to visit us in Chipinga and if I could arrange meetings for him. To be quite honest I was not overjoyed but it was one of those situations where I felt that I could not refuse, and so it was that Ndaba came to stay. We arranged an evening meeting for him in Chipinga and one of the congregants requested that we have it at her home.

When we met him, we discovered that he was an educated man with quite a story to tell. He had grown up in a Methodist Manse as his father was a Minister. He had also been privileged to receive a university education and often mixed with the 'white' missionaries on the mission stations where his father was ministering. As a result, he was quite comfortable in both 'black' and 'white' circles.

However, despite growing up in a 'Christian' home he had not committed his life to Christ. Yet he was still very involved in the 'Church,' and even became the youth leader. Somewhere along the line he had become 'radicalised,' most likely at university, and began encouraging the young people in his father's church to join in the 'liberation struggle.' He had become a 'terrorist' recruiter and he operated from his father's Methodist Church.

Praise God, one day he was wonderfully converted, and as a result began to try and undo the harm that he had done. Sadly, he met with a lot of opposition and was ultimately forced to leave the church as his changed position was not accepted. As we listened to his story, we were all encouraged and praised God for what He had done in Ndaba's life. In fact, the lady in whose house the meeting was held, had this to say to Ndaba before we left, **"How come you took so long to come and tell us your story?"**

As I had also arranged to take him down to Middle Sabi for a meeting, I was very encouraged by her response, and the response of others who were at the meeting that night. Sometime before I had asked Chris and Maureen Triegaardt to arrange a meeting for him. However, like me, when I phoned Chris, he was not overjoyed at the prospect of Ndaba's visit and our conversation went something like this,

"Hi Chris, I would like to bring a special guest preacher with me this week by the name of Ndaba ------ . Would that be alright?" I asked.

Chris replied, **"No problem AB, I will speak to my 'boss boy" and I am sure that he will be able to arrange some accommodation down in the compound."**

I responded, **"No, Chris that is not what I meant, he is not that sort of preacher. I am bringing him down to speak at one of our meetings, and would** like you to accommodate him in your house."

There was a long pause and finally Chris said, **"OK, he will have to sleep in the outside room where you normally sleep, you and Mally and the boys will sleep indoors."**

When we arrived Chris's greeting was rather subdued, and he also managed, I suspect on purpose, to be late for lunch. He finally arrived after we had all finished eating! But in spite of the initial difficulties, things changed dramatically before we returned to Chipinga. In fact, it was 'Ndaba' this and 'Chris' that, as Ndaba had been fully accepted amongst us.

The next day we went to the meeting arranged at a local farmers home. Maureen had phoned every farmer in the valley as she always did, however, this was a very special occasion as most of them would never have sat under the ministry of a 'black' man before! As a result, we were amazed when one of the other farmers suggested that we have it at their home and were interested to see who would in fact attend the service that morning.

When we arrived, we were told that we would be having the meeting on the lawn and surprisingly, it was the biggest turnout that we ever had at a meeting in Middle Sabi. Most of those who attended were Afrikaners and a lot of them were members of the DRC, in theory at least, however, sadly many if not most were not 'saved.'

After leading a short time of praise and worship on my piano accordion, we opened in prayer, and having introduced Ndaba, I handed the meeting over to him. The message he preached could not have been more appropriate for the people that he addressed that day. He challenged the 'white' people of South Africa and Rhodesia to turn back to their God and start serving Him as the Voortrekkers had done, many years before.

He referred to the battle of Blood River which took place in Natal, in South Africa, on the 16th December 1838. On that day just over 140 years before, a force of around 15,000 Zulus, had been sent by Dingane the Zulu king, to attack a group of Voortrekkers on the banks of the Ncome River. This particular 'trek,' was composed of 470 men, women, and children and was led by Andies Pretorious. Just before the battle commenced, the Voortrekkers, gathered in the centre of the enclosure, called a 'laager,' surrounded by their wagons, and prayed. Guided by their staunch Christian faith they prayed for salvation, and victory. In spite of the huge Zulu force, in answer to their prayers, the Boers had a decisive victory, which they believed was down to God's intervention.

At the end of the battle that day, something like 3000 Zulus lay dead, but only 3 of the Voortrekkers had been wounded, and none of their party had been killed. I understand that before the battle, Sarel Cilliers issued a proclamation which said, **"We stand here before the Holy God of heaven and earth, to make a vow to Him that, if He will protect us and give our enemy into our hand, we shall keep this day and date every year as a day of thanksgiving like a Sabbath, and that we shall build a house to His honour wherever it should please Him, and that we will also tell our children that they should share in that with us in memory for future generations. For the honour of His name will be glorified by giving Him the fame and honour for the victory."**

As a result of the amazing Voortrekker victory, the 16th of December became known as the Day of the Vow. In time the Blood River Monument and Museum Complex was constructed consisting of 64 Ox wagons in 'laager' formation, cast in bronze, with a small Chapel constructed in the form of a wagon. In more recent days a long overdue memorial has been constructed in honour of the brave Zulu warriors that died that day.

Now on that memorable day in Middle Sabi, our guest speaker Ndaba Musa challenged a predominately Afrikaner farming congregation, who were all descended from the Voortrekkers, to return to the Day of the Vow. He said that if the South Africans and Rhodesians would once again call out to Almighty God in the way those Voortrekkers had done on the 16th December 1838, they would be amazed at what God would do. It was a really challenging message and I am sure that not one of those farmers went away untouched by what God had laid on the preacher's heart that day.

Although I am not a descendant of the Voortrekkers, I was also touched by what he had to say. In fact, I determined that the very next time we crossed over the border into South Africa we had to make a point of visiting the site of the battle of Blood River. I am grateful that we were able to do this and I will never forget our visit. It was a place where Almighty God heard and answered the prayers of those who trusted in Him!

By the time we left Middle Sabi the following day, the relationship between Chris and Ndaba had really softened and all in all it proved to be a most enjoyable and productive visit. After his visit to

Chipinga and Middle Sabi we had the pleasure of his company one last time when we met up again in Chipinga.

I was in the town centre not far from where we lived when I saw him, and went to speak to him. He had been given permission by the government to visit the 'Protected Villages' they had set up in the rural areas. In fact, they were so keen for him to visit these areas that they had even provided him with free transport. He was in Chipinga waiting for his 'transport' to one of these villages.

Because the villages were vulnerable to visits from the "terrorists" the government came up with the idea of building 'protected villages' in the tribal areas. By moving the people into these villages, the idea was to deny these combatants food and provisions. It also provided a measure of protection and Ndaba had obtained permission to visit them. On these visits he was able to share his change of heart with these villages and it gave him a wonderful opportunity to share the message of salvation with them and their protectors.

As it was nearly lunchtime, I asked him whether he had time to come and eat lunch with us. He said that he would be happy to do that, but that he was not on his own as he had two other men with him. Having confirmed that it would be some time before the 'transport' left town I invited them all home for lunch. As our servant was also a 'cook' who had a number of specialities which he loved to present to us, it was not too much of a burden on my good wife to be suddenly presented with three guests for lunch. As a result, Ndaba and his friends were very welcome at our home. When we sat down to eat Ndaba was quite at home, but his two companions were well out of their depth. As soon as we finished the first course, they quickly excused themselves from the table in spite of the fact that I had advised them that we had a desert as well. Ndaba was quite at home at our table but his friends were very uncomfortable. Had I known how uncomfortable they would be, we could all have quite easily eaten outside under the trees. Soon after our meal they were on their way and it was the last time that I had the pleasure of meeting with him.

The trip down to Middle Sabi with Ndaba, was a special trip, which I believe took place on a Sunday. We were still travelling to the valley every month and having our series of four meetings. On one of these occasions a number of people responded to the Gospel, the evening just before we were due to travel home. One of them was the husband of a lady who had attended on a regular basis right from the start.

His wife Stella attended all the meetings but he had not been to Church since the end of the second world war. During the war he had served in the South African Army and after being demobbed he went to Church but was turned away and denied entry because he was still wearing his uniform. His Church was the Dutch Reformed Church and many of the Afrikaners had not forgotten the Boer War and wanted nothing to do with the British. As a result, they had been very much against South Africa entering the war on the side of the British, and opposed any Afrikaner who served in the army. As a result of his rejection that day our friend had never darkened a Church door since, except possibly to attend a wedding or a funeral.

Yet, much to our surprise and pleasure, on this

particular evening he was seated alongside his wife in our 'Gospel meeting.' It was even more thrilling to see him raise his hand to commit his life to The Lord Jesus when I made the appeal. Instead of calling him aside that evening, I felt that I needed to go around and visit him in his home. Despite the fact that we were due to leave for home in the morning, I arranged to visit Max du Preez before we left. Early that morning before he reported for work, we prayed together and he asked Jesus to be his Lord and Saviour.

Not long afterwards, we were thrilled to discover that he had been promoted to head up the farming operations of Middle Sabi Enterprises. This quasi-Government body had a large farm in the valley, which employed a very large labour force. Sadly, the accommodation that Middle Sabi Enterprises provided for their large labour force was truly shameful. One of the first things that Max did as Manager, which gave indisputable evidence to his conversion to Christ, was to order the construction of better houses for his workers. Praise God, when Jesus comes into our lives, we are a 'new creation,' we live differently and care for our 'neighbours.'

After praying for Max and Stella that morning I left their home praising God for His wonderful favour and hurried around to Chris and Maureen's home to pick up my family. I was fully aware that it was getting late and we needed to catch the convoy which was now operating from the Estate to the main road. Yet in spite of my efforts, when we arrived at the assembly point the convoy had already left. We had to get home that day and so I put my foot down and set off in pursuit.

Our destination was the junction where we

would pick up the convoy from Birchenough Bridge to take us through to Chipinga. As we sped down the road, we passed Richard Hotchkiss travelling home in a Police Reserve Landrover having just come off duty. I believe that it was Maureen Triegaardt who had led them to The Lord, and since then Richard and Sannie had become regulars at our meetings. It can be taken as read that Richard was very surprised to see us travelling down the road without an escort.

Believing that we had already missed the convoy, when we arrived at the junction I failed to stop and just carried on towards Chipinga. As it turned out, we had not missed that convoy at all, as it had not arrived. But it failed to register in my mind that if the police reserve guys were still at the crossroads, which they were, the convoy was still awaited. With my foot down I sped down the road and was really surprised when we arrived in Chipinga to find that the town was very quiet. The reason was obvious, the morning convoy that we ought to have been on, had still not arrived in town!

Back in Middle Sabi, just before Richard arrived home, a message came through on the radio that a 'lone vehicle' had been ambushed. As he had just seen us go past on our own, and not part of the morning convoy, he concluded that it could possibly be us and he was really worried until he received some further information.

What happened, was that an ambush had been set up to attack the convoy. I was later told that it was one of the best positioned ambushes that were ever established during the whole conflict. However, one of the combatants had let off a round by mistake, just as a military vehicle was travelling past on the road below. As their position had now been compromised, they had no option but to attack this lone vehicle which they did with some force. In spite of that, praise God, I understand that no one was killed and The Lord God had watched over us by taking us home safely.

Around about this time I attended a 'security briefing' where the Member in Charge of the BSAP in Chipinga spoke to the residents about the threat to the town. He concluded by saying that if any of those present made regular trips out of town and wanted to speak to him personally, he would be happy to advise us. As I made numerous trips outside the town, I took him up on his suggestion. I started our conversation something like this, **"Good afternoon, Sir, my name is AB Robertson and I am the Pastor of the local Assembly of God congregation in Chipinga. I was at the 'security briefing' the other day and thought that I would take advantage of your invitation to have a chat with you. You said that you would be happy to advise us if we made frequent trips out of town into the surrounding area. I frequently travel out of town visiting the Tea Estates, Coffee farms, Middle Sabi and so on."**

He said, **"Good afternoon Mr. Robertson, you realise, of course, that as a Minister of a local church congregation in this town you are definitely a target for the terrorists. If they managed to kill you it would not only have an effect on your family, but also upon the congregation that you serve and even upon the wider community as well. ----"**

After a short conversation I thanked him for his advice and returned home. After returning home I considered what he had said, in particular what he had said about me being a 'target!' As a result, for a short while, I was not all that enthusiastic about venturing out of town. Nevertheless, that soon passed as I had a job to do, and nothing was going to stop me, and I continued as I had done before, but never forgot what he had to say.

A Presbyterian Minister friend, had volunteered as an Army Chaplain and had come under fire as he was returning from one of his stints in the army. He said, **"It was quite a shock to realise that someone wanted to kill me."**

Moving on from there, one of the farmers that I got to know was a member of the DRC where my friend Danie Haasbroek's was the minister. I cannot remember why, but one day I ended up visiting him on his farm. Whilst in conversation with him he began to complain about his Minister, and after listening to him for a short while I said, **"Do you pray for your minister?"**

The farmer replied, **"Pray for him, he is supposed to pray for us."**

It is so sad that many Church goers are not 'born-again,' and as a result they do not understand the 'spiritual battle' that 'believers' are involved in. For them the 'church' is more like a club, and the 'minister' is just an employee of the 'members.' That is not what I understand about 'church' as The Lord Jesus is the 'head' of the 'church' and we are all 'members of 'His body.' We need to pray for each other, and especially for those who are in leadership in the church that we attend. If the Minister is 'boring' do not complain to the rest of the congregation, rather tell it all to The Lord. If he needs to be 'born-again' or filled with the Holy

Spirit, pray for him as it is amazing what God can do, as He does answer prayer!

One day I was invited to visit another farmer who lived some distance out of Chipinga. I would need to stay the night, and I was asked to bring along my piano accordion, as they were going to have a 'braai' that evening. It was a lovely night and we all sat outside under a blazing electric light around a large fire where the meat was being cooked. I am sure that I had never been to a 'braai' where there was so much meat! There were ordinary sausages, boerewors, lamb chops, pork chops, steak, burgers, in fact it was a real feast. I am pretty sure that there was also 'sadza' and gravy, and mealies roasted in the fire, as a 'braai' needed all of that to round things off.

While the meat was cooking, I was playing the piano accordion and leading the family in some wonderful songs of praise. I was amazed at the wonderful opportunities that The Lord gave me as many if not most of those around the 'braai' that evening were not 'born-again' believers in The Lord Jesus Christ! However, sitting outside the house, under a bright electric light, and possibly visible for many miles, was not really what a man considered by the police to be a 'target,' ought to have been doing. However, God was so good, I survived another day!

Unbeknown to me because of our frequent trips out into the country around Chipinga, Neil Gibbs and others had become very concerned for our welfare. As a result, sometime during my first year a Chevrolet Apache pickup was purchased for my use in the area. This lovely pickup had been the pride and joy of Roland Pletts' father who had recently passed away. It must have been manufactured between 1955 and 1960 but it was in mint condition when I received the vehicle. Once it had been delivered, in order to give me some protection from land mines, and the danger of attack, I took it to the local garage. They attached bullet proof windows, steel plating to the doors and underneath the cab to transform it into an 'armoured car!' After that it became my 'pride and joy' as I loved driving around in my Chev!

But during that first year I became well known at the garage as my Peugeot 304 was playing up. It seemed that every time I went on a trip, when I returned, or even whilst I was still away, I had to take it in for repairs. It had become quite dangerous as on one occasion when I was on the convoy the car failed. On this occasion the convoy commander took pity on me and gave me a tow so that I could get home. What they did for us was not the norm, as a failed motor car could put the whole convoy in danger, but God was good to me. However, the mechanics were never able to put their finger on the problem and it was not long before the car was back again, in the garage.

As a result, the next time that I visited Umtali I tried to put my name down for a new Datsun Pulsar, the latest car to have broken 'sanctions.' But I was unable to do so as they already had too many names on their list. In fact, in spite of wanting to put my name down, I had never actually seen a Pulsar, and had no idea what the car looked like.

Around about that time, Neil Gibbs arranged for a Ministers' meeting to be held in Gwelo. When they heard that we were coming to Gwelo, Geoff and Dianne Gonifas, who were pastoring the Gwelo

Assembly, invited Mally and I and our two boys to stay with them. I say that Geoff invited us, but it may well have been the other way around. They also had two or it could have been three sons at the time so it was fun for the children as well. As we were going to be travelling a long way, Geoff asked if we could stay over for the weekend and minister in the assembly on the Sunday.

After the Ministers' meeting, I mentioned to Geoff that I had, as yet, not seen a Datsun Pulsar (called a Cherry in the UK) and he suggested that we visit a car sales room in the town the following morning, which was Saturday. When we arrived at the showroom there were two cars on the showroom floor, one was a Pulsar and the other was a Datsun 140Y. When I enquired about the Pulsar the salesman said that I was wasting my time as he had a long list of customers, and only the possibility of a few cars. I then asked why the Datsun 140Y had a sold sign sitting on the back seat and not on the roof? He replied, **"The Datsun 140Y has, in a sense, been sold three times but on two of the occasions the buyer either failed to get a loan or did not return. I am just waiting on the latest purchaser to return and finalise the deal. Why what have you got?"**

I said, **"I have a Peugeot 304 Station Wagon."**

"Look give it until Monday midday and if he hasn't returned bring your car in and we will have a look at it and maybe come up with a deal." Said the Salesman.

I agreed and we then left the showroom and wondered what Monday would bring.

As arranged, I phoned around noon on the Monday morning and learned that the 'buyer' had failed to arrive. I was then requested to bring my car into the showroom and the salesman asked what I wanted for the car? I replied that I would like around R$1,500.00 and then left the car for them to examine. Once they had examined the car the salesman said, **"Your car stopped in the middle of the test drive and we had to push it back to the garage."**

I said, **"Yes, it is a problem that I have had for some time and we have thus far failed to get it fixed."**

The salesman went on to say, **"There is a crack in the windscreen that needs to be repaired and ------."**

He then mentioned some other imperfections in my car before saying that if I was interested, all that they could give me as a trade in on the Datsun 140Y was R$1,700.00. I naturally replied that I was interested, amazed that he was offering me R$200.00 more than I had actually asked. The numbers may not be exact but I was definitely offered more than I requested. God is so good!

We then sat down to work out the details of the transaction. But as I had not come prepared to buy a new car, all of the documents that he requested were in Chipinga! In fact, the only thing that I had to prove who I was turned out to be my AA Card which really did not prove a thing. In spite of that, I walked out of the showroom the owner of a Datsun 140Y and we returned to Chipinga in our new motor car. Having returned home I made sure that all the documentation was sent to the salesman by the following post, praising God for His goodness to me. Hallelujah!

When all this was taking place in Gwelo, Geoff was quite taken aback. We had arrived for the Ministers' meeting in Gwelo in a well-travelled vehicle and travelled home in a new car! This was our **third** brand new car, and as a family we were also amazed at God's provision. Praise God for His wonderful provision, a new Datsun 140Y in addition to our wonderful Chevrolet Apache, The Lord had indeed blessed us abundantly!

When we returned home Steve Bowen was also impressed. His comment was that if people were thinking that our little Assembly was not much to write home about, my new car should make them sit up and take notice!

As mentioned earlier, the farmers in Middle Sabi had done really well. Because the farms were irrigated, they were able to grow two successful crops a year. As a result, some of the farmers had placed managers on their farms like Chris Triegaardt. They then purchased additional farms elsewhere in the country where it was not so hot and moved away. One of these successful farmers who was still living in Middle Sabi not only had two cars, they also possessed two light planes, one for her and one for him! As it happened, we were blessed to be assisted in an emergency by one of these 'flying' farmers and their private aircraft.

This took place when our eldest son Mark was around four years old. We were visiting Middle Sabi when he happened to walk in front of a swing, when one of the children was on it. He was hit with some force on the head and we felt that he should be checked out by a doctor.

After a couple of phone calls, Mark and I were on our way to Chipinga with one of the farmers in his private plane. We were met by one of our congregants at the little Chipinga airstrip and taken to the hospital where Mark was admitted for the night. Once he had been properly checked out, we were able to return to Middle Sabi to the rest of the family as Mally had stayed behind with Matthew.

Sadly, that was not the only incident which involved our 4-year-old son. One evening I was out visiting when I received a distressed phone call from Mally. She explained that Mark was rolling around the floor in agony. I returned home immediately and we both laid hands on Mark and called out to The Lord to touch and heal him. In time the pain receded but returned later on a number of occasions. The doctor told us that he could not be sure, but it was possibly tonsillitis, and we ought to wait until he was older before taking them out. The fact was, that he had no idea what the problem was! It would be a number of years before, much to the surprise to everyone, that we learned that it was kidney stones that were causing our little boy all that pain!

We had a lovely back garden but we needed some sand to make a 'sand pit' for the boys to play in. When I mentioned it to Chris (they had one for their children) he suggested that we could load up with sand from the banks of the Sabi River where there was an abundance. Sometime later I drove down to Middle Sabi and went to the River with Chris and a couple of labourers from the farm where they loaded up the pickup with sand. I then drove very carefully home. What, with the sand, the steel doors, and mine proofing the vehicle was really over-loaded. I had never really understood how heavy 'sand' was until that day!

As previously mentioned, Danie Haasbroek, the Dutch Reformed Minister was the only other 'white' Minister in Chipinga at that time. He and I got on very well and he joined us when we 'broke bread' together with a few of my congregation, to see in the New Year. As Ministers, neither Danie nor I were liable for Army or Police Reserve duties but, one day, he told me that he had volunteered for 'Reaction Stick' duties at the Police Station.

Up till that time I did not know about the 'Reaction Stick' and so he explained it all to me. I learned that the 'Reaction Stick' was a unit composed of four men who were required to be on duty at the Police Station every night and would be the first responders to any attack upon the town. Every evening whilst on duty they were required to go on a patrol around the town in a small pickup truck which had a machine gun mounted on the back. One of the men stayed in the Police Station manning the radio whilst the other two men were fully armed in the front on the vehicle. The machine gunner had some protection, but I was told that the machine gun was liable to jam, and as the vehicle was not protected in any way, all of the men were quite vulnerable. When Danie told me what he was doing, I also felt that I should volunteer. Our duties were not too arduous, as it meant a night on duty around every ten days or so.

The very first night that I was on duty, I met up with Kath Neville who was just coming off duty on the Agric-alert, a radio system set up to connect the farmers to the security forces. If any farmer came under attack, they could contact the police station by radio and alert them so that help could be sent out as soon as possible. That Friday evening Kath and I had a chat before she went off duty and I was thrilled to see her the very next Sunday in church. I am not positive, but it may well have been that very day that she gave her life to The Lord. Praise God He was so gracious.

Before moving to Chipinga, Kath and her husband had worked and lived on the Mount Selinda Mission Station, until it became too dangerous. Mr. Neville had worked in some technical capacity and whilst there they established lasting friendships with the 'mission' staff. As a result, one of the first things that Kath did, after coming to know The Lord as her Saviour, was to write and share her testimony with her former 'missionary' friends. In the months that followed, a number of these same 'missionary' personnel advised her that on returning to the USA they had also come to know Christ as their Saviour and Lord. Praise God, for such wonderful news, however, what a tragedy that these 'missionary' doctors, teachers, etc. had been sent out to Rhodesia before they knew Christ as their own personal Saviour.

Before leaving the "Reaction Stick', I would like to share one last incident which took place one night whilst I was having a meal in the canteen at the Police Station. A group of Police Reservists who were based in town were arguing about Ian Smith, the Prime Minister. Some of the comments were very derogatory, so much so, that I felt that I had to say something, resulting in me standing to my feet and reminding them of the importance of praying for those who rule over us. I reminded them that it was not an easy thing to lead a nation and that our Prime Minister's situation was very difficult. When I had had my say, which I felt at the time was really anointed by God, the discussion came to an end.

I am not sure whether my comments had

anything to do with it, but before I left Chipinga there were four Policemen (regulars and reservists) in the congregation and one 'batman' who worked for one of the officers, for which I praised God.

It was lovely to have seen Kath Neville come to The Lord, possibly to some degree as a result of my joining the REACTION STICK, however as I have already mentioned Kath did not keep the news to herself. One of the ladies that was touched by Kath's testimony was a lady by the name of Tilly Davy. Her husband was the manager of Chibuku Brewery and they had an active social life often entertaining people in their home.

Sometime after Kath got saved her friend Tilly Davy ended up in hospital and she asked me to visit her, which I was pleased to do. When Tilly told me that she was unable to sleep in hospital, I asked her if she had asked God to help her sleep. She replied that she did not know how to pray and I replied that prayer is when we 'speak' to God and it is just the same as when we speak to each other. That night Tilly asked God to help her to go to sleep and had a wonderful night's sleep.

She was not in hospital long before she was able to go home and the next Sunday she was in church. We had a guest speaker that weekend, none other than Paddy McCoun, who we got to know in QueQue. That morning, he spoke about his own weaknesses and how much he depended upon The Lord. His message touched Tilly's heart as she had always thought that she was just not good enough to be a Christian. When she heard Paddy say that he was not good enough, and his only hope was in Jesus, something clicked deep within her and that Sunday she asked Jesus to be her Lord and Saviour.

When she gave her heart to The Lord, Tilly was serious. The next time they had a 'dinner party,' with all her husband's business associates at their home, before they started to eat, she called the company to attention and said, **"Before we start can we just give thanks."**

Our new convert, Tilly, was a larger-than-life character who wore big dangling earrings and very large necklaces and so when I began to teach on the subject of 'wives' as mentioned in the epistle of Peter she was a little concerned. Among other things Peter said,

"Wives, likewise, be submissive to your own husbands, ----------. Do not let your adornment be merely outward – arranging the hair, wearing gold, or putting on fine apparel – rather let it be the hidden person of the heart, with the incorruptible beauty of a gentle and quite spirit, which is very precious in the sight of God." 1 Peter 3.1,3-4

After one Bible study she came to me and said, **"I have changed so much since I gave my life to Jesus that if I change any-more my husband will not recognise me. If I stop wearing necklaces and earrings ----."**
I assured her that God understood her situation clearly and that she should ask The Lord how she could win her husband to The Lord. I told her to allow The Lord to lead her step by step. He would show her the way.

This next incident took place during the following year when we had our own premises, but as we are talking about Tilly, we will discuss it here. She ran the local "Cubs" and asked whether we could have their annual church service in the Assembly instead of in the Anglican Church. Naturally I was overjoyed and on that day the church was filled to overflowing with the Cubs and their parents. It was a really special time and Tilly was truly proving that she meant business with God. Praise His Holy Name!

It was during our first year in Chipinga that I was honoured to be invited to be the grooms-man for my good friend Malcolm Fraser when he and Riana got married. Another one of my friends, Alan Keeling, was asked to be the best man. Malcolm was very generous and paid for a new suit, shoes and tie so that I fitted in with Alan and himself. I already possessed a perfectly good suit, but I never argued when he volunteered to bless me in such a way. As already mentioned elsewhere in my story, these two men had been a blessing to me in so many ways in the past.

Although the whole time that we lived in Chipinga my relationship with Danie Haasbroek the DRC minister was very good, I did have one very difficult moment with him. The thing that almost ended our good working relationship came about as a result of a 'baptism' which we had in the town. On that occasion I baptised six of my congregation by full immersion. They included Steve and Linda Bowen, and at least a couple of ladies that my friend Danie claimed were members of the DRC.

However, all six had either given their lives to Jesus during one of our services or were already committed believers before moving to the town and joining our congregation. I explained that I had not felt the need to contact him before 'baptising' them as these ladies had all made professions of faith in Christ in one of my services. Although he was very annoyed, we continued to be friends.

THE BAPTISM.
From the left: - ------, Badsie Snyders, Kath Neville, ------, Linda and Steve Bowen, AB.

I was aware that Danie valued the work that we were doing in the area in spite of this little difficulty. On one occasion whilst visiting Middle Sabi he informed Chris and Maureen that the only place where he received true 'Christian fellowship' was when he visited anyone of our congregation. When he visited any of his congregation all they talked about was the 'crops' the 'animals' or the 'weather' but when he visited anyone of our congregation, he was able to speak about God and the Bible! Praise God for such a commendation, hallelujah!

Around about this time I began a Bible Study on the dangers of the Occult and week after week I presented one aspect of 'occultic' practice that we ought to avoid as Christians. My studies were based upon what God had instructed Moses where He said,

"There shall not be found among you anyone who makes his son or his daughter pass through the fire, or one who practices witchcraft, or a soothsayer; or one who interprets omens, or a sorcerer; or one who conjures spells, or a medium, or a spiritist, or one who calls up the dead." Deuteronomy 18.10-11

There was no doubt in my mind that most Christians were ignorant of the dangers of the 'Occult' and many were totally unaware of what constituted the 'Occult!' However, as I look back on those Bible studies, I know that I continued to deal with this subject for far too long. I was brought to my senses and determined to move on to a new subject when I heard 'aunty' Lena Coetzee, make the following comment, as she was leaving our home after the Bible study, **"It seems that EVERYTHING is wrong"**
The following week we moved on to a new series of Bible studies much to the relief of my congregation. Although over the years, I have spoken of the dangers of the Occult on many occasions, as part of a 'Bible study' or 'message' I have never done such a lengthy series again.

The Bible is an amazing book and there is so

much to learn both from the life of The Lord Jesus Christ and from those who followed Him. In addition, it is vital that we do not ignore the Old Testament as it is full of amazing stories from beginning to end. In fact, you cannot really understand the New Testament unless you first get to grips with the Old. The Old Testament reveals how God Created the heavens and the earth, and how Mankind was Created in the image of God. It then reveals how Adam and Eve were tempted and the terrible consequences of the Fall of Man because of sin. Unless we know the beginning, we cannot really understand why we all need a Saviour, Jesus Christ, and why He had to suffer and die a terrible death on the Cross for our sins. Praise God for His wonderful Word!

One of the things that we studied in Chipinga was,

"THE FIRST PRINCIPLES OF THE DOCTRINE OF CHRIST."

This series of seven studies is taken from the book of Hebrews where we read,

"Therefore, leaving the discussion of the elementary principles of Christ, let us go on to perfection, not laying again the foundation of repentance from dead works and of faith towards God, of the doctrine of baptisms, of laying on of hands, of resurrection of the dead, and of eternal judgement, and this we will do if God permits." Hebrews 6.1-3

In this portion of Scripture, we are reminded of seven basic principles which are: -

1) THE DOCTRINE OF REPENTANCE FROM DEAD WORKS.
2) THE DOCTRINE OF FAITH TOWARDS GOD.
3) THE DOCTRINE OF BAPTISMS.
4) THE DOCTRINE OF THE LAYING ON OF HANDS.
5) THE DOCTRINE OF THE RESURRECTION OF THE DEAD.
6) THE DOCTRINE OF ETERNAL JUDGEMENT.
7) THE DOCTRINE OF GOING ON TO PERFECTION.

Naturally when we studied BAPTISM IN WATER, I encouraged all those who had not been baptised to obey the commandment of The Lord and be baptised. As a result, we had a number of baptisms whilst I was in Chipinga in addition to the one that I have already mentioned. Each one was thrilling and it was wonderful to listen to the amazing testimonies that those being baptised shared with us before going into the water.

When we studied the BAPTISM IN THE HOLY SPIRIT, I made sure that I was available to pray for all those who desired to be filled with the Holy Spirit. However, aunty Lena, who I have already mentioned, was not baptised in the Holy Spirit when we prayed for her. As she left for home, I encouraged her to believe God and have confidence that she would be filled with the Holy Spirit as promised by Almighty God.

We were thus all interested when she attended the next meeting and told us that she had a story to tell. She told us that while having a shower the very next morning after we had prayed for her, the Holy Spirit had come upon her and she found herself speaking in an unknown tongue. Praise God, The Lord was definitely at work and we rejoiced with her in what The Lord had accomplished in her life. Hallelujah!

I am not sure when it was, but Mr. and Mrs. Swindells, a lovely older couple, started to attend our services. They were both well established 'Pentecostal' believers, and lived just outside Chipinga. He was the chief engineer on New Year's Gift Tea Estate, the producers of 'Tanganda Tea.' On one occasion whilst visiting them on the estate I was privileged to be given a guided tour around the factory where the tea was processed. It was a real eye opener to discover how the green tea leaves were processed before being packed up and shipped to the consumer. Tanganda Tea was the well-known brand that could be found in almost every Rhodesian home, be they black or white.

As he showed me around, he told me that before 'sanctions' were imposed by the British Government, and then adopted by the United Nations, all our tea making machinery had been imported from India. But, due to 'sanctions,' because they were no longer able to import the machinery, it all had to be manufactured in the estate workshops which my friend managed. As I took in the responsibility that now rested on his shoulders my next question was related to how large a workforce was under his control.

He explained that because of the war, he was now the only 'European' working in the workshops. In the past there had been a number of others, but he was now on his own. He had been forced to train up his own 'African' workers to do the job. I expressed my amazement as all 'white' Rhodesians were under the impression that the 'African' was not capable of that type of work. In order to prove to me that what he was saying was true, he took me into his workshop and showed me some of the work that these men had done under his supervision. I was truly amazed as I examined the precision engineering that they had been responsible for producing. As a result, my 'racial' prejudice took another bashing. Praise God, The Lord was continuing to change me.

Chipinga and the surrounding districts were the major Tea producing areas of the country and boasted a number of big tea estates. I am forever grateful to have seen the vast acreages of tea growing in the area as it was a sight that I will never forget. I have often thought about my visits to these amazing estates where I saw whole hillsides covered with beautifully manicured tea bushes.

Before we leave this lovely couple, I need to mention another incident that involved members of the Dutch Reformed Church. I do not know how it came about but I had been requested to sing The Lord's Prayer in Afrikaans at a local wedding. Although I speak a little Afrikaans, I am by no means bi-lingual and so when I was asked to sing **"DIE HERE IS MY HERDER"** I was decidedly nervous. As it happened the Swindell's daughter, married to a minister, and an excellent musician was visiting at the time. She offered to accompany me and teach me the song in Afrikaans.

We made excellent progress and I was getting more and more confident when she told me that she would be leaving on the Friday which was the day before the wedding. I was shocked as I knew of no one else who would be able to accompany me and thus I would be singing the song at this local wedding unaccompanied. The day dawned and I sang my song as requested and hopefully it was a blessing. I am not sure however, as it was the first and only time that I was ever requested to sing at a DRC wedding! It seems that my story is full of first- and last-time accounts!

However, in addition to growing tea in the area, more and more farmers had started planting coffee. So much so that a large coffee processing factory had been constructed in the town. It was explained to me that when a farmer planted coffee, he had to lay out a very large amount of money as the first real harvest could only be reaped after five years. As a result, all the coffee farmers owed a considerable amount to the banks. It was an expensive crop to grow but when fully established the rewards were considerable.

As a result of the success of 'coffee' in the area, one of the people from our congregation who was a beef farmer decided to plant some. He was not prepared to get into debt and managed to plant the crop and look after it for around three years. Yet, when it came to the final two years before harvest, he decided he would need a loan from the bank to see him through. Sadly, the bank was not interested and he failed to get a loan and the whole project failed. He felt at the time that had he asked for more money at the beginning of the project he would possibly have received the loan. No matter what the reason, his venture into coffee farming was not a success.

One day I was visiting another farmer who had ventured into coffee and he exclaimed that he needed someone to teach him about Bible Prophecy as he really had no idea what it all meant. Although I had given many Bible Studies on the subject, I responded to his statement by saying, **"Well, I am no expert --------."**

However, before I was able to finish what I was saying, he interrupted me and said, **"Well, I need an expert!"**

Sadly, that was that, the conversation was closed. He never gave me the opportunity to share what I knew. What a mistake, it taught me a great lesson that day and I have never responded that way again. I am sure that I would have been able to help him a great deal, but my words denied me that opportunity.

As a result of intensive negotiations between the Rhodesian Front Government of Ian Smith and the various political leaders in the country the first universal suffrage elections were held in Rhodesia in April 1979. The government had made it quite clear that provided ZANU(PF) the party of Robert Mugabe who were supported by the Chinese Communist Party, and ZAPU(PF) the party of Joshua Nkomo who were financed by the communists of the Soviet Union, were prepared to lay down their weapons they also could participate. However, they were not prepared to lay down their weapons.

The agreement that had been reached gave the former, mainly white electorate, the opportunity to vote as before, and elect 28 representatives to the White Roll of the new 100 seat parliament. In addition, they were able to cast a second vote to elect 72 'black' representatives to parliament on the Common Roll, with the rest of the population for the new 'black' majority government.

On the day of the election, we went to the polling station at the District Commissioners offices. In the street outside, the supporters of the two main political parties in the area had gathered. They were ZANU headed up by the Reverend Ndabaningi Sithole whose base was in the Chipinga area and the UANC the party of Bishop Abel Muzorewa. The representatives of these two parties danced and sang all day in the street outside. They moved backwards and forwards keeping out of each other's way the whole day and there was a spirit of real joy and excitement in the air. Although we all expected trouble there was none and the elections went off peacefully all over the country.

The UANC won 51 of the available seats and were thus able to establish the first black majority government in the country. As a result, our new Prime Minister became Bishop Able Muzorewa, and the name of our country was changed to Zimbabwe/Rhodesia. Sadly, the African leaders of the British Commonwealth refused to accept the result of the elections and Margaret Thatcher the British Prime Minister accepted their advice and likewise rejected the results of a fair and free election. An election where there was no intimidation and the people were free to make their own decisions.

The African leaders and the British government failed to appreciate what had taken place and chose not to accept the result unless the two terrorist organisations were included. No one took note of the fact that they could have participated had they only been willing to lay down their arms.

Leaving the 'political' situation, you may remember that a few years before coming to Chipinga I produced a series of Bible Studies on 'THE FAMILY' which I preached in our Assemblies all around the country! Well, as we had a number of young families in the fellowship, I decided to deal with this subject whilst in Chipinga. However, I had barely completed the series, taking time to stress the importance of giving children love, instruction, and discipline when I was given a book by one of the people in the congregation entitled,

DARE TO DISCIPLINE By James C. Dobson

We were given the book just as we were about to leave on holiday and were encouraged to put it into practice, as it seemed that they felt that our children were out of control. I was very aware of our responsibility and found it difficult to understand where they felt we had failed. Some of the meetings were held in our home and I would always be leading. As a result, Mally had her hands full with two children to look after, but in spite of this our sons were always well-behaved. Sadly, it appeared that not everyone agreed and hence the 'book.'

Let me make it very clear, the book is a classic, and I was happy to read it, but was surprised that there were those who felt that our children were out of hand. The book is still available and I highly recommend it to you.

As we approached the end of our first year in Chipinga I really needed a holiday. While on duty at the Police Station one of the Reaction Stick members advised me that as a 'policeman' I may be entitled to use holiday accommodation owned by the South African Police as there was an agreement between the two Police Forces. I thought that it was worth a try and made enquiries and, praise God, my request was accepted.

We planned to leave first thing on the Monday morning on a much-needed holiday. As we were hoping to attend some services whilst we were away, I made sure that I took a suit. But when I looked at my lovely new suit, and new shoes, (given to me by my friend Malcolm) I felt that it would be better to leave them as they could get damaged whilst we were away.

You can imagine how I felt when I was presented with a major problem, just before the Sunday morning service, on the day before we were due to go on holiday! That morning I was advised by a representative of the Church of England, that from the following Sunday we would no longer be able to use their premises. As we were leaving for South Africa the next morning, there was nothing that I could do. I called a few of the men together after the service and advised them that I was leaving the problem in their hands. To be clear, I left the problem in the hands of God, and these capable men, and thought nothing more about it as I needed to get away.

That morning we set out bright and early and completed the first stretch of our journey with the 'convoy' to Birchenough Bridge without any trouble. But, on arrival at this point we were told that there had been an incident on the road to Fort Victoria, and there would be no convoy travelling that way until it was safe to do so. The thought of travelling back to Chipinga was out of the question, we were not going to retrace our steps, we were on holiday. As a result, we continued our journey travelling the long way round, via Umtali and Salisbury.

Somewhere along the way I must have contacted Neil Gibbs as they invited us to spend the night with them before continuing our journey to the border and South Africa. Whilst staying with Neil and Marge I remember speaking to Neil about my sons, who were four years old and under and he replied, **"AB when you have small kids you have small problems. However, when you have big kids then you have big problems."**

Although I include his words, I have to say that our sons were never a 'problem.' They have always been a credit to Mally and I and we were so pleased that The Lord chose to give them to us.

When we finally crossed the border into South Africa our initial destination was to visit the memorial of the battle of Blood River. It was a sobering thing to try and visualise that small group of Voortrekkers being confronted by 15,000 Zulu warriors in full battle regalia. That, amazing God-given victory, on the 16th of December 1838, resulted in the death of 3000 Zulu warriors and the beginning of the decline in the power of the Zulu kingdom. We walked around the 64 bronze Ox wagons in 'laager' formation, and viewed the small Chapel constructed in the form of a wagon. As we did so we considered the words of Ndaba once again, the question was, would Rhodesians and South Africans once again call out to God to save them or would they continue to ignore the God who made them?

THE MEMORIAL AT BLOOD RIVER

On our visit to Natal, we arranged to visit Rodney and Ann Woodley and their family. We first met them when we were in QueQue and he was working as a Tsetse Control officer out beyond Gokwe which was some miles from QueQue on a very rough gravel road. Every month in order to do his job, the family spent 3 weeks in the bush living in a tent. They then came back to Gokwe for a week's rest where they had a house. During their week off they did their best to visit us in QueQue and attend our meetings.

The Tsetse Control department had to stop their activities as it was too dangerous to operate out in the bush and Rodney had to find a new job. It so happened that at that time Ann inherited a Sugar Farm in Natal on the KwaZulu border and they moved to South Africa. When we visited Rodney had some rather disturbing stories to relate about what was happening in KwaZulu and as a result he had made provision to protect his family.

When we were there, a large sugar cane field that had already been reaped, was being burned so that a new crop could grow more easily. I decided to accompany Rodney when he went to check on the progress being made by his workers. I was always interested in the different farming activities and was keen to learn about Sugar Cane. Our son Mark asked if he could accompany us while Mally and Matthew stayed with Ann and the rest of her family.

We travelled down a rough farm road that was on the side of a hill. The fields of reaped sugar cane were up the hill on our right, and down the hill on our left. Just as we approached the area where the burning was taking place, the wind suddenly changed, and we found ourselves enveloped by smoke. It was so bad that we could not see and breathing was very difficult. Praise God, Rod had the presence of mind to put his hand out of the window and make sure that he could feel the sugar cane as he continued to drive along the road and to safety. Had he not done that, he would not have known where the road was, and we could have left the road and tumbled down the hill. I was naturally not only concerned for myself but also for our young son, Mark. Praise God, we survived to tell the tale.

After a pleasant visit with the Woodley's and their family we were on our way again. Our final destination was Port Edward where we had been privileged to rent a thatched cottage for our holiday from the South African Police Association at a very reasonable rate. When we arrived, we were thrilled to discover that there was a lovely lagoon nearby and everything else that a holiday by the sea can provide for land-locked Rhodesians.

Sadly, Mark had one of his attacks just before we arrived, and was in real agony once again. Praise God, it passed away and he was able to enjoy his holiday. We all enjoyed the lagoon and had a wonderful relaxed holiday. While there we met up with Nadine 'Hopkins' and her doctor husband and their two delightful little boys. Nadine had been nursing in Salisbury and been a good friend of Cassie Perioli and in fellowship at McChlery Avenue.

Sadly, all too soon our well-deserved holiday was over, and we were heading back home. But we were greatly refreshed and ready for the challenges that lay ahead. While waiting for the convoy at Birchenough Bridge, we must have met up with Chris and Maureen as instead of going straight home we ended up spending the night with them at their home in Middle Sabi.

That evening we received a phone call from Rod and Ellie Hein who warned us that while we were away our home had been burgled. They did not let us know earlier as they had not wanted the news to spoil our holiday. They had been alerted by the neighbours who had found our clothes and other items scattered from the back of the house all the way to the back fence. It appeared that the thieves had been disturbed and must have left in a hurry.

Naturally, we were disappointed, however, I replied that nothing was going to spoil our holiday as God had blessed us with a wonderful break. We returned home the next day to a house that had been burgled and although a lot had been stolen nothing was of great value. However, among the things that were stolen were the new suit and new shoes that had been provided for me for the wedding of Malcolm and Riana Fraser. In hind sight it appears that I ought to have taken them with me! In spite of this, we were not prepared to have the benefits of our holiday spoiled, as whilst we had been away, we had been so wonderfully refreshed and blessed.

During the month that we were away the members of the pioneer Assembly and in particular Rod and Ellie Hein had not been idle. A new place of worship had been secured which belonged to the Herevormede Kerk, an offshoot of the DRC, who owned a lovely church building in Chipinga. In the past it had only ever been used once a month for services, but due to changed circumstances brought on by the war, and other developments, the building was no longer being used.

We were given exclusive use of the building, the only requirement being that we kept it in good repair. Although there was no electricity in the building, as it had only been used in daylight hours, we arranged for the building to be connected to the electricity supply and had lights installed. It was a wonderful surprise to come home and find that we now had a place of our own. However, it was not a complete surprise, but rather a confirmation about what The Lord had shown me right at the beginning. When we had first moved to Chipinga and driven past the building I had distinctly felt The Lord put it in my heart that we would one day be using that building. Praise God, He had confirmed His unspoken Word!

However, the surprises were not finished! The house next door, number 203 Ferreira Street had a gate in the fence leading to the church. It was up for sale and we moved in next door. This small fellowship was prepared to make a commitment to purchase this house so that we would not have to move again. We soon moved into a modern house with a large garden right next to our place of worship. Thinking back upon what happened in QueQue, I should have listened to my 'small' congregation and had the faith to purchase the house they recommended at the time. Sadly, it appeared that my congregation had more 'faith' than their minister!

For some Ministers, the thought of living in the house next door to the church would fill them with misgivings, however we really enjoyed our new home in Chipinga. It was so much easier to organise tea/coffee and fellowship between the services on a Sunday morning. It was also easier for Mally to handle our growing family as the arrival of our third child was getting closer every day.

One day I had a phone call from one of the ladies in the town who had started attending our services. She said something like this, **"Before attending your services I felt that I was a Christian, however, since I started to attend, I just do not know where I stand any more with God. Since you are responsible for causing me to be unsure, I think you ought to help me get myself sorted out!"**

That afternoon Mally was leading a ladies' meeting at our home and so I suggested that she meet me at the church and we could discuss her 'problem.' When she arrived this is basically the story that she told me, **"When I was a girl, about 16 years old, we had a visit from an 'evangelist' who spoke at our local Dutch Reformed Church. As a result of what he preached that evening, when I arrived home, I got on my knees and asked The Lord Jesus to come into my heart. So where does that leave me now?"**

Having heard what she had to say about what happened that evening so many years before, I asked her a few questions. What I discovered was that she had never told anyone about her commitment to Christ basically right up to the present day. As a result, over the years she had just grown cold until she had begun to attend our services a short while before.

After discussing her situation for a little while I suggested that possibly the best thing to do was to start all over again. Having made that suggestion, I then proceeded to show her the 'way of salvation' by referring her to a number of verses in the Bible. Having done that, we prayed together and she asked The Lord to forgive her and come into her heart once again. After we had prayed, I showed her a few more Scriptures and then explained to her the importance of telling others what she had done that afternoon. I showed her the verse which states,

"--- if you confess with your mouth The Lord Jesus and believe in your heart that God raised Him from the dead, you will be saved." Romans 10.9

We then crossed over to our house where she proceeded to walk into our sitting room and tell all the ladies present that she had given her life to Jesus. We were thrilled to see that whatever doubts she had had previously, from then on, her doubts were gone as she knew that she was 'born-again.'

Now moving on from there, I have always been happy to entertain visiting preachers in whatever Assembly I have been in, as their 'ministry' will naturally be different from my own, enriching my local congregation. As a result, when I was phoned by Ron Davies who asked if he could bring Ray Belfield, a visiting British AOG Minister to Chipinga I was very happy to oblige. This minister, his wife and family were on a 'World Missions' trip paid for by some well-wisher. During all the years that he had been in the Ministry he had always been an enthusiastic supporter of World Missions and he now had the opportunity to see in person what was happening around the world where British AOG Missionaries were labouring.

Because of the war it was considered unwise for the whole family to travel with him to Rhodesia and so he travelled alone and the family remained in South Africa. He had visited Ron and Dorothy Davies who were British Missionaries doing an amazing work in Rhodesia with Global Literature Lifeline. But although Ray was keen to visit some of the 'tribal' areas of the country this was not possible because of the war. As a result, Ron believed that the next best thing was to visit Chipinga a small border town. In addition to arranging a few special meetings, because it is such a beautiful part of the country, we did our best to show them the tea estates, coffee farms, and so on, in the area.

Despite a couple of difficulties, the visit was a great success and we were really blessed by their ministry and friendship and I count it a privilege to have known both of these men and their wives. Before he left, Ray encouraged us to remain in Chipinga as he could see that The Lord was using us there. He also promised to arrange a preaching tour for us if we were ever to visit the UK. His visit to Chipinga was surely ordained by God and we established a friendship that would last for the rest of his life.

Among the other people who joined us in Chipinga were Johan (Jannie) and Dawn Barnard. We had got to know them in Umtali and Jannie had secured work on a Wattle Estate outside Chipinga. They were not able to be with us as often as some but were a real blessing when they came. Jannie had a lovely voice and played the guitar. One day he sang a song by the Gaithers called '**I HAVE RETURNED'** and I include the first verse and chorus,

I HAVE RETURNED TO THE GOD OF MY CHILDHOOD,
TO THE SAME SIMPLE FAITH AS A CHILD I ONCE KNEW,
LIKE A PRODIGAL SON I'VE LONGED FOR MY LOVED ONES,
FOR THE COMFORTS OF HOME AND THE GOD I OUTGREW.
I HAVE RETURNED TO THE GOD OF MY CHILDHOOD,
BETHLEHEM'S BABE, THE PROPHET'S MESSIAH,
HE'S JESUS TO ME, ETERNAL DEITY!
PRAISE HIS NAME, I HAVE RETURNED.

I have never forgotten how blessed I was, listening to Jannie sing that song! Would to God the many 'backsliders' who populate our towns and cities would RETURN before it is too late. Jesus said He would return and HE WILL DO JUST THAT, and most Bible believing Christians believe that the TIME for Him TO RETURN cannot be very far away. We need to get right with God, as time is surely running out!

I praise God for Jannie and Dawn who went on some years later to serve The Lord ministering to the tribal people who lived on the shores of Lake Kariba. Praise God for such people as this!

We continued to minister the Word of God to the people of Middle Sabi on a regular basis and God continued to honour His Word. One evening I was ministering to a packed 'house meeting' on the subject of 'REPENTANCE FROM DEAD WORKS,' when a farmer, who had never attended our meetings before, wept his way to salvation. It was wonderful to see this man, who was a very successful farmer come to The Lord in tears in the presence of all who knew him.

His wife was a dedicated Roman Catholic but attended the ladies' meetings on a regular basis. Her husband, according to Chris Triegaardt, would have been the 'Mayor' of Middle Sabi had there been such a post as he was so well respected in the community. That night he very clearly committed his life to Christ.

In spite of that, only a few days later I saw him in Chipinga and crossed the road to talk with him, but he avoided speaking to me. The following month he failed to attend any of the meetings and we were quite concerned for both him and his wife. It seemed that he had decided not to follow up on the decision that he had made in tears the month before. But God had other plans, He had not given up on him!

In fact, it was not long after this that he was kicked by a horse and was flown to hospital in Salisbury in great pain. A call went out to pray for him as nothing seemed to be helping with the pain racking his body. Then suddenly the pain went and, lying in hospital, he 'knew' that God had touched him and healed him, and soon afterwards he was discharged and back at home.

On my next trip to Middle Sabi I decided to visit him on his farm to see how he was doing. When I arrived at their home, he had other visitors, but as soon as he saw me, he left them and came to talk to me. He told me what God had done for him and he said that he would be attending the meeting that night. From then on, he was really keen and even attended some early morning prayer meetings that we had in the valley. But one evening he confessed to me that he was finding it difficult to serve The Lord to which I responded, **"You surely do not want to be kicked by a horse again, do you? Keep close to Jesus, there is no other way to go."**

He agreed that he did not want to be kicked by a horse again, in order to wake him up, and things continued until they announced that they were leaving. They were putting a manager on their farm and they had purchased a dairy farm just outside Salisbury where they would now be living. The dairy farm they purchased was, from what I was told, the most productive farm in the country with the cows being milked three times a day. He was definitely doing well and they also owned a ranch in another part of the country.

I was concerned that he should find a suitable place of worship when they moved. It would do him no good if he attended the Roman Catholic Church with his wife and I was really concerned that he came under sound Christian teaching. At the time I had an Assembly of God magazine with a list of our churches on the back and decided to give it to him. As I did not want to destroy the magazine by tearing the back page off, I gave him the whole issue. Sadly, that particular issue included an article dealing with the errors of the Roman Catholic Church which although true was not appreciated by his wife.

Some years later, I did have the opportunity to visit the farm outside Salisbury, but it was not to visit him and his wife, it was to visit another couple who worked for him. The farm was, as I have already mentioned the very best dairy farm in the country and it was wonderful to be able to visit. Sadly, we lost contact, however I do hope that he and his wife eventually found a Bible-believing church to be part of and that they both went on with The Lord.

Being out on a limb in Chipinga it was a wonderful blessing for us to travel to various AOG ministers' meetings which were held from time to time. One such meeting was held at THE GOLDEN MILE Hotel just outside QueQue. We were quite impressed that Neil Gibbs had arranged it at this hotel which was around halfway between Salisbury and Bulawayo. What impressed us more than anything was that the costs were to be met by the National Development Fund. This was a particular blessing to my wife who had sacrificed much as we served The Lord in different parts of the country.

At these meetings we were able to get to know new members of the 'team' and have fellowship with one another. They were important as they helped to keep the unity of a growing ministry right across the land. Sadly, they were always over all too soon and we were once more heading back home. I might add that on this occasion I still had the same car that I arrived with!

As Mally and I had different blood groups, having children could present problems. Thankfully, the birth of Mark caused no difficulties at all, for which we praised God. After the birth of Mark my wife was given certain injections which were supposed to assist and the birth of Matthew also took place without any problems, for which we again praised God. However, when she fell pregnant with Jonathan things became a little more difficult.

Our Doctor in Chipinga advised us to seek the assistance of a Specialist in Salisbury. As a result, a few weeks before the baby was due Mally moved up to Salisbury and stayed with Malcolm and Riana Fraser. Due to the difficulties which greatly increase the nearer you get to the expected birth date the Specialist decided to induce the birth a few days early. The date that he selected was the 4th July 1979, and the baby would require a blood transfusion immediately after birth otherwise he would die. Our little boy would have all his blood removed, and replaced by blood that was more compatible with his needs.

As the time drew near, I drove up to Salisbury and left Mally in the kind care of Malcolm and Riana Fraser. They lived very close to the hospital and so if anything changed, she could be there very quickly. I also left her with the car so that she would be able to get to other appointments without difficulty. As a result, I needed transport to get back home to Chipinga which was quite some distance away.

I am not too sure how this happened but I agreed to drive a car back to Umtali that had been repaired in Salisbury. Although Umtali is still a long way from Chipinga I would at least be part way home.

Having picked up the car, I drove it back at my normal speed of around 70 mph (maybe less as it had just been repaired) and delivered it to a garage in Umtali. I later learned that after examining the car, the mechanic came to the conclusion that it was a miracle that I had made it to Umtali alive. One of the wheels of the 'repaired' vehicle had not been bolted on properly. In fact, there were only two bolts out of the four that should have been there, and they had not been properly tightened. I was told that had I hit a bump of any kind the wheel could have come off and I would have been involved in a major accident. God is so good to me, praise His name, I lived to continue to preach God's wonderful Word!

Having arrived in Umtali, I am not too sure how I travelled the rest of the way back to Chipinga but I most likely managed to get a lift. Of course, when I arrived home, I was able to travel around in my lovely mine and bullet-proof Chevy Apache. I planned to drive my 'tank' up to Salisbury before our new baby was due to be born. But on the day appointed, I was waiting for the convoy to leave when it began to rain. That ought not to have been a problem, but when it rained and I discovered that the windscreen wipers were not working. There was no time to fix the wipers before the convoy departed and although I was offered the loan of a car by someone in our congregation, for various reasons, I declined to accept his offer.

God was so good as another light aircraft owner came to my rescue. He was the owner of a local service station and, although not a member of my congregation, he had attended a few of our services and I believe that he was born-again. He came to my rescue again some years later but that story will be told in due time. He took me all the way to Salisbury in his plane and drove me to the hospital from the airfield in his car. I arrived in time to be present when Jonathan made his way into the world. Although I failed to be present for the birth of our first two sons, praise God, I was at least there for the birth of one of my children in spite of having to travel over 300 miles to get there!

We were so blessed to have the medical assistance that we needed and God gave us another lovely son. When Mark was born just on four years before, all our medical expenses were met in QueQue and we had nothing to pay. Less than two years later when Matthew was born in Umtali we had a small fee to pay but when Jonathan was born in Salisbury we were presented with a large bill. Yet, knowing that I was a Minister of the Gospel, and not likely to be in receipt of a large income, the Specialist graciously wrote on the bottom of the bill something like the following, **"Pay as much as you can."**

This was difficult, as although we really did not have the money to pay, he had presented me with a problem. If he had chosen not to give us a bill, I would have graciously received his 'gift' with thanksgiving to The Lord. But this man chose to give me a bill, clearly showing me the cost of the treatment that we had received. As a result, I felt obliged to pay, and when I sent in my cheque sometime later, I wrote on the bill something like the following, **"Thank you so much for all that you have done for us, we are so very thankful to you and to God. Thank you also for giving us the option to pay as little or as much as we chose, however the Bible says, "The labourer is worthy of his hire." As a result, I enclose a cheque for the full** amount.

Thank you so much.
Alan, Mally and Jonathan Robertson

Praise God, we are the servants of the living God, we are not beggars! We ought not to go around and 'ask' unbelievers to give us a 'special price' because it 'is for the Church!' We ought not to expect the 'world' to subsidise the work of God. That Specialist was an 'unbeliever' and if he had chosen not to charge us, I would have accepted it as from The Lord but he sent me a 'bill' and so I paid it. He had blessed us with his expertise and we praised God for him, however, we were the people of the LIVING GOD and The Lord GOD is our provider. Hallelujah!

The next story is so very sad and happened very close to the end of hostilities that one has to wonder why it happened at all. We were visiting Middle Sabi once again when Maureen had a very worrying phone call from her parents the evening before we were due to return to Chipinga. They were very concerned and asked for prayer as they were sure that there were terrorists on their farm in Odzi. They were farming in an area between Umtali and Inyazura on the way to Salisbury. We all prayed for them that night, but we had to leave early the next morning to catch the convoy back to Chipinga.

Sadly, the following morning when Maureen's father went out to the lands, he was confronted by a group of terrorists who shot him down in cold blood. The security forces were on the farm very soon afterwards but it was too late to save her dad. We learned later that he had given his heart to The Lord and was talking about getting baptised as soon as it could be arranged. As a result, although the funeral would be taken by the new Dutch Reformed minister in Umtali I was asked to say a few words on behalf of the family at the funeral as his two daughters and their families were part of my congregation. Sadly, the lovely born-again, spirit filled Dominee, that I had known in Umtali had moved on and the new 'Dominee' was not at all keen on 'Pentecostals.'

I spoke to the Dominee before the service and was given to understand that after he finished, I would be given an opportunity to say a few words. The funeral proceeded and the Dominee concluded what he had to say at the grave side and moved away without mentioning my contribution at all. I realised that unless I stepped forward immediately everyone would move away very quickly and so I took the bull by the horns and stepped forward. It was a difficult situation as I felt like a gate crasher, however, in spite of that I said a few words on behalf of the rest of the family and I trust that I mentioned what I knew about his decision for Christ before he died. Praise God, we will all be meeting again at the feet of Jesus in the days that are ahead.

I do not blame this man for his attitude as if we are 'shepherds' of the flock we need to protect those in our charge from 'false teaching.' Sad to say, although his predecessor knew me to be a 'man of God,' and not a 'false teacher,' this man did not know me at all. The previous Dominee had the same experiences as I had as he was 'born-again' and 'filled with the Holy Spirit.' Sadly, this man had obviously not, and as a result he considered me to be in error. He was only trying to protect his flock and should rather have said, "NO" to any participation of mine instead of behaving as he did. However, he is of course forgiven!

Sadly, in spite of the success of the first 'one man one vote' elections in the history of Rhodesia and the formation of a new government under the leadership of Bishop Abel Muzorewa there was a problem. Although the Conservative Government of Margaret Thatcher were at first sympathetic to the changed circumstances, they later rejected the result. There was a Commonwealth heads of state meeting in Lusaka in Zambia which totally rejected the outcome of the elections and as a result the new Zimbabwe/Rhodesian government was not accepted on the world stage.

The British Government instituted the Lancaster House conference in England where a new agreement was finally thrashed out. This entailed new elections which would include Zanu (PF) and ZAPU (PF) who would be allowed to enter the country fully armed. Large Marquees were erected and British Policemen were brought over to 'keep an eye' on these armed men.

As a result, these new elections took place in an atmosphere of fear. There was no joy in Chipinga during the elections such as we had seen the previous year. The people were decidedly fearful. It was widely believed that under cover of darkness the men that the British Policemen were supposed to be keeping an eye on went into the countryside and warned the people of the consequences of not voting for their leaders. They threatened to continue the war if not elected into office. In addition, some wise person commented that the 'white' population had been, **"Deceived by their own** propaganda."

We really did not believe that the people would vote for Zanu (PF) or Zapu (PF). We knew that they were the ones who had abducted their children and murdered their people! Why would they 'vote' for them? However, they did!!

I was watching TV when the results were announced and it took some time for the result to penetrate my mind. As a result of the outcome of the elections, I knew that we would now definitely be leaving Zimbabwe/Rhodesia sometime in the future. I went away to pray and felt that The Lord drew my attention to a particular verse which was,

"The words of his mouth were smoother than butter, but war was in his heart; his words were softer than oil, yet they were drawn swords." Psalm 55.21

The news was greeted by many initially with disbelief, and many made plans to leave the country. Most of us were really shocked by the result but nevertheless we had to get on with the job on hand.

Neil Gibbs who was, at that time, the leader of 'the work' was involved it what he called the 'NOW IS THE HOUR' crusade which he took all around the country. When he came to Chipinga he came with a music group called "HARVEST TIME COUNTRY GOSPEL SINGERS." Most of the six men who made up the group had family in the area and so that was a great draw card for the special meeting held in town.

The school hall was packed to overflowing with around 200 people in attendance which was around one out of every five of the 'white' residents living in the entire area. Sadly, when Tim King wrote his very good book "IN SEARCH OF OPHIR" on the History of the Assemblies of God in Rhodesia/Zimbabwe, he misunderstood me and said that 200 people got saved. But what I really meant was that over 200 people attended the meeting that night! Praise God a number of people did commit their lives to Christ as it was an exceptional meeting. One of those who came to Christ was the daughter of Richard and Sannie Hotchkiss from Middle Sabi. Quite recently Shereen, now Thompson, told me that she gave her heart to The Lord that night and that it was my wife Mally who prayed with her after the meeting. Praise God, Shereen and her husband continue to serve The Lord to this day.

No Church will see people coming to Christ without having to deal with a few problems as time goes on and that was the same with our Assembly in Chipinga. I have purposely avoided including some of these stories as I love and respect the people concerned. Yet, just because I have excluded them does not mean that they did not happen. When we preach the Gospel the enemy of our souls will do everything in his power to destroy us and sadly sometimes, we even allow him to use us if we are foolish enough to let our guard down. May the good Lord help us to walk together in love and unity at all times.

As I felt that my time was up in the area, I had asked for a move and we were due to leave for Bulawayo in a matter of months. Mike Howard, who had been keen to move to Chipinga for some time, was due to take my place. I had delayed moving until I felt that the Assembly was to some degree established, but felt that it was now time to move in spite of there being no 'recognised' leaders in the Assembly. I was sure that it was too soon to recognise Elders; however, I felt that we could recognise 'deacons' as we had some very good men in the fellowship.

As a result, I presented a number of names to the Assembly as potential 'deacons' and said that unless there was any objection, we would be recognising them as 'deacons in the Assembly the following week. If the congregation had any problem with any of them, they should approach me before the following week. The names that I put forward that day were Steve Bowen, Rod Hein, Simon Rhodes, Errol Lobb, and Jannie Barnard. It is amazing to record that from this small Assembly **all of these men** were later to go into full time ministry. I was thrilled to leave a team of excellent, dedicated men, to assist the incoming minister when I left.

Nevertheless, I had one very interesting phone call when word got out in that small community that we would be recognising 'deacons' in the Chipinga Assembly. The lady was a member of the DRC and phoned and asked me the following question, **"When you appoint 'deacons' in the church do you take into account how they behave outside the church as well as how they behave inside the church?**

I replied that of course we consider their whole life, inside and outside the church!

The men that were recognised as deacons in Chipinga that day were exceptional. They and their wives continue to serve God to the present day. I consider it a real privilege to have had a small part in their spiritual journey. Thank you!

FOUR OF THE FIVE DEACONS AND THEIR WIVES WHO LATER WENT INTO THE MINISTRY.
Simon & Rina Rhodes, Errol & Davril Lobb, Steve & Linda Bowen, & Jannie & Dawn Barnard. Sadly, I do not have a good photo of Rod & Ellie Hein at this time.

The day for us to leave Chipinga was at hand. It had been an amazing two years. Many people had come to know The Lord as Saviour and a functioning, self-supporting Assembly had been established. Two National elections had taken place during that time changing the whole situation in the country. The war had come to an end, however, what did the future hold? Only God knew!

It was at the beginning of October 1980 that we once again headed for South Africa to take a much-needed holiday. We would not be returning to Chipinga but would go straight to Bulawayo to take on the Pastorate of Bethshan Tabernacle. As previously agreed, Mike Howard moved to the town to replace us in Chipinga and we were confident that he would do a good job as he was already well-known and loved by a number of the members of the congregation.

As I close this chapter of my life, I have to say a BIG THANK YOU TO GOD for giving me the privilege of ministering in Chipinga. I am also so thankful for the part my late wife Mally played during those two eventful years. It was her encouragement that enabled me to survive that first difficult year and I am indebted to her for staying by my side as we moved from place to place. Thank you Mally!

I hope that you have enjoyed the story so far? The final part of my story LIVING UNDER FIVE FLAGS continues in Book number three.

www.ingramcontent.com/pod-product-compliance
Lightning Source LLC
Chambersburg PA
CBHW040106120526
44588CB00039B/2756